TUNNEL-MASTER
and
ARSONIST
of the
GREAT WAR
The Norton-Griffiths Story

GW00468192

TUNNEL-MASTER
and
ARSONIST
of the
GREAT WAR

The Norton-Griffiths Story

by

TONY BRIDGLAND
and
ANNE MORGAN

Pen & Sword
MILITARY

First published in Great Britain in 2003 by LEO COOPER
Republished in this format in 2021 by
Pen & Sword Military
an imprint of
Pen & Sword Books Ltd
Yorkshire – Philadelphia

ISBN 978 1 39901 604 9

A CIP catalogue record for this book is available from the British Library.

Typeset in Sabon by Phoenix Typesetting

Printed in the UK by CPI Group (UK) Ltd, Croydon, CR0 4YY.

Pen & Sword Books Limited incorporates the imprints of Atlas,
Archaeology, Aviation, Discovery, Family History, Fiction, History,
Maritime, Military, Military Classics, Politics, Select, Transport, True
Crime, Air World, Frontline Publishing, Leo Cooper, Remember When,
Seaforth Publishing, The Praetorian Press, Wharncliffe Local History,
Wharncliffe Transport, Wharncliffe True Crime and White Owl.

For a complete list of Pen & Sword titles please contact

PEN & SWORD BOOKS LIMITED
47 Church Street, Barnsley, South Yorkshire, S70 2AS, England
E-mail: enquiries@pen-and-sword.co.uk
Website: www.pen-and-sword.co.uk

Or
PEN AND SWORD BOOKS
1950 Lawrence Rd, Havertown, PA 19083, USA
E-mail: Uspen-and-sword@casematepublishers.com
Website: www.penandswordbooks.com

Contents

Acknowledgments   vii

1   The Boy Jack   1

2   South Africa   8

3   The Lure of Gold   16

4   Doctor Jim   23

5   The Raid   30

6   With Honey's Scouts in Mashonaland   36

7   Another Crossroads   54

8   A Decisive Encounter in Zanzibar   57

9   Back to Africa   62

10   A Marriage, a Mine and a Railway   82

11   'Empire Jack'   93

12   When Duty Calls   104

13   Hill 60 Goes Up   129

14   Bring up the Ammonal   142

15   Code Name – Deep Water   146

16   Green Light for the Big Blow   169

17   Operation Arson   179

18   The Greatest Man-Made Earthquake   203

19   Trouble   218

20   The Flame Goes Out   227

     Appendix   237

     Bibliography   238

     Index   239

Acknowledgments

To research the remarkable century-old adventures, scattered worldwide, of this man of much action and few written words, required a very special kind of dedication. Perhaps such dedication could only have been applied by someone who possesses a special kind of relationship with the subject of that research.

Sir John Norton-Griffiths' granddaughter, Anne Morgan, never knew him, but she has lived all her life with his story. Nursing deep feelings that to research that story was a family privilege – even a duty – she set out to do it. She travelled thousands of miles, to all corners of the globe. She wandered through the African bush, often alone, pored over archives in London, Somerset, Cairo, Johannesburg and Harare, rattled over stony desert tracks in ramshackle buses, spoke to tribal chiefs and elders, climbed skyscrapers in Canada, and explored old abandoned First World War tunnels under the mud of Flanders and the Somme. Together with her private family papers, the product of those perambulations was sufficient to fill a car-boot full of ring-binders, every one crammed with enough material to take it to bursting point.

I was honoured to be asked to be the co-author of this book, which is based in the main on Anne's research, plus, of course, the usual kind help that a writer can expect from the Public Record Office and the Imperial War Museum. The more I delved into archives, the more I was convinced that I had been given the easier part, such was the sheer wealth of information that Anne had amassed.

Jack was exasperatingly parsimonious with his ink, at least

until the time came to keep a War Diary, and therefore some parts of his earlier life may seem to be a little disjointed. Nevertheless, I have tried to construct as smooth a tale as possible. With that apologia, I trust that it will be felt that I have done justice to Anne – and to her remarkable grandfather.

Finally, I would like to thank Umashanie Reddy of Natal University and Timothy Kimber for help they provided in adding a little historical colour to the early passages, Michael Ward for his invaluable assistance with the illustrations, my editor Tom Hartman for applying his usual gentle discipline and my wife and family for their patient forbearance during my long absences on the project.

Tony Bridgland,
Rye,
East Sussex.   December 2002.

I would like to express my thanks to Peter Barton for his indefatigable encouragement, our shared research and his documentary film which did so much to reawaken interest in my grandfather's career; to Jaime Ashworth for many hours spent in the Public Record Office on my behalf; Robert Milne for taking me to Doornkopf and 'showing' me, on the ground, the history of the Jameson Raid; Gwyneth C.D. Jones for turning up trumps with the building permit for the Dominion Trust Building; Dan Parker for sharing his experience of the Nile and work on the second heightening of the Aswan Dam; to Mott Macdonald for allowing me to pore over their archives on Aswan where I found a treasure: the Specifications for the second heightening; to the Under-Secretary, Chairman and Officials of the Nile Water Section of the Ministry of Public Works and Water for receiving me with kindness; to Mahatma Gandhi's grandson, H.E. Gopalkrishna Gandhi, for extending the grapevine of information to E.S. Reddy and Uma Mesthine, both hives of information on recruiting labour for the railways. I especially want to thank my brother Dr Michael Norton-Griffiths for his patience, encouragement, critique and burrowing on the internet for morsels of information; also my cousin Jeremy Thorpe for giving me access to various family papers; to Tony for his willingness, enthusiasm and skill with which he wove his superior knowledge of the history of the epoch into the story of my grandfather while maintaining the spirit and flavour of my original effort; lastly, posthumously, my grandmother for her memoirs without which there would have been no story.

Anne Morgan,
Montgaudry,   November 2002.
France

1

THE BOY JACK

It was sometime in the summer of 1874 that a strange little figure was to be seen toddling down a leafy Gloucestershire lane. He was quite alone and he wore a determined look on his chubby face, which peered with obvious difficulty from beneath the brim of a gentleman's top-hat. He would surely have merited a second glance from any passer-by, for he was also enshrouded in the voluminous folds of a grown man's frock coat, the tails of which had been black but a few minutes since but were now sandy-grey as they trailed behind him on the ground. The coat was growing heavy and he was growing tired. He had covered half a mile since leaving the house in Nailsworth, but there were still another three miles to go to Stroud railway station.

A couple of hundred yards behind him ran a woman, in her thirties, holding up her long skirts for better speed. Her face was flushed pink with running and a tress of dark hair had escaped from her carefully coiffed bun to swing across her face. She was the lad's mother. "Jack! Jack!" she cried. She had only popped into the house for a minute to arrange some flowers in a vase. The boy had been playing happily on the grass as she had gathered them from the garden. But when she came back there was only a collection of scattered toys and no Jack. She ran next door to the Vicarage. No, they hadn't seen him. But some workmen had spotted him heading out of the gate. They pointed down the lane. At last she caught up with the would-be three-year-old truant and swept him up into her arms, gently scolding him. He protested loudly in red-faced infant rage as she carried him home, kicking his feet and bawling that he wanted to go to work in London on the train like his father.

This, and several other anecdotes that have survived the passage of time, were telling portents of the character which the adult Jack Norton Griffiths would eventually display. There was the occasion his sister Annie had just managed to grab his ankles, in the nick of time, to prevent him from falling head first down a well, and another when she had pulled him up over the balcony, late at night, as he returned from some boyish escapade to tumble fully clothed into his bed and feign sleep just before his irate father burst into the room exuding high-voiced Welsh fury and brandishing a cane.

Jack's family found themselves constantly on the move, taking up residence wherever their father, a tall stern dark-bearded man, could earn a good living as a Clerk of Works, mainly renovating large houses and churches to a high standard. The majestic piles of Gloucestershire, Sussex, where Griffiths senior worked the magic of his craft on Glyndebourne House of opera fame, Berkshire, Warwickshire, London and Somerset, where Jack was born at West Quantoxhead on 13 July 1871, all saw the coming and going of the Griffiths family. Maybe these peregrinations in his formative years were one root cause of the restlessness which was to possess Jack from his teens onwards.

If the family had a base at all, although they rarely visited it, it was high in the Brecon Beacons in Wales, where they had lived for many generations. Indeed, Jack's father John had started out on his working life in that area, as a partner with *his* father Thomas. Together they had built the market-place in Brecon. Throughout the 1850s and '60s John Griffiths had driven for many a mile behind the swinging rumps of a pair of heavy horses hauling a wagon laden with sand, timber or Welsh slate bearing the legend on its smartly painted side "T. Griffiths & Son, Builders and Timber Merchants – Llanspyddid." And it is easy to imagine a knickerbockered young Jack sitting beside a stream in the bracken-clad hills during one of the family's later sabbaticals, brooding, tossing stones into the clear water which rushed on its way to Newport far below, where it would become a sullen ribbon, silky-black with coal-dust from the Valleys.

By the time old Thomas died in 1867, John had resolved to try to better himself. Soon, he was proud to be able to place the letters MCWA after his name, which told the world he was no longer a simple builder but a professional Clerk of Works. And with such status came a superior line of work. But there was a sadness in his soul. Not only had his first wife, Mary Winstone, died at 31 in 1858, but their only son did not survive infancy. He married Juliet Avery in 1863 and she had first borne him twin daughters, Annie and Fanny, the following year. Fanny was one day to marry the illegitimate son of Napoleon III. Then came two boys, Arthur and Frank, both of whom died in childhood, and another girl Nelly, born in 1868. Finally, came John Norton, otherwise known as Jack, and diplomatically named after the architect who was in charge of the project at St. Audries, West Quantoxhead, Somerset, in 1871. At the behest of Fate, therefore, John Norton Griffiths was to be the only son of the four sired by his father to make it into adulthood.

Ironically, this was in all probability why father and son experienced for years much difficulty in seeing eye to eye. That John, although sad and stern and given to a hot temper, loved his son is beyond doubt. And perhaps it was natural that John, self-promoted from jobbing builder to Clerk of Works on high-class projects, should see that to become an architect was to have ascended to the apex of the construction industry's hierarchical pyramid. With his Victorian middle-class ambition for his family, that was the position for his son that he saw in his mind's eye, for the only son he had, and on whose youthful shoulders therefore everything rested if his father's dreams were ever to materialize. After all, had he not paid an architect the compliment of naming the lad after him? Unfortunately, the teenage Jack never came to share the same dream. His horizons were far, far wider than that.

By late 1874 work began to proliferate in and around London, which put paid to the family's nomadic existence for a number of years. Eventually they found themselves living at 'The Acacias', a big old-fashioned house in King Street, Hammersmith, which in those days was a small town still more or less in the country, although the tramway running through the middle of it was a sure sign of its imminent absorption into London proper.

'The Acacias'? Here was another omen pointing to Jack's future. In time he would be looking at the flat tops of thousands of them as they spangled some African plain, stretching away into the distance as far as the eye could see.

His parents tried very hard to see that Jack started life with a decent education. First a Dr Dolby who had a small grammar school in Edmonton, and then a Mr Bewsher, who ran Collet House Preparatory School in the basement of his house in Hammersmith and whose dozen or so pupils were intended to proceed eventually to St Paul's School, tried to work their educational skills on a reluctant Jack. But he showed not the slightest interest in books or study. He was in perpetual trouble with his masters, as was testified by the several sheets of paper that he always carried in his pocket for insertion into the seat of his trousers whenever a cane was produced. Sport was his only interest, it seemed, especially swimming or rowing on the Thames. Eventually, a frustrated Mr Bewsher euphemistically invited Mrs Griffiths to take Jack away, suggesting that perhaps private tuition would produce better results. But after just one term the tutor wrote to Mrs Griffiths saying that he felt unable to accept his fees because Jack had never turned up for lessons.

Needless to say, his father's rage knew no limits and Jack was wise enough to give him a wide berth. His sister Annie, together with his other sisters and their mother, always conspired to cover up for him wherever possible. Many years later she wrote, "He was always on something of his own – on the Thames boating or swimming at the baths, sports of some kind, or with his friends finding out about life for himself and getting into scrapes, although he had a marvellous knack of avoiding the dire results. He easily made many good friends and was always good company."

It was his exceptional natural ability to make instant friends and be 'good company' which was to serve him so well. One such boyhood friend was a German cobbler. His name is not recorded, but he was probably befriended during one of Jack's absences from his tutor. This man must have succeeded in instilling some practical knowledge where more than one professional educationalist had failed with Latin verbs, because the boy suddenly appeared to have acquired the skills of half-soling and heeling. And he was so keen to demonstrate it that soon he was persuading the family, several friends and sundry visitors besides,

4

to let him mend their shoes in return for some suitable remuneration.

Another friend was Percy Kimber, a couple of years older than Jack and son of the MP for Wandsworth. We do not know exactly how the pair came to meet. Perhaps they had been schoolmates together at Collet House. Percy was in all likelihood a frequent illicit rowing or swimming companion and he was to be a major catalyst when the first major crossroads of Destiny appeared in Jack's life.

Meantime, the determined John Griffiths had managed, through a friend, to introduce Jack to a firm of architects, Messrs Wetherby & Jones of Cockspur Street, just off Trafalgar Square. The boy had, of course, little to show by way of formal education and it appears that his position as trainee draughtsman, without any payment of the usual premium, was obtained purely on the strength of his personality. In short, both Mr Wetherby and Mr Jones 'took a shine' to him. And he tried hard, very honestly, to become a draughtsman. But life on an office stool soon became unbearable for him, although his affable employers were pleased to make every allowance for his shortcomings.

Sadly for them it wasn't to last and they were to receive a poor dividend for the kindness they had invested in him. One day, after he had spent but a short while at Wetherby & Jones, and on an apparent impulse, he took French leave, strolled over to Knightsbridge Barracks, told a sergeant some suitable lies about his age and enlisted as a trooper in the Royal Horse Guards! The next time his family were to see him, he would be clad in his dashing dark blue uniform with a red stripe down the side of his long narrow trousers and sporting the wispy sproutings of a youthful military moustache. He did very well at Riding School and won a Cup to prove it, which skill was to be another great asset to him later. And, astonishingly, his father was no longer angry with him. Quite miraculously, his unbending approach turned to one of pride. "Come home, Jack," wrote sister Annie, "Father is proud of you now." But the army clearly suited Jack and his father now came to realize that his efforts to steer the boy into a career which clearly held little interest for him had been short-sighted and unwise.

Again it wasn't to last, even though Jack revelled in the army life. Because something even more exciting and appealing soon came along. After less than a year as a soldier of the Queen, he wrote to his father from King's Lynn, where he was stationed, to say that he was being bought out of the army. Percy Kimber had come back into his life.

Percy's father, Sir Henry, owned a firm known as the Natal Land and Colonisation Company Ltd. He had set it up in 1861 in partnership with his brother to exploit the growing interest in emigration to South Africa, and in particular the area around the hinterland of Durban. The aim was to assist young men who wanted to go out and try their hand at sheep farming on the Company's estate at Dargle. After one year, if all went well, the young man was set up with fifty acres of his own and a £150 loan to get him going. Kimber's most prestigious client thus far had made the seventy-day voyage eighteen years before, also to try his hand at farming. He was none other than Cecil Rhodes, who was in poor health at the time and was hoping that a sub-tropical climate would be better for him than the damp mists of his native Hertfordshire, where his doctor had noted on his medical records 'Only Six Months to Live'. Rhodes, though, had not been intending to farm on Sir Henry's estate but on his own brother's land at Umkomaas, on the beautiful coast south of Durban, who was trying, not very successfully, to grow cotton. Although Jack had no way of knowing it at the time, this was the man whose unshakeable ambitions were to shape his own adventures within a few years.

Percy Kimber had been badgering his father for some time to be allowed to go himself, but the older man, who as far as is known never visited South Africa himself, was reluctant to see his son go pioneering on his own. And John Griffiths, for his part, was against his son leaving the army now that he had at long last found his niche. Ever a firm believer in 'working your way up' in life, he exhorted Jack to stay and do that in the army. He probably imagined his son as being a Colonel at least. Alas, although he was indeed to be one day, it was not to be achieved in any conventional way and it would not be in John's lifetime.

We can only assume that Sir Henry Kimber was the subject of considerable pressure from two very determined young men in that year of 1888. It would be all right if Percy were accompa-

6

nied by Jack, they argued. They could make a go of it together. Surely he could see that. And so on. It was probably a case of 'anything for a quiet life' when Sir Henry finally relented as he drew out his cheque-book to purchase Trooper John Norton Griffiths' release from the army. And the two youths were soon aboard a ship ploughing its way southwards through the Atlantic.

2

SOUTH AFRICA

Vasco da Gama may have performed a major feat of exploration in landing at the Cape of Good Hope on 22 November 1497 on the way to Calicut in his tiny carrack *Saõ Gabriel* with her crew of ex-convicts, but little immediate interest was shown by Europeans in the land he had discovered. The Cape became a convenient place for the ships of the Dutch East India Company to obtain fresh water and provisions on the long voyage to the Orient, but that was about the limit of its perceived importance.

Even a couple of centuries later the scant population consisted merely of the indigenous people, hunter-gatherer bushmen and Hottentots, and a small colony of Dutch farmers, called Boers, who had settled there. There seems to have been little friction between the two communities, but each must have considered the other to be very strange, at least in the beginning. The diminutive tawny-skinned Hottentots, whose antecedence still remains somewhat of a mystery, were peaceful herders who lived in conical tents covered with ox-hides. They dressed in animal skins and spoke in a bizarre language consisting largely of tongue clicking, while the tall, pale-faced, bearded Dutchmen wore woollen caps, made wooden houses, shot birds with muskets, stuck pipes in their mouths and blew smoke out of them. They were content to plough their fields and tend their cattle. But when these Dutchmen attempted to spread eastwards from the Cape in the late 1770s they encountered for the first time a race of people who resented their presence – Bantus. The result was the first of what became known as the Kaffir Wars, which were to splash the pages of South African history with blood for the next hundred years. To add to the discomfiture of the Dutchmen, this first Kaffir War was scarcely over when their peaceful rural existence at the Cape was disturbed by some unwelcome visitors – the English. And England, at that time, was embroiled in war with the French.

Holland was a French possession and ally. Indeed, Napoleon Bonaparte's brother Louis became King of Holland. Given the strong Dutch connection at the Cape, Britain had seen a distinct possibility that this situation could lead to a blockade of the route to their own possessions in India, Australia and the Far East. Without more ado, she sent troops to seize the Colony, and retained it after the wars, for which the Dutch were paid £6 million compensation. Emigration from Britain to the Cape increased, heralding a rapid and extensive British expansion and dominance in Africa.

Friction between the English and the Boers soon arose. Local government was reformed and English was made the official language in the courts. But the main reason for Boer resentment was the abolition of slavery in 1834. Although staunchly religious, and never far from a Bible from which most of them could freely quote, they saw nothing wrong in slavery and considered that they had been deprived of their 'property', i.e. about 30,000 Africans and Malay slaves, despite having been granted £3 million compensation for their loss, which was about a third of what they wanted. This uneasy situation triggered the Great Trek, the mass emigration of 10,000 Boers to settle in the interior, where they could live under their own laws, unmolested by the English intruders.

With their families and possessions in rude carts pulled by oxen, the *voortrekkers* headed north across the high open plateau of the bleak Karoo Desert, and onwards across the Orange and Vaal Rivers, where they founded the Orange Free State and Transvaal, creating an 800-mile gap between themselves and the overbearing British. Some crossed the Drakensberg mountains and entered what is now Natal. Britain's immediate reaction was to pass laws which extended her jurisdiction well beyond the Vaal River. Unable to shake off what they saw as foreign intrusion in their affairs, the resentful Boers clashed again and again with the British, although they were defeated each time in skirmishes at Port Natal (now Durban), Zwartkopjes and Boomplaats.

However, the expense of maintaining these new far-flung corners of the Empire, with apparently little to show in return, soon prompted a change of attitude in London, which resulted in the signing of the Sand River Convention in 1852. This gave the Boers, at last, the freedom they craved. The Transvaal was officially named the South African Republic and two years later it was joined in independence by its neighbour, Orange Free State.

For a while Britain was content to leave these fledgling republics to their own devices, but the discovery of diamonds in the Griqualand West (Kimberley) region in the late 1860s brought about yet another change in her posture. Orange Free State, Transvaal and the local Griquas themselves all claimed ownership of the mineral rights. But in the end these disputes were effectively settled in London by the Disraeli Government, which abruptly annexed the South African Republic to the British Empire in 1877 on the flimsy grounds that its independence was a menace to peace in Britain's other South African possessions. Understandably, the Boers' hatred of the British boiled over yet again and they took up arms.

Disraeli fell from power in 1880, to be replaced by the liberal Gladstone, who had long felt that the annexation of the South African Republic had been an injustice which should be rectified. In one of the first moves of his new Government, he was in the process of negotiating with the Boer leaders, hoping to reach a peaceful solution that would be satisfactory to all sides, when his efforts were pre-empted, with long-reaching and disastrous results, by the impatient Boers themselves. In December 1880, in what became known as the First Boer War, they revolted. In the course of this, a detachment of 500 British troops of the Northamptonshire Regiment, King's Royal Rifles and Scots Fusiliers under General Sir George Coley, was attacked and soundly defeated in the so-called Battle of Majuba Hill at the northern tip of Natal, on 27 February 1881, with Coley losing his life. Gladstone considered that such a mere skirmish, however humiliating, should not deflect him from his policy of restoring independence to the South African Republic. This was finalized, with the provisos that no treaties could be made with foreign countries without the approval of Great Britain, and that 'white men should have full liberty to reside in any part of the republic, to trade in it, and to be liable to pay the same taxes only as those exacted from the citizens of the republic'. The amateurish drafting of the wording of this instrument would be the cause of much violence later.

At home, Gladstone was roundly criticized for his appeasement, and for leaving Majuba Hill unavenged, by those who considered that the prestige of the Empire had been damaged. The jubilant Boers, for their part, considered that their victory had been won by force of arms and took every opportunity to anger the British by reminding them of the name – Majuba Hill. They convinced themselves that what they had been able to do once they could do again. However, nineteen years to the very day after the battle in which General Coley was killed the words 'Majuba Hill' were to be loudly hurled back at them from the lips of vengeful British troops at two other places simultaneously – Paardeberg and Ladysmith.

For Great Britain, the late nineteenth century was a time of high empire, with the scramble for Africa taking centre stage. And the British possessed no greater Imperialist than a man named Cecil Rhodes. He was born in 1853, one of six sons of the vicar at Bishop's Stortford, Hertfordshire. Dogged by poor health, he was prevented from following the professional career he planned and had been sent to South Africa to join his brother Herbert in the hope that the climate would prove beneficial to his weak lungs. But when he arrived there in 1870 he found that Herbert had abandoned the quest for cotton and had left for Kimberley in search of diamonds. Herbert had returned, brimming with stories about the riches to be found across the veldt beyond Basutoland. In Kimberley, according to Herbert, a man with good enough eyesight to distinguish a diamond from a pebble could make £100 in a week. Overcome with 'diamond fever', even before they had plucked a single diamond from the dirt, the two brothers took off on the dangerous 600-mile journey back to Kimberley in a cart pulled by oxen, with a pick, two shovels and plenty of books, including a Greek lexicon.

Life in Kimberley was tough and Herbert soon left, but Cecil persevered, gradually advancing from being a speculative digger to the millionaire owner of several claims, employing others to do the digging. From his shrewd business manoeuvres sprang the famous De Beers Consolidated Mines Ltd. Kimberley soon boasted the biggest man-made hole in the world – 3,500 feet deep and half a mile across – in which 40,000 men toiled 'like black ants'. It was owned by Rhodes' rival, a man named Barnato. Nonetheless, by 1891 Cecil had acquired it, and in so doing he made De Beers the owner of 90% of the world's diamond production. However, although revelling in the cut and thrust of business and the champagne lifestyle that came with riches, Rhodes was in the grip of an even stronger obsession. He wanted to paint the map of Africa red for Queen Victoria, with a Cape to Cairo railway running the length of it. To do this, he dreamed of driving northwards, planting the Union Jack everywhere along the way, until he came to the Mediterranean. Indeed, it was said of him that he would have colonised the planets if he could have.

Now well on the way to making his first fortune from diamonds, Rhodes stood for, and was elected to, the Cape Colony parliament in 1881 as the member for Griqualand West, which included Kimberley. Bechuanaland (now Botswana), Cape Colony's immediate neighbour to the north, was the cork which needed to be drawn to open up the bottle of the interior. Possession of this territory would enable the next step towards Cairo to be taken into Mashonaland and Matabeleland (which is now Zimbabwe), and would neatly circumvent the Boer Transvaal. Bringing his talent for political deviousness to the fore, Rhodes persuaded the High Commissioner in Cape Town, Sir Hercules Robinson, to recall the Deputy Commissioner from Bechuanaland in exchange for himself. His object was to have Bechuanaland declared as a British Protectorate. But the Transvaal also coveted this territory. It had in fact moved into the eastern part of it, but withdrew when the British sent up an expeditionary force from the Cape. Rhodes met the President of Transvaal, Paul Kruger, a dour old Boer who was shortly to become a deadly enemy, at a conference on the Vaal River in February 1885. The upshot was that, although Rhodes did not get all his own way, part of Bechuanaland was declared a Crown Colony and part of it did become a British Protectorate. But there was still one man standing in the way of Rhodes' drive northward. His name was King Lobengula.

The nineteenth century had seen Great Britain constantly involved in war all around the globe as her Empire grew. Nowhere was this more so than in Africa where there was a bewildering permutation of combatants; the British, the Boers and several native tribes. Places such as Blood River, where the Boers fought the Zulus in 1838; Hlobane, where the British and the Boers fought side by side against the Zulus; Isandhlwana, where 1,700 infantrymen of the 24th Foot (Northamptons) were massacred by 20,000 Zulus on 22 January 1879; and on the same day Rorke's Drift, where a tiny supply post manned by men of the South Wales Borderers won eleven VCs by holding out against 4,000 Zulus; Ulundi, where the Zulus were finally crushed a few months later, bringing an end to the Ninth Kaffir War and Majuba Hill, where we have already seen that the Boers routed a British force in 1881, are all names that are firmly etched on the bloody pages of South African history, together with a plethora of others where factions of indigenous warriors hurled themselves into battle with their cousins.

Lobengula was the ruler of the Matabele people who, together with the less warlike Mashonas whom they had subjugated, occupied the land that is now Zimbabwe. These tribes were part of the Zulu nation, but had emigrated northwards from Natal in 1823 after their Chief Mzilikazi, who was Lobengula's father, had fallen foul of Shaka, King of the Zulus. Very heavily built with a huge belly, well over six feet tall and 'every ounce a king', Lobengula had sixty-eight wives. Majestically clad in a monkey-skin loincloth, a wideawake hat trimmed with an ostrich feather and often a pair of European socks, he cut an impressive figure. He was scrupulously clean and carried his enormous weight with a stately erect gait. By nature he could be cruel, but it was often mingled with geniality. That said, he was known to like a drink. Hence, perhaps, the geniality. And he seemed to have difficulty in forcing himself to utter a firm "no" even when it would have served his best interests to do so. Such easy-going ways were to lead to his undoing.

Knowing that the only white men the uneducated Lobengula trusted were missionaries, Rhodes, crafty as ever and knowing that President Kruger also had his eye on Mashonaland, sent the son of a missionary, John Moffat, to obtain a 'Treaty of Friendship' with Lobengula in February 1888, and on the strength of this he persuaded the King to grant him mining concessions. As far as Lobengula was concerned, he had merely granted the white man permission to 'dig a big hole'. But he had been duped. He had granted Rhodes' agents 'exclusive power over all metals and minerals in his kingdom, and the authority to expel all other claimants'. In return he was to receive £100 per month plus a thousand rifles with ammunition. But he was not entirely unaware of his mistake. "They come in like wolves without my leave," he said later, "and make roads into my country." These words were enough to make his young Matabele warriors restive, a sign of trouble ahead, for their tendency towards belligerence was never far beneath the surface. But Rhodes was already on his way to England, to press the British Government to grant a Charter to his new British South Africa Company to develop the newly acquired territory. Lobengula wrote to Queen Victoria, "If the Queen hears that I have given away my whole country, it is not so. I do not understand where the dispute is, because I have no knowledge of writing." But it was too late. The Charter was granted in October 1889 and a pioneering expedition set off for Mashonaland to prepare for digging to begin.

Kruger's South African Republic was inhabited mainly by Boers, who were almost exclusively farmers. They were stolid, religious people, although they might be thought today to be unprogressive and backward. And they mistrusted foreigners, especially Englishmen. But their rural contentment was disturbed yet again in 1886 when an Australian scavenger, George Harrison, discovered gold at Landlaagte Farm. It turned out that George had found the main reef, the Golden Arc, on the convex side of which grew up the modern city of Johannesburg that we know today. There were immense quantities of gold under the Rand. Immediately, a great influx of miners and speculators began, and they were chiefly Englishmen. The Boers called them *Uitlanders* (pronounced aitlanders), the Dutch word for 'foreigners' or 'outsiders'. And of course these Uitlanders had every right, thanks to the slapdash drafting of Gladstone's Treaty with the Republic, to reside and work there, subject to paying the same taxes as its citizens.

Within a very short while the gold-fever in the Golden City had reached such a height that it would even have its own Stock Exchange. It was opened on 16 January 1888, a single-storey brick building with a tin roof on Commissioner Street. It was not long before over 300 stockbrokers were all scrambling over each other, trying to make a living from Johannesburg's gold. And in that highly charged environment business was conducted at such a furious pace that trading often continued in the street after the Exchange had closed its doors for the day, with brokers shouting prices above the clamour of a crowd which seemed to be composed of half the population.

This then, was the South Africa towards which Jack Norton Griffiths and his friend Percy Kimber were sailing in that southern hemisphere springtime of October 1888.

Not every teenager in the course of a major adventure has the presence of mind to keep a regular diary of events. The headiness of the adventure itself is enough to preoccupy the young mind without any laborious scribbling at the end of each day. It was one of his shortcomings that Jack was not much of a one for writing down anything, even when it came to letters home, in which filial duty he appears to have been sadly lacking. Therefore, we do not know much in the way of anecdotal detail about his everyday life during his first few years in South Africa.

But some momentous events were taking place there at that time which were to impinge directly on what he did, where he went, and why, and would provide the impetus for his immediate future. We will need to examine these events in order to paint a reasonable picture of his life.

3

THE LURE OF GOLD

It was a strapping young fellow who walked down the gangway when the ship docked in Durban. He was already over six feet tall and strongly built, with clear green eyes which gazed confidently from beneath a head of dark hair. His short time in the army had seen the transformation of Jack the boy into Jack the seventeen-year-old man.

Durban, although as yet still not fully fledged as a port, was already an established outpost of the Empire as one of the coaling stations which were the evenly spread stitches around the globe holding together the threads of the mighty network. A gleaming British cruiser was more often than not to be seen at anchor in the bay, as her bluejackets swarmed ashore to spend their precious hours of liberty carousing in the town's several tin-roofed taverns. Indeed, bar the occasional incongruous stone civic building, bank or church, the corrugated tin-roof was pretty well the standard protection from the elements in Durban as it was all over late-Victorian colonial South Africa. The urban planners had not yet had an opportunity to impose their influence on the town and it had a very loose and random appearance, with many rocky patches, virgin scrub and plenty of coral trees and yuccas in between the scattered tin rooftops.

Cargo traffic was growing too, as Natal developed, and the quayside was beginning to show the bustle of a really busy place, with heaps of coal from the mines up-country around Glencoe and Dundee to feed the hungry boilers of the ships and heavy wagons piled high with material of all descriptions rumbling away from the dockside to their various destinations.

Jack sniffed the mild salty breeze which blew in from the Indian

Ocean. Stepping towards some men who were busy loading a wagon, he asked for directions to Market Square, where the Natal Land & Colonisation Company had its Durban office. The ship's arrival would be known by now all over the town and they were to meet Mr Goodricke, the firm's solicitor there as soon as possible. The two adventurers hoisted their bags on their shoulders and set off up the town. It was only a couple of miles. Goodricke had some papers for them to sign and they needed to arrange some supper and some beds for the night before setting off for Dargle, a few miles up the line past Pietermaritzburg, first thing in the morning. It was the first time that Jack had ever slept in a hotel or under a tin roof. It was to be far from the last.

The healthy outdoor life appealed to Jack, although he found that sub-tropical insects were somewhat less friendly than their distant British cousins. He had always been self-reliant and here he needed to be so more than at any time before. His newly learned skill in handling a horse, thanks to his army training, was put to everyday use. Some days would be spent almost entirely in the saddle as he patrolled the wide acreage of the estate in the sun, wind and sometimes blinding showers of hail, with a Martini-Henry rifle slung on his back and some grub in his bag for lunch, dismounting only to brew a can of tea over a wood fire, to pick up a shot hare or to disentangle a ewe from a mimosa thicket. Almost immediately he became a 'colonial' in his habits and his attitudes. The native workers on the farm respected his firm but tactful ways of getting things done and he turned into his bed each night tired but contented with life as a pioneer.

But, true to form, it was not to last. As had happened already more than once in Jack's short life, and was to happen even more in his future adventures, he got the whiff of something more exciting over the hill and instinctively went for it. And this time the whiff had a strong auriferous flavour to it. It was the scent of gold, wafting over the Drakensberg Mountains from the Transvaal. Indeed, it was powerful enough to waft around the entire planet, drawing brave and adventurous mainly rough-hewn happy-go-lucky characters, like moths to a lamp-light, from all over Europe, Australia and the United States, where California had worked a similar magic some years before. And for Jack, already sitting only a few days' ride away from such untold riches, the draw was a powerful one.

Taking his leave of his friend Kimber, who, being the heir to the estate, had a good enough reason to resist the call of the gold, Jack packed his belongings again. The nearest rail station would have been at Nottingham Road. At that time the railhead was not far north of Ladysmith, and the Laing's Nek tunnel, which was to connect the line between Natal and Transvaal, was still three years away from completion. Exactly how Jack made the rest of his journey to the Golden City we do not know, but he probably cadged a series of lifts on passing wagons, rather than expend any of his limited funds on stagecoach fares.

Johannesburg, 6,000 feet above sea-level, was at that time little more than a huge mining camp. It had even less of the appearance of an established urbanization than Durban. Only Market Square, a large rectangular open space where a continual train of ox-drawn wagons outspanned, and Commissioner Street were recognizable as formal thoroughfares, where a few wooden shacks were interspersed with vacant lots marked out with pegs. For miles around there were regiments of white bell-tents and rough tumbledown shanties, pens of oxen, mules and horses, empty carts, winding gear and great heaps of spoil. In the heat of day a fog of red-brown dust from the diggings hung over the place, sometimes dense enough to restrict visibility. After dark, flames danced and sparks spiralled into the night-sky from a thousand cooking-fires, around which sat groups of gnarled men in wideawake hats, shirt-sleeves, corduroy trousers and unbuttoned twill waistcoats with revolvers stuck in their belts and their faces flickering in the fire-light as they ate, laughed and squabbled. The nearest approach to what might be called pubs were one or two rough tin-roofed huts, each reeking with stale sweat and the fumes of rough whisky and strong tobacco, where the rowdy company could provide at least some respite after a day's hard work. (Although it was said that the roughness of the locally distilled whisky was the cause of the departure of many to try their luck in Australia.) And the lucky ones might even have been able to afford a few intimate moments with a woman's commercial charms in some dark secluded corner, later to retire with the

18

lingering scent of cheap perfume in their nostrils. There were one or two 'clubs', the most prestigious of which, built by Cecil Rhodes in 1887 near the Stock Exchange on Commissioner Street, was the Rand Club, an eccentric edifice with an imposing entrance with columns of marble, a grand staircase and, of course, a tin roof.

Perhaps understandably, such a gathering of wild men with gold in their eyes could be a dangerous place. Indeed, it was Africa's equivalent to the wild and lawless West of America. One night Jack heard a soft footstep behind him. He turned to see a native. There was the glint of a blade in the man's hand as he jumped to attack the youngster. The ensuing struggle ended with the would-be robber prostrate on the ground, having been soundly thrashed by Jack's strong fists. On another occasion Jack was walking past a hut when he heard the cries of a woman. She was being beaten by her drunken common-law husband. Bursting through the open doorway, Jack threw the man aside and stood in front of the terrified woman until he had calmed down. Her name was Nina Tulloch. History does not record much in the way of intimate details of her subsequent relationship with Jack, but we do know that they became good friends and that Nina was already very sick. Whether or not the cause of her ill-health was the cruelty she had suffered we do not know, but in fact she was dying. Jack and Nina set up home together and when the end came, with poignant chivalry, he married her on her deathbed. He cannot have been more than twenty-two years old when he became a widower. And the remains of a Mrs Nina Griffiths, who died an honest woman, are buried somewhere in Johannesburg.

But we are getting ahead of our story. When Jack arrived in Johannesburg, he quickly discovered that its streets were not exactly paved with gold. Getting your hands on the stuff was far from easy. Rand gold could not be obtained simply by standing up to your knees in the water of a mountain stream, passing silt and gravel through a sieve pan, as it could in other parts of the world. Rand gold was deep in the ground. You had to dig for it. And even when you found it, it was invariably stubbornly encased in hard rock.

Prospectors would sink whatever money they had into a claim, then open it up, hopefully to expose a reef. Then, by dint of much sweat, they would shovel out the ore and pile it up, ready for crushing. It was at that point that many prospectors hit stalemate. They needed a stamp battery for crushing the ore to start the process of turning the dirt into wealth. Such was the demand for this machinery that there was often a twelve-month waiting list for its delivery. During that time there was dynamite, mercury, timber props, cement and various licences to buy, wages to pay and food to be found. Without £10,000 capital, you had little chance of success. And not one in a hundred of them had such backing. Enterprising magnates such as Cecil Rhodes and the cockneys Barney Barnato and Solly Joel, already diamond millionaires, set up banks to finance these under-capitalized mining syndicates.

Barney Barnato, real name Barnett Isaacs, was a former member of a music-hall act, who had also known a tough life as a boxer in the East End of London. Unlike his Kimberley rival Rhodes, Barney was in South Africa purely to make money. He had arrived in Johannesburg from Kimberley in a gilded coach. But he never forgot his roots, and could be found any day of the week on Commissioner Street with a pocket full of sovereigns for stony-broke prospectors. His Consolidated Investments Corporation, known as the 'Johnnies' on the London Stock Exchange, became the largest mining house in Europe. Indeed, it was said that many millions of pounds were made from South African gold in London before a shovelful of ore had been processed in Johannesburg.

Thus was the scene in the Golden City that Jack found when he arrived. He had no access to the capital which could have provided an instant path to riches. £10,000? In all probability, he did not even possess ten shillings. And he needed to eat. Years before, a hard-up Barney Barnato had peddled dodgy cigars in Kimberley to keep together life and limb. Now Jack sold buttons in Johannesburg. And almost certainly he was the grateful recipient of more than one of Barney's sovereigns. But it was Barney's nephew, Solly Joel, who was indirectly responsible for helping Jack over the first major hurdle he encountered on his way up in the Golden City.

Within the span of a couple of years Jack had progressed from reluctant schoolboy to trainee draughtsman to soldier to sheep farmer to expectant gold prospector. But now, with the mature mind which comes only with some experience of life, he realized that what he was lacking was specialized knowledge of some sort, which was essential if he were to pave his way forward. What better than mining? And given his present location, preferably the mining of gold. Soon after his arrival in Johannesburg he had managed to fix himself up with lodgings with a Captain Maynard, a member of the Diggers Committee, and his family in their hut in Marshall's township. Maynard became a father figure to Jack and made him a member of his Club. Which Club is not recorded, but it was there that Jack made contacts which led to landing a much-needed job. Here was further proof of the truth of sister Annie's remark that he made friends easily and was always 'good company'.

In early 1889, thanks to his new connections, Jack became a miner, working alongside the engineers at the mills of the Crown Reef Company and learning about dynamite and tunnelling and a horde of associated activities at their Langlaagte mine. His vocabulary was about to become infused with a host of words peculiar to his new world. Words such as stope, amalgam plate, jack-hammer, placer deposit, hopper, gangue and ore-pass would soon all have special meanings for him, while they would probably have nonplussed Doctor Dolby at his little grammar school in Edmonton. But almost as soon as he had started, disaster struck. The gold ore that was turning up was found to be contaminated with iron pyrites – Fool's Gold! Panic! The price of shares plummeted as investors pulled out. It seemed like the end of the Golden City in general and Crown Reef in particular. And the Boers, who had never been completely convinced of the long-term potential of the Rand in the first place, hence their willingness to let the Uitlanders flood into their country and produce so much sweat while obediently paying their taxes, quietly laughed behind their hands. But Crown Reef was saved, at least for the time being, by the shrewd confidence of Solly Joel, who bought up large slices of its shares, at a rock-bottom price of course.

Solly's confidence was quickly well rewarded. Two engineers from faraway Edinburgh named McArthur and Forrest arrived in Johannesburg. They had recently discovered that cyanide and gold have an affinity for each other. Crushed ore, when amalgamated with cyanide, then passed through zinc and heated to boiling point, delivers the true precious constituent as a black powder. The Rand was saved and Jack's fledgling career with it.

4

DOCTOR JIM

Leander Starr Jameson, a handsome slightly built character with a flamboyant disposition, was a brilliant Edinburgh physician. He had arrived in South Africa in 1878 and set up practice in Kimberley, hoping, like Rhodes, to find that the climate would be beneficial to his weak lungs. Being of similar age, the two soon struck up a friendship, and Jameson came to hero-worship Rhodes, some said in an almost girlish manner. This has stoked many a debate about Rhodes' sexuality . Was he a homosexual? Was he a mysoginist? Or was he simply shy in female company? The answers to the latter questions are almost certainly 'no', because he is known to have said quite firmly to Queen Victoria, "How could I hate a sex of which your Majesty is a member?" Further intrigue is added by the fact that the two friends became house-mates. Be that as it may, Jameson's practice began to flourish. He was dubbed 'Doctor Jim' by the hard-bitten Kimberleyites, with whom he was popular for his breezy bedside manner. "Rub it with a brick," he once told a fanciful woman who had complained of a sore back.

And once, in the course of a hunting trip, he had visited the vastly overweight King Lobengula and cured him of an attack of gout. This successful administration of the white man's medicine was to prove useful later, when the King decided to renege on the mining concession he had granted to Rhodes. Point blank, he refused to allow the pioneer expedition to enter his domain. Playing his cards with his usual adroitness, Rhodes urged Jameson to pay a visit to his old friend and attempt to engineer a change of heart. The doctor was received most hospitably into the royal abode, which by now was crammed with the cases of champagne, whisky and rifles with which various white adventurers had tried to worm their way into his gout-prone Majesty's favour. Jameson's smooth diplomacy won the day, but soon after his departure back to Kimberley, Lobengula changed his mind again. And Jameson's career had begun its departure from doctoring the sick to take on a more aggressive slant. He now began to see himself more as a go-getting imperialist in the Rhodes mould. Whether this was because he had been blinded by the praises heaped upon him by Rhodes or whether it was recklessness or just plain stupidity on his part is a question that has been asked by historians ever since.

Rhodes tried another tack. Rather than provoke Lobengula, whose hawkish warriors were still quietly simmering, by going into Matabeleland itself, he decided to route the expedition to the south of Bulawayo and through the country of the Mashona, a gentler people, and then work northwards to establish themselves beyond the Hunyani River. And time was of the essence, because Rhodes' intelligence told him that the Boers were also planning a northwards trek. "We cannot allow a single Boer to settle north of the Limpopo," he said, "until our position in the north is secure."

Rhodes' Pioneers were recruited at the Cape, drilled and kitted out for the hazardous journey. They were a mixed lot, adventure-mad to the last man - butchers, Americans, bakers, Dutchmen, fresh-faced young cricketers, Jews, Irishmen and rich men's sons from the shires of England who had been exiled 'for putting the scullery-maid in the family way'. Among this motley crowd was a Major Leonard, who kept a diary. With an army officer's trained ability of character assessment, he had already seen the ruthlessness in the two principals of the operation. "As for the Matabele," he wrote, "Rhodes will make short shrift of them if he gets the chance, or if they do not give it to him, he and Jameson between them will make it, as sure as eggs are eggs." Accompanied by two troops of armed police and 300 Bechuana natives to cut new roads, the 192 Pioneers moved out of Macloutsi in the far north-west of Bechuanaland on 27 June 1890 with the famous big-game hunter F.C. Selous at the head of their 117 ox-drawn wagons, two 7-pounder guns and three Maxims, and splashed their way across the Shashi River. By September they had established a fortified outpost in Mashonaland, 400 miles away. Lobengula's 2,000 fierce *impi*, armed now with the rifles the white man had presented to them as well as their familiar short stabbing spears, had watched survey parties from the Pioneers carve up the countryside along the way into prospective farms. These Pioneers were not there purely as soldiers. They had no intention to settle for mere soldiers' pay. As an incentive to enrol, Rhodes had also promised each of them, on completion of the campaign, a farm of 6,000 acres and twenty gold claims. The warriors could have overwhelmed the column if they had wished, despite its artillery, but were under orders to refrain from attack by Lobengula, whom Rhodes had recently taken to England in 'the great *kraal* which pushes through the water', staying at the Berners Hotel, watching a review at Aldershot and dining with Queen Victoria at Windsor Castle.

The Pioneers called their new fort Salisbury, after the British Prime Minister of the day, and at daybreak on 12 September 1890 the Union Flag was planted in what is now Union Square, in what is now Harare, and the surrounding country became known as Rhodesia, now Zimbabwe.

Meanwhile, Rhodes had become Prime Minister of Cape Colony and was displaying a tactful range of policies designed to minimize friction between Briton and Boer (although, of course, with the silent proviso that the Union Flag should predominate everywhere. There was invariably an angle to Rhodes' actions.) Around the Cape this initiative was broadly welcomed on both sides, but in the north it was met with spoiling tactics by the intractable and bigoted Kruger, who was miffed at being beaten to the punch by Rhodes in Mashonaland. He set out to apply the conditions of the Convention he had signed with Gladstone to the very letter. The Uitlanders, it will be remembered, of which Jack Griffiths was now one, had the right to work in the Transvaal subject to paying the same taxes as the Republic's own citizens. But they had no vote. Afrikaans was made the official language, in obvious retaliation for the compulsory use of English at the Cape. Eventually, in 1894 Kruger even closed the 'drifts' on the Vaal River, preventing the transport of supply wagons carrying produce from the Cape, on which he imposed heavy duties. And all the time the helpless unenfranchized Uitlanders were watching the Transvaalers grow rich, as they saw it on their taxes, building up armaments and constructing robust fortresses around the Johannesburg perimeter. And the only conceivable enemy that these defences could be intended to repel was Great Britain. Rhodes began to grow impatient.

Lobengula, too, continued to be difficult. Weak-willed as usual, his prevarications exasperated Rhodes. But in truth the King's basic problem was that he was still having difficulty in restraining his *impi,* who were thirsting to be let off the leash and beat off the white intruders. His Majesty had no objections, however, to his warriors killing Mashonas, which had the effect of this more peaceful offshoot of the Zulu nation looking to the British for protection and somewhat defeated his objective. At last the Matabeles' patience expired and a patrol of Bechuana-land Border Police was fired on near Macloutsi on 5 October 1893, which precipitated a ten-week war. Although the *impi* killed to the last man a patrol sent out to capture Lobengula at the battle of the Shangani River in central Matabeleland, the war was a virtual walkover for the whites and the King, now old and sick, was chased all over the countryside by Doctor Jim's police. While fleeing north, he died soon after Shangani of smallpox and starvation, and with the loss of their King, the Matabele gave up their struggle to oust the British intruders, at least for the time being. Another half a million square miles of Africa had been painted red, and by the end of January 1894 over 900 new farm rights had been granted in it, nearly 10,000 gold claims had been registered and over 100,000 cattle, the very livelihood of Matabele and Mashona alike, had been stolen by the white man.

Discontent among the Uitlanders continued to fester under President Kruger's turning of the vindictive screw. The stubborn, Scripture-quoting Kruger, or Oom Paul (Uncle Paul) as he was known to his loyal compatriots, was as tough as old boots. He cut an impressive figure in a frock coat and top hat, with his big pale face adorned with lamb-chop whiskers, wispy beard and wide-set little black eyes. He constantly spat, always carried a Bible and, when he got off a train, the crowds waiting on the plat-form to see him would have to wait for him to emerge until he finished the chapter he was reading in the Good Book. He had once famously amputated his own thumb with a knife after a shooting accident while hunting on the veldt, far from professional medical attention, and soused the stump in turpentine to arrest the gangrene. He had been a childhood *voortrekker* and now, sixty years later, he was still striving to extricate the people of his tiny republic of rough farmers from British interference.

That, in truth, was the sum total of Kruger's aims. But he had none of the subtlety of Rhodes. Even one of his own right-hand men, Doctor Leyds, once described his master as 'an ignorant, narrow-minded, pig-headed, irascible old Boer'. And his policy towards the Uitlanders has to be seen as a victory for asininity. They had been promised, back in 1881, 'the protection of the law, and all then privileges attendant thereon'. As we have seen, they had dutifully paid their taxes, but still had no vote. The Americans had gone to war 120 years before, boiling under the self-same grievance. Dutch was the only language allowed in schools and courts. Nepotism and corruption reigned, with monopolies and concessions for dynamite, coal and transport adding much expense not only to mining itself but to the general cost of living. Uitlanders were denied the right to trial by a properly constituted jury, and the maladministration of justice by minor officials caused much discontent. But rather than trying to convert them into useful citizens of the Transvaal, Kruger continued to deny them what might be called today basic human rights. Even President Brand of the Orange Free State had advised him, years before, to make friends with these miners, but he clung to his obstinate opinions, saying that "the goose that laid the golden egg should never be allowed to cackle". As far as Oom Paul was concerned these Uitlanders were the scum of the earth. They had foisted themselves on his country without showing the slightest loyalty towards it, and although they had enriched his treasury tenfold in as many years they had also enriched themselves. So why should they now clamour for representation in his *volksraad* (parliament)?

The Uitlanders' leaders formed themselves into a Reform Committee and organized a petition bearing thousands of signatures to be presented in Pretoria, hopefully to remedy their position, but it was treated with contempt. And a warrant had been issued for the arrest of F.W. Moneypenny, editor of the pro-Uitlander *Johannesburg Star*. It was clear that sooner or later the pot would boil over and there would be a revolt. And Rhodes, who had long since thought of himself as Queen Victoria's Attorney-in-Africa, was determined to foment matters and set out to make it happen sooner rather than later.

By forcing the issue of the Uitlanders' plight, he would naturally bring matters to a head between himself and Kruger. The Imperial Government would then have to intervene and make a settlement. That was the plan, the motives for which, said Rhodes, were to force Kruger to agree to free trade between all the South African states, from which would emerge "a customs union, railway amalgamation and, ultimately, federation". No doubt he then muttered under his breath, "and it will all be painted red". He had obtained a strip of land near the Bechuanaland border, ostensibly for the building of a railway, with the right to keep an armed force there, officially for the protection of the construction parties. Jameson, whose military prowess, at least in the eyes of Rhodes and himself, had been considerably enhanced by his hollow victory over Lobengula, was dispatched to take command of these 600 men, who were mostly from the Bechuanaland Border Police and the Mashonaland Mounted Police. They were led by some exuberant scatter-brained young Guards officers seconded for police work, whose fondness of champagne was to have disastrous effects.

Then, financed by Rhodes and his wealthy mine-owning friends, arms and ammunition began to be smuggled into Johannesburg hidden in Standard Oil drums or concealed under coal sacks in preparation for the uprising of the Uitlanders planned by the Reform Committee at secretive meetings at the Rand Club. The trigger for this revolt was to be an invasion of the Transvaal by Jameson's force, which would march on Johannesburg, 176 miles inside the border, by which tactic it would both surprise Kruger's commandos and split them at the same time. At last help seemed to be on the way for the distressed men, women and children of the Uitlanders. And to prove it, there was now a considerable stack of rifles and boxes of ammunition cached deep in the bowels of the mine at Robinson Deep, which was immediately next door to Crown Reef, where the youthful Jack Griffiths had first learned about stopes, gangues and jack-hammers.

By now, six years on, he had been promoted. He was now a twenty-four-year-old sub-manager at the Tharsis Gold Mining Company, a small concern at Paardekraal about four miles to the west, near to the very spot where the Australian scavenger George Harrison had first struck gold.

5

THE RAID

Pitsani, a small dusty outpost on the south-east Bechuanaland-Transvaal border comprising a handful of tin-roofed buildings, a single telegraph wire, some tents and a parade ground, was going to be one of the jumping-off points for the Raid. Mafeking was the other, twenty-five miles to the south. At Pitsani, on the sweltering Sunday afternoon of 29 December 1895, Jameson was pacing up and down outside his tent, deep in thought, kicking his boots in the sand. A clutch of coded telegrams had come in from Johannesburg, followed finally by the arrival of a special messenger in a state of some agitation. The Uitlanders' leaders wanted to call the whole thing off . . . you must not invade . . . the 'revolutionaries' had decided they were not in a position to revolt . . . in fact, they were dead against it . . . sorry, but they were not ready . . . it would be a fiasco. This, after all the preparation that had been done, and with his men now all keyed up for action, was galling. What an anti-climax. Jameson was both angry at this 'funking' and uncertain what to do next.

Finally he came to a decision. They were going in! If those damned fellows in Johannesburg would not rise up of their own accord, as had been agreed, he would have to force them to do it. And with his six hundred trusty troopers he would lick Kruger's commandos at the same time.

Bugles blew and the grey-suited troopers mounted up. It was very quiet as they waited to move off, with just an occasional snicker from a horse or a jingle of harness to break the silence while a hot wind off the Kalahari hummed in the single telegraph wire, the poles of which stretched away like stitches across the endless blanket of flat pale landscape.

Jameson stepped from his tent, clad in a fawn-coloured riding coat and a felt hat, and mounted a handsome black stallion. Clearly he was nervous, but all the same he managed a stirring announcement outlining the righteousness of their mission. Then, in the failing light, another bugle sound, three cheers for Queen Victoria, and the slouch-hatted column trotted off down the rutted track towards the border. Jameson had ordered them to travel light, but they had a cask of Cape brandy for the men and several cases of champagne for the officers carefully stacked in a mule cart. Six Maxims and three field guns rumbled along in a cloud of dust at the rear. Their brass-bound barrels, glinting in the moonlight, finally vanished into the gloom and they were gone.

That the Jameson Raid was doomed to be a charade as a military operation was clear from the outset. In the first place its timing had been postponed for no other reason than not to interfere with the racing calendar, and then, after a drunken weekend at Pitsani, there was much desertion. Thus the column was already depleted by several dozen before it even reached the Transvaal border. Jameson called a halt at Malmani (now Ottoshoop) to cut the telegraph wires, and therefore Kruger's lines of communication, it being imperative for them to reach as far as possible into the Transvaal before he had time to mobilize his commandos. It was said later that the troopers detailed to do the cutting (legend has it that they were members of G Troop under a Captain Gosling) were so drunk that they cut the wires of a fence instead, burying the ends carefully in the sand.

Oom Paul had built up an extensive secret service over the years. Indeed, it included in its spies several Uitlanders, and therefore double agents. But it was anything but secret, and became the butt of much ribaldry on the British side. The British, for their part, had adopted an almost puerile approach to the operation's security. Communications had been carried out under a melodramatic system of mysterious code words, reminiscent of some cloak-and-dagger yarn in the *Boy's Own Paper*. The plot itself had the code names 'the flotation' and 'the polo tournament', and one telegram between two of the Reform Committee's ringleaders read –'Have seen Saufinder, mitzdruse to schaffiger bleimass absolutely that Chairman hablohner on flotation no request or letter is hobelspane as anlegspan is ausgerodet as previously angelstern.'

Be these things as they may, the fact was that Kruger *did* know about the incursion onto his territory. And he was prepared for it.

Jameson had planned to be in Johannesburg in three days, but progress had been very slow. For one thing, the remounts provided at Malan's Farm had turned out to be coach horses which needed a rest every few hours before they could continue. Two Uitlanders arrived on bicycles out from Zeerust and, in a final attempt to avert disaster, urged him to turn back, saying that all was now well in Johannesburg and that Kruger had finally bowed to their demands. This was untrue. The simple fact was that the Uitlanders had decided that on balance they were doing very nicely as things stood, thank you, and that it would be better not to rock the boat. In any event, Jameson ignored them and pressed on relentlessly. Some would say recklessly. So recklessly, in fact, that he threw away, with brash pantomime light-heartedness, a trump card which two days later could have saved him from much ignominy. He released a hostage. And what a hostage! It was a Lieutenant Sarel Johannes Eloff, who was the grandson of President Kruger himself! Jameson's officers arrested him as they passed Boon's Store on New Year's Eve. He was released on the promise that he would remain in the store for two hours after the column had departed. Jameson, with a laugh, called back over his shoulder as he rode away, telling Eloff that his rifle would be returned to him in Pretoria.

The third day arrived and they were still several miles from their objective, when the first attack was made by the burghers. Here was a preview of the hit-and-run tactics which would be used with such great effect by the commandos in the Second Boer War, and caused so much pain to the most highly disciplined army in the world, of which calibre Jameson's column was decidedly not. Even the famous tight red square, so victorious for centuries around the globe, often against far superior odds, was at a loss when faced with a highly mobile and frequently invisible enemy. This had been proved at Majuba. Now the Transvaaler snipers, flitting from cover to cover, spent the day at target practice, harrying Jameson's tail-end and calmly picking off any slouch-hatted grey-suited stragglers who happened to appear in the sights of their Mausers.

They kept this up for two more days and nights, giving the troopers no time to sleep nor even eat, until at last they had them surrounded near a whitewashed farmstead, by a kopje called Doornkop, just half a dozen miles from Johannesburg.

The Raiders had spent the previous night pegged down in a swamp by the Boers' fire, with their carts and ambulance wagons drawn up in a circle, while they lay prone in the brown parched grass, firing blindly over their saddles into the dark nothingness.

Came the dawn and Jameson managed to get a message through to the men in Johannesburg, whose headgear wheels and great shining heaps of slag were clearly in view, forming a giant incongruous ulcer on the beautiful open countryside, with stark iron chimneys already pouring grey smoke into a clear African morning. Indeed, the very nearest ones were well within the range of a Lee-Metford rifle. They had had a couple of skirmishes (went the stiff-upper-lipped message) and were all fine, but they could do with a little help if it could be spared. Not a single volunteer came out to their rescue and the Boers continued to pick them off. By eight o'clock, now faced by the Staats Artillerie to boot, it was clear that the Raid was going nowhere and sixty-five troopers lay dead or wounded. A white flag appeared on the end of a rifle to flutter above the Raiders' position. It was not, as has been said, a white shirt torn from the back of a dead trooper, nor was it the borrowed pinafore of a young African servant girl. It was the apron of an old Hottentot *tanta*, or mammy, who happened to be at the kraal and was probably nonplussed by all the fuss going on around her.

The firing ceased and, as if by magic, the encircling burghers materialized, rising from the long silvery grass and from behind boulders and termite mounds. They advanced towards their exhausted and famished prisoners, with Mausers at the hip and watch-chains swinging from their waistcoat pockets. Some had come straight from New Year's celebrations and were still in their black Sunday best. They disarmed the Raiders and searched their baggage. In a tin box they found the telegrams received by Jameson at Pitsani. But they were, of course, in code. The code-book itself lay with a heap of empty champagne bottles.

The captured raiders were held overnight at the Old Magistrates Court at Krugersdorp. An eye-witness described the scene as they arrived: "On they went to the market square and there dismounted. Some of them fell asleep at once at their horses' feet. Jameson and his officers were ushered into the Courthouse on the edge of the square, where the defeated doctor made his way into a corner and sat down in a veritable stupor of despair. Baskets of food were brought in but Jameson would not eat and provisions were given to the troops in the square. General Cronje meanwhile was holding an inquiry in the courthouse."

By 3 January the raiders were all securely imprisoned, crammed thirty to a cell with their food brought in buckets, while a sorrowful Jameson was in the *tronk* (jail) at Pretoria. Many hundreds of miles away at the Cape, Cecil Rhodes had had a heart attack and resigned as Prime Minister. And 'Kaiser Bill', the German Emperor, had sent his famous telegram, fired off in a fit of pique after being kept waiting for meetings with Prime Minister Salisbury at Cowes Week on two consecutive days:

I express my sincere congratulations that, supported by your people without appealing for the help of friendly Powers, you have succeeded by your own energetic action against armed bands which invaded your country as disturbers of the peace and have thus been able to restore peace and safeguard the independence of the country against attacks from outside.

Salisbury apologized, but the Kaiser continued to carp long afterwards, bringing forth a growl from the Prime Minister to diplomat Baron Hermann von Eckardstein, "Your Kaiser seems to forget that I do not work for the King of Prussia, but for the Queen of England." A malignant ulcer had been created, which would continue to fester for nearly twenty years before it burst with a catastrophic explosion.

What was Oom Paul going to do with his guests? He decided that here was a golden opportunity to humiliate the British even further. With mocking magnanimity, he sent them back to Britain for trial. After three weeks penned in some wool sheds at Volksrust railway station, near the Natal border, they were taken down to Durban and shipped aboard the *Harlech Castle*.

But there was no such mercy for the leaders of the Reform Committee, who included Frank Rhodes, Cecil's brother, and Solly Joel. They were convicted of treason and sentenced to death. Solly lost no time while awaiting his fate. He and his uncle Barney Barnato presented Kruger with a magnificent pair of stone lions, which grace the President's residence to this day. The gesture was enough to mollify the stony-faced old Boer, who reduced the sentences to fines of £25,000 each.

Jack Griffiths was arrested too, although the reasons are unclear. His name did not appear in the list of Jameson's arrested officers and troopers, which a delighted Kruger was only too pleased to note was published in London. So what had he done to deserve it? Some people are known to have watched the final action from the headgear of the Durban Deep mine at Roodepoort. It is unlikely that they would have been Boers. And it is not difficult to imagine that one of them could have been Jack, armed with one of the Robinson Deep's Lee-Metfords, just in case, perched high on a clumsy edifice made of heavy baulks of timber and scaffolding, with a couple of bandoliers slung across his shoulders. He may even have taken the odd pot-shot at the fleeting glimpse of a brown waistcoat. Given the character that we know him to have been, it is more than likely that he had been one of the few Uitlanders who had remained in favour of the Raid, and was probably known to and was recognized by the Zarps, Kruger's policemen.

Whatever the facts surrounding Jack's arrest may have been, we do know that he was given twenty-four hours to leave the country, no doubt full of gratitude, yet again, to the power of the Joel gold sovereigns.

6

WITH HONEY'S SCOUTS IN MASHONALAND

The train hissed to a halt at the border station of Volksrust. Jack and the two black-macintoshed Zarps climbed out onto the platform and made their way to the ticket office, where they stood by, watching over his shoulder as he purchased a one-way ticket to Durban. They were going back to Jo'burg on the next train up, and were making doubly sure that he would be travelling in the opposite direction. At first he had been unsure of his destination. He had had a close shave after the Jameson Raid, it was true, but on the whole the eight years that he had spent in South Africa had been one hell of an adventure, with hardly a thought of England. So perhaps it was now time to go home with his skin intact.

Hardly a word was spoken as they stood side by side waiting for his train. When it arrived he heaved his bags into the guard's van and climbed into his seat. The train snorted off into the Laing's Nek tunnel, emerged with a shrill whistle at the other end through a billow of smoke and began to click-clack its way down the gradient, picking its way between the Natal kopjes. He sat looking pensively through the rain-striped window as the brooding mass of Majuba slid by on his right, looming black against the grey sky.

Newcastle, Ladysmith, where a crowd of leave-bound rowdy soldiers got on in the middle of a hailstorm, Colenso, Estcourt and Nottingham Road, where he had said good-bye to Percy Kimber seven years before, were all little tin-roofed places almost unheard of in the wider world. In four years' time they were to be world famous.

The Durban dockside was a hive of activity. A business-like squadron of armed men in slouch-hats, with their baggage, carts, crates of supplies and 140 horses, were on the wharf waiting to board a ship, the *Arab*, which was moving into the harbour.

Apparently there had been trouble in Mashonaland. As soon as Jameson's Rhodesian police had turned their backs to embark on their disastrous Raid, the Matabele had seized the opportunity to rebel and reclaim some of their land and cattle, without which they had endured considerable suffering. And now the Mashona had joined them in arms; just for once the two factions found themselves on the same side, their age-old enmity forgotten for the time being. If Rhodes were to keep the prize he had won for Queen Victoria, something serious had to be done. With his entire police force in prison, he had commissioned a Lieutenant-Colonel Alderson to recruit a force capable of putting down this rebellion. And this was that force, on its way up to Beira, then a tiny fever-ridden port-settlement in Portuguese East Africa, from where they would advance to Salisbury. Learning what was going on from one of the men, Jack quickly sought out Alderson. Thoughts of England were instantly put out of mind. There was more adventure in the offing! When the *Arab* backed away from the dockside and steamed out into the Bay of Natal Jack Griffiths was leaning on her rail, chatting with Alderson, as they watched Durban receding in the distance. It was a 600-mile, three-day steam to Beira. But before they had gone very far the Colonel's expert eye had summed up his new acquaintance very well. Alderson had gone ashore from the *Arab* in Durban to have lunch with the Chartered Company's agent and to collect mail. Two telegrams awaited him. One was from the chief staff officer in Bulawayo, directing him to assume supreme command of all armed men in Mashonaland on arriving in that country, the other from Judge Vincent in Salisbury, informing him that a Mr Honey and twelve volunteers would be joining him at Beira. Wilfred Honey, who had founded the Standard Bank in Salisbury, had raised a force of Scouts, a party of men especially assigned to probe ahead of the main column as it advanced through hostile country. Theirs would be a dangerous task and Alderson was confident that the young man he had just met would be a valuable asset to them. And so, as the *Arab* worked her way up the

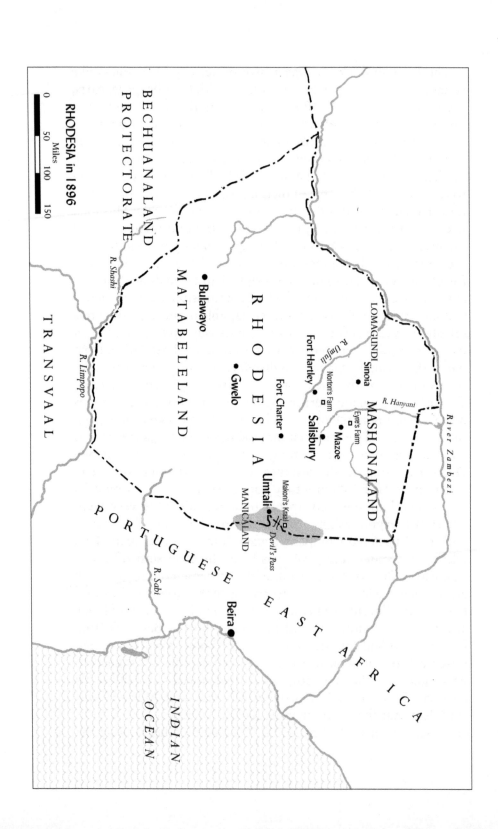

Miles
0
50
100
150

BECHUANALAND
PROTECTORATE

TRANSVAAL

R. Shashi

R. Limpopo

MATABELELAND

● Bulawayo

● Gwelo

R H O D E S I A

Fort Charter ●

Fort Hartley ●

LOMAGUNDI

Sinoia ●

R. Umfuli

Norton's Farm □

Salisbury ●

Eyre's Farm □

● Mazoe

MASHONALAND

R. Hanyani

River Zambezi

Makoni's Kraal □

Umtali ●

MANICALAND

Devil's Pass

PORTUGUESE

R. Sabi

Beira ●

E A S T

A F R I C A

INDIAN
OCEAN

coasts of Natal and Mozambique, it was agreed that Alderson would introduce Jack to a Lieutenant Wilfred Honey in Beira, who was in need of a fellow of his stamp. Once more, the ability to 'make friends and be good company' was standing Jack in good stead.

Honey, as the owner of a Salisbury bank, naturally had a vested interest in quelling the rebellion. He had several other men with him, all standing on the jetty waiting for the *Arab* to come alongside. Alderson and Jack joined them and they all trooped off to a private room at Honey's hotel to discuss the operation. It was agreed that the volunteers would be paid ten shillings a day, plus clothes and rations, and Jack was signed on as the sergeant of Honey's Scouts. Today they would be called commandos. The other signatories were Troopers N. Fielders, J. Ross, W. Simpson, W. Drubble, F. Todd, Sam Schuster, Price, Ayling, Nias, Urquhart, Renchen, Reeves, and an eager youth who appeared to be little more than a teenager, Philip Botha. Honey handed command to a Major Jenner, with Captain A.J. Godley as staff officer, Captain Roach as intelligence officer, and a medical officer with an appropriate but grisly name – Surgeon Captain Saw. It was 9 July 1896.

At that time, thanks to an Anglo-Portuguese Treaty of 1891, the Beira-Salisbury railway was under construction by a British firm headed by Sir George Pauling, to give Rhodesia access to a seaport. But only the first 100 miles had been completed, the railhead being at Chimoio in the eastern Manicaland uplands some way short of the Rhodesian border. The horses, many of which were only partially broken, were skittish, and it was some time before they were all entrained and on their way, chugging through the flat swampy bushlands around Beira. It was unhealthy country, ripe for malaria and blackwater fever, which were taking a heavy toll of life among the Europeans. It was said that a life was lost for every sleeper laid on that railway, mainly to fever, but there were other dangers too. Lion roamed freely in great numbers, having yet to be decimated by hunters. There is a story that a European fitter, sleeping with his boots on outside his tent, lost them both and part of his own heel to a hungry lion one night.

At Chimoio they were met by forty-five wagons drawn by

teams of fractious mules, for there were no oxen, the rinderpest having killed them all off. Here gangs of mud-splattered native labourers toiled in the winter rain with picks and shovels, levelling the new track and laying sleepers under the watchful eyes of British engineers and supervisors draped in green groundsheets. Others came behind them, bearing lengths of rail in great calipers, sixteen to a team. It was clearly a slow, laborious business. With his mining experience, it was all of great interest to Jack, and he took note of the technique. It would come in useful to him one day.

The 200-mile wagon track over the Manicaland highlands was fairly good. The heat was not excessive, it being winter, and although there had been some rain, the road, where there was a road at all, was not badly rutted. The order of travel, dictated by Alderson's Mashonaland Field Force Order No. 9, dated 27 July 1896, was most important if the column were to avoid any surprise attack. Honey's Scouts were to proceed generally from two to four miles ahead of the advanced guard of the main party under Alderson. They pressed on through the bush. Nothing much happened at first, except that they saw three lions one day. Neither side disturbed the other and the three beasts simply gazed disinterestedly at their party as it passed. At nightfall they drew their wagons into a diamond shape, tied the mules and horses to the dissel-booms and placed a Maxim and a 7-pounder at alternate corners.

Cautiously they crossed the border at Umtali, now called Mutare, but were met with immediate trouble from Chief Makoni, who was holding Devil's Pass with his *impi*. There was a short sharp engagement, which ended in Makoni's kraal being destroyed. Although the Scouts made the mistake of firing on some 'friendlies' at one point, it seems that no lasting harm was done because Alderson recorded that the first fight of the Mashonaland Field Force had ended very satisfactorily.

Uncharacteristically for him, Jack began to keep a diary, although it lasted for only three weeks. It was written in a small note-book, using a purple indelible pencil. The first entry was dated 29 September 1896, at Charter, now a small town fifty miles south of Harare. Then it was a tiny garrison composed of a mere twenty men.

Dear Mother, Nell and Annie, A wagon arrived here bringing mail from Bulawayo, on its way to Salisbury. I take advantage to write. We're laagered. No news. Waiting for the remaining part of our column before proceeding to Mashayamombe's. Frightfully monotonous. Reading when we can get books to read. They are still fighting and having rough times at Mazoe – losing some men. A private wagon belonging to a Beyenhout brought some things on speck. But what a price! Whisky £2 10s 0d a bottle. Cigarettes two shillings a packet.

On ten shillings a day he could not have afforded much whisky. But on the other hand a week's pay would have bought him, at that time, a 16,000-acre spread of good farmland, with so many settlers wanting to get out.

30 September 1896   A very enjoyable evening. Sat around the camp fire, took turns singing songs. I was persuaded to get up and sing, which they seemed to appreciate. There was a fight. I was referee. One man was knocked out. I've heard from all sides that Mashayamombe's is a very strong place indeed. And I am afraid that some of us will rest in peace there, or depart for pink clouds. I hope not.

1 October 1896   Another, but more private smoking concert was given over at the C laager to wish Captain Stricklin goodbye, he having resigned as O/C of the Charter. I thought the singing was rather poor.

Eventually Alderson's wagons turned up from Gwelo with the awaited supplies – fourteen days' rations and 200 rounds of ammunition for the big gun. By now he had amassed a force of 500 men. They moved out on 5 October, heading for the kraal of Mashayamombe, who was considered to be the ringleader of the Mashona Rebellion. This part of Africa, on either side of the Umfuli River, sixty miles from Salisbury, was dotted with great rocky kopjes – heaps of massive boulders, holed with many caves and recesses. The rest of the scenery consisted of tracts of forest and scrub. It was a perfect place for hide-and-seek.

Mashayamombe had been causing trouble all winter and had

already beaten off a patrol of the Natal Troop under Captain J.F. Taylor in June. An Indian storekeeper was murdered and two European prospectors were seized, bound hand and foot and thrown into the Umfuli. Whether they were dead or alive was never established. He had even besieged Captain the Hon C.J. White's patrol at Hartley Hill during July. Alderson planned a pincer movement. Honey's Scouts, under Major Jenner at Fort Charter, were to attack from the south, driving the rebels from their kraals towards Mashayamombe's, where the main force would be waiting for the kill.

The Mashona peoples' kraals were composed of wattle and daub huts. There were usually between twenty-five and a hundred of them to each community. In their gardens they grew sweet potatoes, mealies, kaffir-corn, pumpkins and monkey-nuts. Sometimes, if there were a *vlei*, or pan, nearby they would make it into a rice-bed. To add to their security, they would build stone walls between the outcrops of rock surrounding the kraal, turning it into an excellent refuge. In fact, it was a fortress.

> On the 6th we outspanned about six miles from Charter. 4pm on the Gazu River. Very forested. After off-saddling, Honey and self went for a bath and discovered a lovely deep place about 200 yards long. I jumped for joy and immediately undressed for a good swim. Swimming quietly along. A shout from Skeed, our guide. "For God's sake look out! Crocodiles!" I made for the bank as hard as I could and was just in time to escape the jaws of a rather small croc. Narrow escape. The rivers in these parts are full of them. Horses in at 6 pm. Dinner at 7. Army & Navy rations. Nice bread and tea.

Now the countryside was flatter, its even contours broken only by rocky kopjes, a favourite resting place for lion. It was spring-time and the ground cover was already taking on a parched brownness. Flat-topped acacia trees sprang from the red earth, stretching for mile after mile like a limitless park. Here and there an elephant or giraffe browsed among their thorny branches. And antelope in their hundreds stood grazing, always at a safe distance. This was the favourite hunting ground of the famous big game hunter Frank Courtenay Selous, who had led Rhodes' first Pioneer Expedition into Lobengula's land. Honey had been taken sick and it fell to Sergeant Jack to lead the Scouts.

7 October 1896   Soft ground and clumps of trees etc. We proceed to advance. On arriving at pools found 3 little holes. Two we used for horses . . . the other and best one was kept for drinking. This consisted of 25% mud, 15% reeds, and 60% water. Anyhow this had to do as it was quite dark and we could not go on to better water. So we had to quench our thirst with this, which also had to do for cooking, but we were all very thankful for it. Lights out at 8.30. Going to sleep. Good night all. Reveille 4.15 tomorrow'.

8 October 1896   The Scouts under myself left the laager ½ an hour before orders to find out way and whereabouts we were. The guide here was utterly useless. I sent back ½ section every mile to lead the column on. I came across the mule road and discovered by scouting the country that we were within 3 miles of the mine. Sent back and reported this and waited till the column came up. We then proceeded to the mine and laagered. The mine was completely deserted of course. Two men and a Cape boy being recently murdered here and their bodies thrown down the shaft of the mine. Four other men escaped. We saw the blood marks where the men had been murdered. Found plenty of jam, butter and a few other luxuries which the niggers had left. Came in very handy. The quartz here was very rich, showing visible gold. The troops were highly interested, each trying to obtain a specimen. We started ahead again to find our next water and distance. Found water and good grazing 5 miles from our last outspan. On the way to this water we had to ride hard at times to miss a very big grass fire raging across the country. Getting scorched and almost burned in some places. When I reached the water, I put a sentry ½ a mile ahead to keep a sharp lookout as we are only about 2 miles away from the place where the Natal troops on their previous visit here had to off-load their kit and dump their provisions to lighten their wagons so as to hasten their retreat.

On the night of 9 October Jenner made contact by exchanging red and white lamp flashes with Alderson and a joint attack was made the next day. Sections of the Salisbury Rifles, the Mounted Infantry and Native Contingents were sent in to clear Mashayamombe's protective kopjes. The kraals were torched.

Great flames leaped into the sky from the tinder-dry thatched huts as screaming men, women and children ran, terrified, into the caves. Then, wherever a cave could be located, it was blown up.

9 October 1896 Left laager 5.45.am. Proceeded about 8 miles, when Major Jenner, who was riding along with me leading the column, espied a kraal in the distance. Major Jenner, myself and other scouts immediately called in as they were flanking either side of me. Also a ½ section galloped around the kraal to gain an idea of the best place for an attack. We then advanced, Major J and self, rushing thru opening in a strong stone wall, but alas after this [illegible] we found the niggers had retreated to stronger place. Left here and proceeded at 2 pm. At 4.20 one of the ½ sections of scouts flanking on my right were fired on from the kopjes. Strongly fortified. We were all proceeding across an open space towards the kopjes, expecting to find niggers. Closed my men in immediately and dismounted them, leaving 3 holding the horses. All told we were about 50 men dismounted. We then chased up side of kopje fighting hard + a goodly [illegible] fire from the enemy. We drove them out and continued chasing them across very rocky country. Very woody and full of kopjes, killing a great number. Bullets whizzing all around us.

The whole of the men divided into three distinct sections. Lieutenant Eustace was shot thru ankle and one man amongst other narrow escapes receiving a bullet right through his helmet taking off the hair on his head. But we gave them very little chance of stopping to [illegible]. We then espied another kraal on a high kopje. We all advanced from different directions, pouring in deadly vollies [sic]. This we took, completely routing enemy, burning the kraal, about twenty-five big huts. Continued chore until dark, shooting & killing the whole time. This is the commencement of a range of country, nothing else but steep honeycomb kopjes and mountains full of caves. Mashaya-mombe's country. Dogs, fowls etc being burned alive in the huts. No time to set them free. We returned to our laager after sunset very tired and sopping wet with perspiration. Had grub.

About 7.30 we saw the signal rockets of the other part of the column which has come straight from Salisbury. By the rockets we should say they were about 10 miles off – about 300 men and horses. I am too tired to give a more descriptive account of over

3 hours' continual climbing rocky kopjes, fighting – hard work I assure you. A very [illegible] Sergeant Jack with bullets whizzing all around you- & they sound very peculiar. We start tomorrow at 6 am to advance and attack at the same time.

Orders by Major A.V. Jenner, DSO commanding column 10 October 1896:

Orderly officer Lt S.C.C. Tounsend.

Reveille 4.45 am.

Rifle Company + 7-pounder. Scouts + Maxim will parade at 6.30 am –

½ day's rations to be carried in the wallets. Greatcoats & waterproof sheet will not be carried.

By order, H.E. Vernon. Capt.

10 October 1896   With about 70 men left laager at 6 am, detailed to take kopjes each side of the drift & where the wagons had to go through & burning two kraals which had been deserted. We held the kopjes while the column passed through. It seemed as if we were entering a regular maze of kopjes and hills.

If they had been occupied by niggers it would have been a deadly place to have entered. Of course we, the scouts, were a good way ahead and on each side of us some 200 yds out were a section of men dismounted, walking and climbing along to see if there were any niggers. About 8.30 we came in contact with the Scouts of the main column under Colonel Alderson and some 20 minutes later met the whole column, about 400 men all told – 200 of his column were then engaged attacking Mashayamombe's principal kraal and caves. We laagered to give the horses and mules water and food. I could hear the firing of the attacking party who were some 600 yds away About one o'clock we heard a tremendous report and could see a great deal of smoke, dust etc. This turned out to be a big charge of dynamite they lowered into a cave in which the niggers had taken refuge. They were firing from it on the troops. As far as I can ascertain they blew the cave to blazes. If so, it must have killed a good number. The men then returned to their column, bringing 3 wounded men with them. We stayed where we first laagered for the whole day. I expect we shall get some more fighting tomorrow. Going to have a wash now. We have just caught two goats. The boys are killing them for dinner. A change from corned beef.

45

11 October 1896 We left laager at about 7.30 am after waiting about an hour for the Col. and his column. The scouts under myself leading Jenner's column down through the kopjes towards the drift or entrance as it were into Mashayamombe's country. The other columns riding up and scouting the kopjes and keeping in touch with us on the road. We reached the drift without anything happening, but could hear firing on the right side of the road. Here the Colonel joined us and some 200 troops & when they moved off in the direction of the firing, Major J. telling me to take 4 men and go with them, leaving the others with the guns on the drift. Waiting for orders after proceeding some ½ a mile down the river where all the kraals are situated. The Colonel sent a Mr Harding who knows the kraals very well, & my 4 men & myself ahead to find out the exact spot of fighting. Myself and two men were riding through a pass between the kopjes on all sides, when rounding a kopje on the riverside (with caves and kopjes facing us from the other side of the river) we were suddenly fired upon – one bullet nearly knocking Botha from his horse, but fortunately only grazed him. Ordered all to dismount, gave Harding our 3 horses and gave order to return fire into the kopjes, picking out holes of caves, Harding in meantime retiring with horses and we doing the same thing, but firing away the whole time until we got under cover and returned to the Colonel's column. We then marched on and attacked Mashayamombe's kraal. Here, we had a very hot time of it, a strong fire being returned. Fighting until 4 pm when we returned to our laager. Several men were hit this day, one white man being shot dead. Trapped by a calf tied up at the bottom of a kopje. He, thinking it was loose, went up to drive it away. By doing this, the enemy drew him under the opening of one of their caves. As soon as he arrived where the calf was, he received a bullet right through the chest.

12 October 1896 This was a day of hard fighting. Marching from laager at 7.30 we no sooner arrived within 300 yards of the same kopje when a heavy fire was opened on us. The column took up position the same as yesterday with the men on a kopje facing the enemy, the river running in between. Captain McMahon with the Irish column attacked on the right face, got down into the open. Here the fire was so strong that he and his men had to take cover behind some small rocks dotting up here and there out of the ground. For five hours he could neither advance nor retreat. As soon as any of the men showed themselves to the enemy, they were either killed or seriously wounded, one man receiving a bullet right through his helmet. The men brought the Maxim and 2 seven-pounders into action, pouring in a continuous fire. The Irish column were enabled to get up to our kopje and assist with keeping up the fire from there. After this, Major Jenner & his men & scouts under myself were ordered to work around by the left face & attack the rear of the enemy's position. This was rather a dangerous task. We managed to cross the river when on the other side we discovered we should have to gallop between two of the enemy's kopjes, about ¼ mile in order to get to the back. So when we were all ready we spurred and galloped through under a pretty strong fire. 3 of the horses were shot dead but no men hit. We then got to the rear & Major J & myself and one scout & the adjutant started creeping up under cover to see position of enemy. This took a good hour. Suddenly a fire was opened on us. Time to beat a retreat. Major J ordered us to dismount and put the horses into a safe position & sent word to Colonel that no chance of attacking kopje unless losing several men. Colonel sent order to attack, burn kraal and retire. We all extended a skirmishing order and the Col on his side opened a heavy fire & finished up with 3 seven-pounder shots. This was the signal for our attack to commence. Major J called out "Advance my boys!" Double time emerged out of thicket of cover and as hard as possible across the open – some 300 yards to clear. Here, unfortunately, hidden by some thick bush, was a small but steep kopje to our right, from where a strong and steady fire was opened upon us. Before we reached the kopje what we were making for & from what also a steady fire was pouring on us. It took us some 3 minutes to gain the other side and during this time 3 men were hit & one poor little fox terrier who was with us was shot right through the shoulder & dropped dead in front of me. Poor little thing, he died like a soldier, anyhow. Previous to the charge, Major J said to me, "Griffiths, I want you to keep with me." (Here I may state that, so I am told, he has formed a very high opinion of me.) When we arrived at the bottom of the kopje, which was very steep, we took cover under some rocks to get wind, Major J. telling me to keep up a steady fire with my men on the kopje to the right, from where we got the surprise from. While doing this, pouring in independent fire, young Botha, one of my men who was next to me, touching me in fact, received an explosive bullet in his forehead, almost taking the top of his head off. The poor youngster, only

19 years old, dropped dead, past all assistance or aid. It was a terrible sight to see him lying dead. One of our best Scouts, always willing, plucky & I never had to tell him twice to do a thing. God help any Mashonas if I could have had any within reach of my hand then. When we saw he was quite dead I left him there for the time being and Major J & myself & scouts led the soldiers up the kopje, forced our way into the kraal losing two more men & wounding several. After searching some men all done in a few seconds, we pretended to retire when several niggers jumped out of the caves to take aim at our supposed retreat, were promptly bowled over by our men, one nigger getting 7 bullets in him. Good luck to the black devil. We then set light to the huts and obeyed the Col's orders to retire.

Over this attack I must remark that it was surprising to see that more of our men were not killed. The fire was simply terrible from the enemy and it's the day I shall never forget till my dying day. Each man during that attack, I am sure, felt he was near his death. Thank God not more were shot & thank God I was saved. Myself and 3 others carried poor Botha back until we met the ambulance corps. At 6 o'clock we buried him. Honey had been well enough to read the burial service. Then we made a rough cross & put it upon his grave.

When we were charging up the kopje, some 20 or 30 niggers charged down on the right, this coming under the notice of the Colonel & were promptly mown down by the Maxim. I am too tired to write more tonight and am also upset over poor Botha. It was only a few days ago that he recvd a telegram of his sister's death and this is the 2nd son who has been shot in this country & his father is dangerously ill in the Salisbury hospital.

13, 14 and 15 October 1896   . . . seeking fresh [illegible], bad for horses. Very bad coats & very scarce & frightfully hot.

16 October 1896   Continued trekking. Sent Steven & ½ a troop detail for special duty with myself and 5 other men to follow up a kaffir footprint which was seen. After riding across country for some distance we came upon a sch . . . [illegible] lately occupied by niggers. Myself and F . . . went up the hill and burned same and returned to the others. Came to a good size spruit where we saw lion spoor but couldn't find lions. Continued some 2 miles alongside of water and came across another temporary kraal with 13 huts. My men burnt them and we then made in the direction

48

of where the laager was supposed to be made. Found them after hours of riding. Had grub my boy cooked, a good sleep, then went down for a bath.

17 October 1896 Continued trekking. After going some 8 miles we came up to the Hunyani River. On the march, one of the Scouts belonging to Col. Alderson's column was fetched up on a stretcher & put in ambulance wagon having had a fall off his horse while chasing two niggers which he saw whilst out scouting, he having fallen with his chest on a stone. Nothing serious. We laagered by the river which is big and very pretty. Off-saddled, had scoff. Then 2 hours sleep. Went for a swim. Previous to anyone swimming, the river where the bathing was to take place was dynamited, a charge being thrown in. The surface of the water was covered with dead fish. We all then plunged in, bringing fish to the bank. Splendid eating & quite a treat. Enjoyed my dinner so much. We fried them in a pan. The particulars of Norton's murder by kaffirs is very terrible to hear. One of the other columns relayed me the facts.

18 October 1896 Both the Colonel's and our laager moved off today at 6 am. The Colonel's column continuing towards Reform where Eyre was murdered some 20 or 30 miles off. 4 sections of scouts under myself also 30 of native contingent left laager at 6 am to patrol the Hunyani River to look for kraals. About 3 miles down river we came to Selous' old camping ground, the river here being very pretty indeed and very wide, reminding me in some parts of me dear old [Thames?]. Here we are into lovely country, very flat indeed but very wooded and full of all kinds of game. Small and big buck, great buffalo etc etc. We the Scouts went ahead. I dodged off myself into the thicket & had some good shooting, killing amongst others a splendid Cessily buck. I was so interested in chasing the game that when I came to look about me, I hardly knew in which direction to go, for nothing to guide me, high trees all around. I should like to spend a month here shooting. No wonder Selous chose this spot. We off-saddled by the river about 10.45 am after riding since six. Turned horses loose, knee-haltered to graze and had our grub. I took my 'billy' off saddle and cooked some tea of which Major J and others partook as well & pitched into the Corned Beef and Bread. After an hour's rest saddled up and proceeded on our way home. Came across a section of Colonel Alderson's column who had lost themselves while out flanking. Their officer declared, "Thank God we have met you." He also said he had lost two of his men in the bush. Their horses were all done up after galloping about all day. We then fired the 7-pounder twice as a signal for the other two, which was heard by them. They found our laager almost at sundown. It is a terrible thing to be lost in the veldt. Many have been lost and died dreadful deaths. We saw no niggers whatever during the day, nor any signs of them. Had soup, fried fish for dinner, rice, treacle, off to sleep very tired. So is my horse who is rather footsore after chasing buck over stony ground.

19–24 October These six days we have been trekking, going through lovely country full of all sorts of game. One day shooting an ostrich. Having good sport. Yesterday I shot a porcupine. On 21 October we laagered at Eyre's Farm, awaiting the Natal troop with provisions from Salisbury. Mr Eyre, the owner of the farm, is acting as our guide. He is a very nice man indeed. I knew him in the early days in Johannesburg. His brother was murdered on the farm by the Mashonas while he was away. He has been trying to find the body, but cannot do so, only seeing the blood stains. I expect the Mashona have taken the body away. The Colonel's column went out to some kraals some 7 or 9 miles away, the niggers who are supposed to have murdered Arthur Eyre. We (Honey's column) were left in to have a rest this time having done most of the fighting hitherto. So, not going, I cannot say really what happened.

They found that all the niggers from these kraals had gone into a cave, with only two small openings. While trying to get at them Captain Furnancou, of Salisbury Volunteers, was shot in the leg. They put 5 charges of dynamite into the two entrances & completely, it seems, entombed them. I hope so. Returning to the laager about 4 o'clock bringing this Furnancou with them, who I am sorry to say died shortly afterwards from loss of blood. His death cast quite a gloom as he was a very popular officer indeed. The following morning his funeral took place. The Salisbury Volunteers made the firing party over his grave, all the buglers blowing during the process. Yesterday the Natal troop arrived with the provisions, having had a quiet trip & unmolested, not seeing any signs of niggers whatever. I went over to see the Colonel previous to his departure for Salisbury, to meet Rhodes who is expected there. He was very well . . . & was of great service to Major Jenner, who had spoken highly of me. He said if I

50

wanted to join a new police force he would recommend me for a commission. I of course thanked him and said I would join if I did get a commission. Otherwise, I would like to remain with the troops while in the country.

This morning we left at 6 am for the Mazoe district. We trekked on till about 10 am when we laagered at a place I found for the column. This generally is my duty, going ahead and finding a good place with water, good grazing etc. It is sometimes a difficult job to find both of these. We have no grain whatever for the horses. Poor devils have to live on grass, so we cannot do long treks owing to this. Also the mules wouldn't stand it. Our new [illegible] Highfield seems a good sort, an Inniskilling Dragoon. I hope we shall come across niggers soon.

25 October 1896   Wrote to Mother & Arthur yesterday & sent into Salisbury with the Colonel's column.

Mashayamombe knew the countryside like the back of his hand, of course. He had many strongholds along the banks of the Umfuli and began to flit from one to the other, frustrating Alderson's attempts to corner him. In the end the Mashonaland Field Force withdrew and proceeded on its way.

Alderson came under much criticism for his failure to nail Mashayamombe, whose morale was boosted no end by his success in holding out. When the rains came he returned to his kraal with those of his people who had survived Alderson's dynamite in their caves to rebuild their huts and replant their mealies and pumpkins.

It was decided to establish a fort close to the kraal so as to keep a close eye on the wily old Chief. It would eventually be manned by Rhodes' British South Africa Police and was called Fort Martin, after Sir Richard Martin, the Commandant-General and Imperial Deputy Commissioner. A steep-sided kopje about a mile from the kraal was selected. It had enough space on its flat top for some tents and wattle and daub buildings, and a seven-pounder gun was mounted on its highest point, permanently trained on Mashayamombe's kraal. It was fired from time to time to remind the tribesmen of its presence, and in return came sporadic rifle shots from the kraal.

Captain R.C. Nesbitt, VC, of the BSAP, was very impressed

with Fort Martin when he took over on 20 February 1897. "It is very healthy," he wrote, "being splendidly situated, very high . . . it is impregnable and the best possible place." Jack, too, was full of praise for it, even to the point of making a sketch of it. (The original can be seen in the Harare National Archives.)

Jack could not have received a more powerful recommendation for a commission in the British South Africa Police than that of Cecil Rhodes himself. And in March 1897 Lieutenant John Griffiths was second-in-command under Nesbitt at Fort Martin when it was attacked by several hundred Mashonas and three of the garrison were killed.

Mashayamombe was known to be still brimming with confidence after his success in evading Alderson, and his strutting behaviour was considered to be an ongoing threat. He could not be allowed to relax and his crops were frequently raided by patrols from the Fort. His people were hungry and so he offered surrender terms, but they were rejected. Angrily, he turned to the offensive and at dawn on 17 March 1897 he attacked the Fort with 400 men. It took three hours of stiff fighting, during which three African policemen were killed before the attack was repelled and the tribesmen returned to their kraal.

At the end of July 1897 a strong force paraded in Cecil Square, Salisbury and marched out against the rebel chief. Once again there was to be a pincer attack, with the 7th Hussars moving up from the south. Jack, now the Sub-Inspector in command at Fort Hartley, received orders from Nesbitt:

Confidential.   Fort Martin,
                                            Thursday, 22 July 1897.
Sub-Insptr Griffiths
Commdg Fort Hartley.

The Salisbury column is to arrive at the Zomba [?] drift, about six miles from Hartley, on the evening of the 22 inst. (today).

The attack on Mashingombi [sic] is to be made on the morning of the 24 inst. at daylight. You will leave a guard of six effective men (Europeans) and four of the native contingent at Fort Hartley, & proceed yourself with the rest of the men and native contingent on the morning of the 23 inst. (Friday) bringing all horses which are fit. Mr Peel is to accompany you, bring wagons

52

with more blankets, mealies, etc. leave 3,000 rounds of ammunition (rifle) and 8,000 (maxim) at Fort Hartley and bring the remainder, also field stretchers if there are any, bring four days rations with you, you must start without fail early on the morning of the 23 inst so as to arrive here on the evening of the same date. When approaching this Fort (before arriving out of the bush) take your mounted and most of dismounted men around by the way of where we get water & come up through bush, so as to prevent if possible the Natives noticing the arrival of reinforcements.

R C Nesbitt. Captain.

At dawn on the 24 July the attack was launched on the unsuspecting tribesmen. Once again the defenders retreated into their caves, leaving their goat's meat and mealies still cooking in big pots over the fires in their kraals. The two sides exchanged fire all day long. Night fell, but the sentries posted all around had a restless time, being constantly fired on. At daybreak a concerted break-out was made from the caves. A number of rebels were shot. Among them was Mashayamombe.

At that point Jack had accumulated two medals and been Mentioned in Despatches several times. But life does not appear to have been the proverbial bed of roses, even after the death of Mashayamombe.

7

ANOTHER CROSSROADS

Lomagundi was in the heart of a wild and lonely district, one of the most disaffected areas, when Jack was sent to establish a permanent station there. It was another fever-stricken spot, and life was one of deadly monotony for him and his thirty N.C.Os and men. Supplies and mail could only be obtained at intervals from Salisbury, about ninety miles away, and sometimes during the rainy season it could mean a three-week wait before a supply wagon could get across the Hunyani. It was difficult to keep the men cheerful and healthy, but Jack, with his characteristic energy, set them to work building smart and comfortable huts and recreation rooms out of poles, thatch and clay, and laying out a flower and vegetable garden. In a few months he had by far the most attractive camp in Rhodesia. Nearby were the celebrated limestone caverns of Sinoia, with their underground lakes of an intensely blue colour – like Capri. He loved to explore these. The camp became a showplace and people would travel out from Salisbury to admire it and be given guided tours around it by Captain Griffiths.

In early December 1897, Jack received a personal letter of praise from his then commanding officer, Colonel the Hon F. Eveleigh de Moleyns. We do not know the details of the incident to which it refers, but it is evident that the Colonel thinks highly of him. Apparently, Jack has completed a successful patrol into the bush and has taken prisoner several tribesmen. But the air has still not yet been cleared of the scent of rebellion, and the Colonel is concerned that Jack has sufficient troops to carry out his immediate tasks.

6 December 1897.
Dear Griffiths, I congratulate you on the excellent work you have done – and done quietly which I gather from your report with little or no shooting – nothing could be more satisfactory. I am very glad to hear the patrol had no fever, that is what I was afraid of.

You say nothing about an escort for your prisoners in your second report which I got this morning – as I suppose you still want it, am sending out 20 Black Watch to you this afternoon unless in the meantime Eastwood who is back at Mazoe tells me that you don't want it.

Very truly yours, F de Moleyns.
P.S. The 20 Black Watch will take rations for the trip out and home.

On the same day, 6 December 1897, a letter of recommendation from James Robertson, Acting Under Secretary at Salisbury, led to Jack's appointment as Justice of the Peace for Mashonaland, to take effect as from 23 February 1898. He was now charged with enforcment of all 'Laws Ordinances and Proclamations for the preservation of the Public Peace . . . for the quiet rule and government of the people of Mashonaland . . . and to chastise and punish all persons that offend against those Laws; and to cause to come before you all those who, to any one or more of our People, concerning their Bodies or the firing of their houses, have used threats to find sufficient security for the peace of their good Behaviour towards our Sovereign Lady the Queen and her People . . . to apprehend or cause to be apprehended all persons committing any crime, or Rioting, Brawling or otherwise disturbing the Public Peace . . . and detaining in Prison all Felons, Rioters, Vagrants and offenders of what kind and nature whatsoever, according to the Law.'

Here we are approaching another crossroads in Jack's life. He is an officer on active service commanding a station of the British South Africa Police and he is a Justice of the Peace. On top of all of which he has somehow found the time to register a gold claim in Rhodesia. Now he has received a communication from Acting Commandant Gosling.

5 July 1898 – Salisbury. To O/C Lo Magundi.
Find out at once quietly and send in special runners as soon as possible, whether the native contingent at your station would be prepared to mobilise here and be marched under their own officers to Uganda, Central Africa, for active service. It is possible that the Government would give a bonus of £5 at the end of the rising of course men would be sent back to their homes after-wards, free. A suitable kit will be provided. Your answer is expected in three days time from the 6 inst and you must treat the whole matter as entirely confidential. It is a broad question that requires delicate handling and I rely on your doing your best with secrecy and success. This is not to be taken as an order to move boys until further orders. A Gosling. Actg. Comdt.

Evidently, although there was trouble brewing farther north in Uganda, it does not appear that Jack or any of his men went there. He had a lot on his plate at the time and was probably pondering on what to do next in the furtherance of his career, such as it was. There was still the unfinished business of making his fortune, which he had been forced to abandon following the Jameson Raid, and the likelihood is that he was planning to return to gold-mining – hence the Rhodesian claim that he had registered. But then things were taken out of his hands by Fate, which dictated what his next move would be, overruling any decision to which he may have come. A telegram arrived from England:

Father passed away. Hurry home. Mother distraught. Nelly.

Jack had not been home for eleven years and he had little idea why he should suddenly find himself to be in such a frantic hurry to get there now. His hot-tempered disciplinarian father now lay dead in his grave many thousands of miles away. They had never been close, in fact they had been quite distant despite the old man's half-hearted attempts to patch things up after Jack had joined the army. There was nothing more that could be done about that. But clearly his mother and sisters felt that they needed his presence to console them in their grief. And so he hurried.

8

A DECISIVE ENCOUNTER
IN ZANZIBAR

He threw some things into a couple of bags, jumped on a horse and galloped off into the bush towards the railhead at Umtali. (We must assume that he paused in Salisbury to take leave of his various superiors.) It would be another two months yet before Locomotive No.1 'Cecil J Rhodes', hauling two tenders piled high with logs for its boiler, would snort into Salisbury bearing a placard on its giant headlamp proclaiming "Now we shan't be long to Cairo", to complete the link from Rhodesia to the Indian Ocean. And Umtali was 200 miles away – several days' ride for a lone man on a horse. But years of patrolling this wild country had left Jack in little fear of it and he knew how to conduct himself safely through it. He may even have been able to hitch a ride for part of the way on one of the Hollywood-style stage-coaches which still ran until 1899, swaying sickeningly on great leather suspension straps, hauled by a team of six sweating horses, all driven by a man holding two fists full of reins, who, it was said, could flick a fly from one of their ears with his whip.

The last time Jack had seen Umtali it had been nothing but a collection of thatched huts with a footpath running down the middle and a 'hotel' which consisted of a single-roomed window-less wattle and daub shed with a thatched roof. But now it was a railhead, thanks to the expertise, blood and sweat of Sir George Pauling's construction crews and had assumed the natural importance of such a place. The footpath had grown into a wide main street, with half a dozen street-lights fuelled by paraffin. It now boasted a couple of stores with the proprietors' names proudly sign-written outside, and a telegraph wire. It even had its very own tramway, running the length of the main street, and of course a station.

Jack bought his ticket, settled down on the hard wooden seat in the long narrow carriage and the train steamed off in a shower of smoke and sparks, down into the marshlands of Mozambique. There were several delays en route, one where the heavy rains had caused a bad 'wash out', causing the line's bed to disappear, leaving the rails in mid-air. That necessitated a wait of forty-eight hours before repairs were complete. Elephant and buffalo wandering on the line caused other minor hold-ups. Consequently, on arriving at Beira, he found the ship that he had intended to board had already sailed. Therefore he caught a tramp steamer up to Zanzibar, that being the next nearest port in south–east Africa where he might find a fast voyage home.

Gwladys Wood was twenty-six. She had taken a break from her promising career as a singer in London (coached by Otto Goldschmidt - the husband of the legendary Jenny Lind) to visit her brother Guy, an accountant in Johannesburg, accompanied by her mother. She was semi-engaged to a Mr White, although she felt no love for him, which was beginning to depress her. And her Victorian mother's insistence that she would never find a better catch at twenty-six years old did not add to her peace of mind. Now they were on their way home aboard the SS *Kanzler*, which was due to stop over for three days at Zanzibar.

We must let her tell in her own words what happened to her there. In doing so, we take a pause from our story of the wild events, the blood, the violence and the danger which constituted the life of a male colonial Victorian to look at three crucial days in the life of a genteel Victorian young lady through her own eyes. Her romanticism may make for an incongruous tint on the palette of our story, but it will speak reams about the character that was John Norton Griffiths, her 'beautiful wild Welshman who was to dazzle her for the next thirty years with his stormy green eyes'. No one came to know him better than Gwladys.

I was glad of the break in our journey back to the harsh reality of life in London. Whether to pursue my career as a singer or marry a man I didn't love. I was 26, an impossible choice.

This quaint old Arab town from where Livingstone, fifty years ago, set off into the dark interior of Africa, allowed me to live my illusion a while longer. We were staying with a friend of my brother's who had a house in the centre of town. He sent a man to meet us off the ship. The man, who wore a long white gown and a fez, and looked half African and half Arab, led us through streets so narrow that two donkeys could barely pass each other. My nose wrinkled at the smells emanating from open drains. At ten o'clock in the morning it was already quite hot. Donkeys roamed freely and fed on garbage piled in any open space. Women swathed from head to toe in black, glided silently past, a parcel or a jar of water on their heads. A stream of porters carrying our luggage, one piece apiece on their heads, brought up the rear. We made quite a procession. After ten minutes we came to a massive brass-studded wooden door set in a blank wall. I looked up. No windows overlooked the street. The house, if this was a house, looked ill kept, the wall pock-marked. A sleepy-looking donkey was tied to a ring in the wall.

The major-domo, if that is what he was, banged three times on the door with his stick. A small window in the door slid aside and a dark face peered at us from behind a grille. The doors immediately swung open and we entered a cool paradise. Rooms led off a central courtyard whose stone floors were still damp from a recent washing. Green plants and sweet-smelling jasmine spilled from huge earthenware pots. The slim white trunk of a paw-paw tree rose up by a coral-stone wall like a beanstalk searching the blue sky far above. Red and orange bougainvillea spilled over the top to cascade down the wall. On each floor, a gallery overlooked the central courtyard. At the top of the house a flat roof was laid out with comfortable cane chairs, where we sat in the evening cool.

Our host bent over my mother's hand. He turned to me with a broad smile: "Welcome to my humble abode. You must be tired from your journey."

A servant offered us tall glasses of cool mango juice from a tray. I gulped mine, thirsty from the long hot walk. Then we were shown to our rooms.

The window of my room overlooked the courtyard. It had a stone seat on which I sat. I folded my arms on the pretty carved wooden balustrade and stared into the courtyard below. I was still feeling depressed about the choice I felt unable to make. Mr White had followed us from Johannesburg, boring me with his insistence. Mama approved. "He has a promising career. Good family. A friend of your brother's. You'll never do better than that in London. You're too old." I sighed. Her approval somehow made him seem even less interesting.

Suddenly there was a commotion downstairs. I heard the front door swing open, slam shut. Footsteps. Voices. A deep male voice I hadn't heard before. I tensed on my stone seat, leaned a little further out over the yard.

A tall slim man strode into the courtyard. He carried a mongoose on his shoulder and a parakeet on his finger. He was of course in whites with an open shirt and panama hat and was the handsomest man I had ever seen. I fell in love with him at that moment. He always said that when I sang to him that evening on the flat roof at the top of the house, he said to himself, "That's the only girl I'll ever marry." So you see, the damage was done quickly. That was 22 March 1899.

We had three wonderful days in Zanzibar while he moved heaven and earth to get a passage on the *Kanzler*. I learned he was coming home after eleven years in Africa, fighting in wars and prospecting for gold.

Somehow, he had met Mr White, who told him he had two ladies to look after on the voyage and would he look after the old lady while he looked after the young one! We had rather a painful evening where we handed each others' letters back and Mr White left the ship leaving his berth to my future husband. We sailed on 25 March. He was the most attractive creature you can imagine, the wildest spirits and the wildest ideas of what projects he was going to do in Rhodesia and full of the most priceless stories of his adventures.

We reached Aden on 31 March and landed to drive out and see the tanks by moonlight. The road wound round and round to the top of a hill where huge water tanks stood under palm trees, and the twinkling lights of the town were spread out below. It was the most romantic spot I could imagine. He and I went together by carriage, and came back early in the morning of 1 April, an ecstatically happy couple ready to face anything provided we did it together. I said nothing to Mother that night, but he faced her in the morning. She told him we were both mad but she could not help relenting. She was so fond of him and he handled her so wonderfully. From that day, he changed from a purely happy-go-lucky individual to a man with a purpose. We planned to live in Rhodesia which of course was agony to Mother.

But again Fate was to insist that it had other plans.

9

BACK TO AFRICA

For all their happiness together, the next two years were agony for Jack and Gwladys. For one thing Jack had no money to speak of, but he did have his Rhodesian gold-mine claim and he knew that the gold was there to be had. He formed the Rhodesian Mining & Development Company, with himself as Managing Director, and persuaded Sir Sydney Shippard, of the Chartered Company, to be its Chairman, hoping that some financial backing would be forthcoming from that direction for its development.

"You will make a very bad poor man's wife and I will make a very bad poor woman's husband," he told Gwladys. "We will have to wait to be married. But don't worry. I am determined to make a success of my company. The gold is there. All I have to do is to find someone to finance me."

Their heady days up the Red Sea and through the Mediterranean came to an end when the *Kanzler* docked at Naples, where Gwladys' Uncle Charlie had come down to meet them. He took one look at his nephew-in-law-to-be and his face fell. Jack's luggage, hurriedly thrown together at Lomagundi, was all tied up with string, and his biggest bag burst open at Customs, pouring forth the most amazing collection of junk! It was not an auspicious start to his integration with the Woods.

But he continued to dazzle Gwladys with his wonderful ideas of what life would be like for them. "My friend will lend me horses to ride, and you my darling will appear in the Row, driven in a pony and trap and I will ride beside you in a Buffalo Bill hat." Reality was very different. He still hankered after the freedom of life colonial style, and his mother, Gwladys decided, was a most difficult person who was nothing but a trial to her son. To make matters worse, her own family were all praying that the couple would soon tire of one another. But they prayed in vain.

Jack was becoming perturbed about the future. He simply had to get his hands on that gold which he knew lay 5,000 miles away. Cecil Rhodes had given him a letter of introduction to the directors of the Chartered Company, which governed Rhodesia, and in mid-1899 Jack went back there. No financial backing had been forthcoming either from Sir Sydney Shippard or from the Duke of Abercorn, the figurehead chairman of the Chartered Company. He would have to 'go it alone'. Gwladys was in despair as she longed to go with him, but he would have to live rough, 'up country', while he developed his claims. It would be no life for a woman. And so Gwladys was left behind to wait, no doubt discomfited by the "We told you so" and "Thank God for that" remarks of her family.

"I still wonder how he stuck to his guns," she wrote many years later, "but his character had deepened so much with the promises he had made to me that nothing would deter him from his purpose."

In southern Africa the relationship between the British and the Boers had festered for years, but now matters were coming to a head. The murder by the Zarps of an Uitlander boilermaker, Tom Edgar, had heightened the tension dramatically. Edgar, who stood six and a half feet tall, was an inoffensive hard-working sort of character according to those who knew him. He had been out for a drink with his mates and was returning home at about midnight to his tin-roofed bungalow in a little alley near the Salisbury Mine when he heard a voice say, "Voetsak", which is a very insulting expression in Afrikaans. It was one of his neighbours, a man named Foster, who in fact had been rebuking his dog for relieving itself against the wall of his house. Without bandying words, Edgar clenched his fists and beat him to the ground, whereupon another neighbour, thinking the man was dead, shouted "Police! Police!"

Edgar went indoors and sat on his bed, waiting for the Zarps to arrive. There was a loud rattle at the door, but before Bessie Edgar could open it, it burst open and four large policemen entered. Without making any attempt at an arrest, one drew his revolver and shot Edgar at point-blank range. The policeman, who bore the unlikely name of Jones, was charged with murder, which was later reduced to manslaughter, and, when eventually tried in Johannesburg, was acquitted. The Uitlanders were in uproar. It may have been a relatively minor incident on the wider scale of events, but every snowdrift starts with the first flake.

Throughout the South African winter of 1899 there were loud street demonstrations by the Uitlanders, petitions to Queen Victoria for help and political sparring between Kruger and Sir Alfred Milner, the High Commissioner for South Africa involving veiled threats and counter-threats from both sides, with Kruger objecting vociferously to the build-up of British troops at the Cape and in Natal. It was almost certain, now, that there would be war between the two stubborn sides – one a small republic with a complex and the other a huge Empire with a face to save.

On 25 September a Boer spy in Ladysmith, in northern Natal, reported to Pretoria that the British had moved up large numbers of troops nearer to the border with Transvaal. That seems to have been the needle that finally spurred Kruger into positive action. On 28 September he mobilized his commandos – wagon after wagon and train after long ponderous train arrived at Sandspruit and Volksrust (where Jack had taken his leave of his Zarp escorts three and a half years before) crammed with men and boys with Mausers slung over their waistcoated suits, to set up camp on the Boer side of the border. To the British military mind, they had a strange appearance. Leo Amery of *The Times* hurried to Sandspruit from Pretoria. He reported, "There are no straight lines in the Boer army. For miles the sandy plain was dotted with ponies and oxen and covered wagons; all the paraphernalia of the Great Trek. At night the camp-fires glowed like the lights of a city, and bearded old men sat round the fires singing Dutch psalms with their wives and children."

Kruger now delivered his famous ultimatum. It must have astounded Conyngham Greene, the British Agent in Pretoria, when he opened the envelope. Oom Paul's demands were four-fold. One, that Britain should agree to arbitration on all points of mutual difference. Two, that the British troops 'on the borders of this Republic' shall be instantly withdrawn. Three, that all

64

British reinforcements that had arrived since 1 June should be withdrawn from South Africa. Four, that Her Majesty's troops 'which are now on the high seas' should not land in South Africa. And unless Her Majesty's Government complied with these demands within forty-eight hours the Transvaal would 'with great regret, be compelled to regard it as a formal declaration of war'.

It was inconceivable, of course, that such a mighty power could bring itself to bow to the demands of this Ruritanian upstart. And so the British Government ignored them.

Jack was in Salisbury at the time. This war, and he was rightly convinced that war was now imminent, could do nothing but throw his gold-mining plans awry. Not that the underfunded Rhodesian Mining and Development Company was meeting with any noticeable success. He set off immediately for Cape Town, 1,500 miles away, armed with a letter of introduction, this time to Lieutenant-General Sir Charles Warren who was now back with the army after a frustrating and unfruitful time as Chief Commissioner of the Metropolitan Police trying to solve the mystery of the Jack the Ripper murders.

Salisbury, 29 December 1899.
Dear Sir Charles Warren, This is to introduce you to my friend Mr J.N. Griffiths, late of the Second Life Guards and late in charge of scouts in Colonel Alderson's column from which he was recommended for his commission in the BSA Police here in which he served and was a senior Inspector. He was mentioned in dispatches by Sir Richard Martin and has his medal for '96 and '97. He lived for 12 years in the Transvaal and knows parts of it intimately. He wishes to see more service now and to be attached to one of the forces. I am glad you are in Africa again. I am flourishing, but not able now to offer you my personal services as I would like to do.
    Yours faithfully, Joseph M. Orpin.

In no time Jack was offered the command of a squadron of Brabant's Horse, which had been raised by an ex-colleague in the BSA Police, John Brabant, now a Colonel.

Jack and Brabant knew each other well, both having taken part in the attack on Mashayamombe's kraal. Brabant had his

Headquarters at Dordrecht. His men were to be deployed to guard the eastern part of Cape Colony and assist in driving the Boers back from the Stormberg area. But there were further developments in Jack's life before Brabant's Horse saw any major action.

Kruger's ultimatum expired, and on 11 October the Transvaal Government telegraphed all stations with the single word – Oorlog (war). Martial law was proclaimed and the next day General Piet Joubert's burghers rode across the border into Natal near Ingogo, with supporting columns right and left marching through Botha's Pass, Mol's Nek and Wool's Drift. It was probably the largest body of mounted men that Africa had ever seen – 12,000 of them, composed of the Pretoria, Heidelberg, Middleburg, Krugersdorp, Standerton, Wakkerstroom and Ermelo commandos, appearing as "an endless procession of silent misty figures, horsemen, artillery and wagons, filing past in the cold dark night along the winding road where the black shoulder of Majuba stood hunched against the greyer sky".

But they were cold, shivering and morose. The rain had come early that spring, greening the veldt and sprinkling it with pretty daisies. But the downpour had not stopped for days. The burghers were soaked through. They had slept on the mud, unable to find even a few dry sticks to make their cooking fires. Many of their wagons were already falling to pieces, and even their mules, supplied by a sharp contractor, turned out to be weak and miserable bags of bones. On the bright side, they found themselves unopposed. The British had vanished. Newcastle was almost deserted, and Dannhauser, and Dundee. In fact, the *rooineks* had pulled back seventy miles to make their stand at Ladysmith – a dusty tin-roofed garrison town with a few blue gum trees and encircled by looming kopjes. It was unwise strategy because Ladysmith was a besieger's dream.

The first few months of the war went very badly for the British. Their highly disciplined professional army suffered several ignominious defeats at the hands of these farmers mounted on scruffy ponies. In what became known as Black Week, the defeats at Stormberg, Magersfontein and Colenso, plus the knowledge that Kimberley, Ladysmith and Mafeking were all under siege, brought national morale to an unprecedented low. At home, at least, the famous stiff upper-lip was put to a stern test. General Sir Redvers Buller, the Commander-in-Chief, took most of the blame for these debâcles. He was fired.

'Bobs', or Field-Marshal Lord Frederick Sleigh Roberts of Kandahar and Waterford, VC, KP, GCB, GCSI, GCIE, five feet two, aged sixty-seven, veteran of the Indian Mutiny in 1857 and numerous other colonial actions since, was having his breakfast in Dublin when the morning papers arrived, bearing brief cabled news of the defeat at Colenso. There was no mention of the fact that his own son, Freddie, had lost his life there, riddled with Mauser bullets, to earn a posthumous VC.

There cannot have been many Generals who held the affection of their troops as strongly as Bobs, maybe not even Old Nosey Wellington. Julian Ralph of the *Daily Mail* wrote about him, "His army will do anything for him; march longer, starve harder, go without tents, blankets and rum more days and weeks, and die in greater numbers for him than any other man alive."

As he read his newspaper Bobs knew that he had been right all along about Buller. He had been bombarding the War Office for better prosecution of the war long before Colenso. Buller had simply lost his nerve. Of that he was convinced. But there was one other thing that Bobs did not know. He did not know that the War Cabinet had decided to appoint him in Buller's place. But when their telegram arrived he left for London immediately.

On 23 December, a bare week after news of Colenso had reached London, amid thunderous applause from an adoring crowd at Waterloo Station, Bobs departed for Southampton, where he boarded the same *Dunottar Castle* which had borne the unfortunate Buller to the Cape a short while ago. Meantime General Sir Herbert Kitchener, reliever of Gordon at Khartoum and conqueror of the Mahdi at the Battle of Omdurman, was aboard the cruiser HMS *Isis*, belching smoke as she steamed flat out at eighteen knots through the Mediterranean from Alexandria to Malta, where he would transfer to HMS *Dido* for Gibraltar, to rendezvous with the *Dunottar Castle* when she arrived there. The British lion had had its nose bloodied. It was bent on revenge and was sending two of its most famous soldiers to achieve it.

Roberts and Kitchener, who was to be his Chief-of-Staff, had ample time to discuss tactics as the *Dunottar Castle* lurched her way down through the Atlantic. Roberts was sure that the best route to Pretoria would be via Kimberley and Bloemfontein. True, it was farther overland than via Natal. But the country was far less mountainous. And it would also mean that supplies arriving by sea could come through Cape Town, not Durban, thus shortening the journey from home by many hundreds of sea miles. He proposed to ignore Natal, and therefore Ladysmith, for the time being. He would concentrate all his resources on the western front. Failure to do that had been Buller's main mistake. However, with his natural instincts for tact and good man-management, Roberts did not send Buller home. He left him in command on the eastern (Natal) front, to continue to try to turn the Boer tide and push his way into the Transvaal via Majuba.

Unwilling to wait for action with Brabant's Horse and learning that Field-Marshal Roberts was recruiting a number of men to form his personal bodyguard, Jack armed himself with yet another letter of introduction, this time from a gentleman by the name of Laing. Quite who Messrs Orpin and Laing were we do not know, but evidently Jack had continued to work his charms on the 'right' people:

Cotswold Chambers 31 January 1900.

Dear Captain Waterfield,
  This will serve to introduce Captain or Inspector John Norton Griffiths, an officer of the BSA Police, Mashonaland Regiment. Captain Griffiths is one of the best officers of the force and did some very good work during the last campaign in Rhodesia. He has had 14 years [sic] in South Africa, 10 of them in the Transvaal and knows most of the districts of that country, but is most intimate with the district surrounding Johannesburg and Pretoria. If it could be possible, I should like to get him as Lieut. in the Body Guard. He is the most likely man I have met so far and is in my opinion fully qualified for the appointment. I will be responsible for his behaviour.
  Yours faithfully, WJ Laing.

Waterfield immediately sent a message to Jack. "Dear Griffiths, Will you please come up here about 10.30 tomorrow morning and see Lord Roberts. A. Waterfield." At the appointed hour Jack was ushered into the great man's presence and at the end of the interview Bobs not only invited Jack to be in his bodyguard, but appointed him to be its Captain and Adjutant.

On landing at Cape Town, Roberts' first orders had been to build up supplies at Modder River Crossing, to where the British had fallen back after the disastrous Battle of Magersfontein during Black Week. Normally Modder River was a place of idyllic charm, a cool leafy spot, with a couple of tin-roofed, clapboard hotels, favoured by the Kimberleyites for weekends punting on the bullrush-fringed river, away from the dust and sweat in the Big Hole. Now it had become a city of white tents, piles of ammunition and provisions, great heaps of forage, lumbering wagons and thousands of men and horses, oxen and mules. When the Field Marshal arrived there on 9 February 1900 Jack was riding beside him. They were to become fast friends. Many history books, especially those with the late twentieth century obsession for 'political correctness' and a seemingly uncontrollable urge to discredit everything their country's heroes have ever done, snidely describe Bobs as a "ruthless little man with fearsome eyes", or other words to that effect. Of course he was. That was one reason why they made him a Field-Marshal. There is no point in having an army or a navy if it does not set out to win by hook or by crook when the chips are down. But that is not to say that there should not be magnanimity *after* victory, which was both Roberts' and Nelson's watchword. And to Jack, Victorian colonial that he was, Bobs was a 'dear old thing', at least according to Gwladys many years later.

Cecil Rhodes, besieged in Kimberley twenty miles up the railway line, was behaving with petulance. He had not been accorded the importance that he considered was his right. He had looked after his citizens with all due care, allowing the women and children to shelter from the Boer shells underground at the de Beers mine and dispensing benevolence to them however possible. But now he was tired of being ensnared in this windy, dusty, beleaguered town. He was making a nuisance of himself by constantly carping at Colonel Kekewich, in command of the town garrison, and he even threatened Roberts that if he did not make the relief of Kimberley his main priority he would surrender

69

it and its diamonds to the Boers forthwith. Roberts was able to make nightly communication with Kimberley by means of a makeshift signalling apparatus. It was a searchlight taken from HMS *Doris* at Simonstown, and mounted on a railway truck with a venetian blind shutter contraption in front of it. Roberts' reply came to Rhodes by Morse code, shone by the searchlight on to the clouds. "We are coming."

Bobs' trademark was the speed at which his armies moved. It had been his 320-mile march with 10,000 troops in twenty-three days to Kandahar, Afghanistan in the sweltering summer of 1880, which earned him this reputation. At 3 am on 11 February 1900 General Sir John French's cavalry struck out from Modder River in a southerly direction – away from Kimberley – leaving their tents still standing in their orderly rows, gleaming white in the summer moonlight, to deceive the enemy. The only occupants of Modder River were now the First Division, with some heavy artillery, including naval guns, left behind to keep an eye open in case Cronje's burghers were to spring a surprise attack. The cavalry were travelling light, Boer style, with just the clothes they wore and five days' rations. They trotted through the dawn mist, hugging the railway line to give the impression they were being pulled back to Enslin. Then at Honeynest Kloof French swung to the east, barged his way across the flat red sand with its scattered clumps of giant cacti, through the barbed wire fence which was the border between Orange Free State and Cape Colony and clattered into the collection of hovels known as Ramdam. Bivouacking there, they were joined the next day by the Sixth, Seventh, with Roberts, Jack and his bodyguard, and Ninth Divisions, each heralding its approach with a huge cloud of salmon-pink dust on the western horizon. Roberts was about to out-Boer the Boers. He had marched south, then swung east, and now he was about to strike north without losing the slightest momentum. Astonished farmers grabbed their rifles and galloped off to join their commandos, leaving their wives and children undefended at their farms as the *rooinek* army advanced. Pots of coffee were found on kitchen tables, still hot enough to provide a cup for a thirsty Tommy. In one house warm shaving water and an unwiped razor told a tale of panic.

French departed from Ramdam in the middle of the night,

flying northwards at top speed, hampered more by the slow-moving transport columns of their own infantry who were now obstructing their path than by any Boer resistance. By nightfall on 14 February French was north of the Modder and Riet rivers, widely outflanking the Boer trenches around Magersfontein, who in any case were pre-occupied with a well-timed artillery bombardment from the naval guns at Modder River. He set the Lancers and Scots Greys at the thinly held Boer line at Abon's Dam and, without slackening pace, charged straight through it like a giant ploughshare. All that remained now between him and Kimberley was a five-mile-long plain, dotted with wild quince and babel thorn. They charged on, back into Cape Colony and into the besieged town that sat almost on the border. Kimberley had been relieved and it had been almost bloodless. But there was a heavy toll on the cavalry's horses. So heavy, in fact, that the cavalry could not thereafter be considered as an effective fighting force. So hard had been that final five-mile gallop in the fierce heat that many of them collapsed and died, still unfit and green after their long voyage from England. Only a matter of weeks before, some of them had been hauling omnibuses in London.

Meanwhile, thirty-five miles away to the south at Ramdam, Roberts had assembled his huge infantry column. Jack was guarding the Field-Marshal's Headquarters, a wagon marked by a red flag, while inside Bobs wrote his reports and sent telegrams via the telegraph line which unrolled from a great spool on a special cart which followed them everywhere. No doubt Jack found this aspect of his duties somewhat of a bore, but at least he was able to 'work' the odd telegram to Gwladys by courtesy of a co-operative spark-key operator.

They pushed on north-westwards to Waterval Drift. News had come in that, with Kimberley relieved, Cronje had left his trenches at Magersfontein and was fleeing east, obviously to try to save Bloemfontein. He had to be cut off before he could reach there and constitute a major obstacle in Roberts' progress towards Johannesburg.

The Boers were expert in making hurried departures from a laager. But here they broke all records. In a flash, 4,000 men had woken up, saddled up, mounted up and ridden out of

Magersfontein, leaving behind nearly all their personal belongings in their trenches. Led by Cronje, they managed to wriggle their way past General Kelly-Kenny's Sixth Division as it rested among the kopjes. That they were able to do this, on a bright moonlit night, with a five-mile-long train of plodding bullock wagons, says little for the alertness of the British scouts. Roberts set Kitchener and Tucker after him, one each side of the willow-fringed Modder River, while French, having requisitioned some remounts from the Diamond Fields Artillery and De Beers and drank champagne with Rhodes in Kimberley, was now charging hell-for-leather across the parched brown veldt as fast as his makeshift cavalry could gallop to head him off.

But Bobs had made one of his rare mistakes. His lumbering three-mile column of men, wagons and heavy guns was crossing the difficult Waterval Drift when suddenly they were met by a cascade of bullets and shells from the rocky bluffs flanking the Riet River. They had been found by Christiaan de Wet, the immaculate marauder, arch guerrilla of an army of guerrillas, who was to be a thorn in the side of the British for a long time to come, even after the end of the war. Stocky and dapper, in an elegant suit, with a heavy gold watch-chain dangling from his waistcoat, his war correspondence and plans in a smart leather briefcase and a pair of binoculars slung round his neck, his appearance belied his chosen profession – banditry. And he was brilliant at it. With Kimberley relieved, Cronje had headed for Bloemfontein, while one of his colleagues, Ferreira, had melted away towards Mafeking. The other colleague, de Wet, had followed his roving instincts and taken his small but highly efficient band of burghers to roam among the kopjes to hunt for prey. He can hardly have hoped to find a bigger prize - Roberts' baggage, wallowing in the middle of Waterval Drift and he spewed Maxim and Mauser fire down on to the helpless wagons as hard as he could.

From Bobs' point of view his mission was to take Bloemfontein, and that meant getting there before Cronje. Speed, as ever, was vital to Roberts. He reasoned that he had no time to stand and fight de Wet. Therefore he elected to abandon his baggage in the middle of the river and urge more speed from his infantry. He would come to regret this later as he advanced far into the Transvaal, leaving a long chain behind him for his supplies to travel.

The main column halted at 6 am, at Klip Kraal Drift, to rest and take breakfast. The troops now knew that they were about to go into action. They were always fed first. The Field-Marshall and his staff cantered up, immaculate on their giant chargers, and went to where some large 4.7 inch guns were parked. "I want the Naval Brigade to push up another ten miles," said Bobs to Captain Bearcroft, RN. "We have Cronje surrounded, and I want to give the Navy a show." (Long range naval guns had been brought ashore to match the range of the Boers' 'Long Toms'.) Clearly, French's 'part-time' cavalry had got themselves ahead of Cronje and now sat on the other side of the river, forming the other claw to Roberts' pincer, firmly cornering the old fox. It was at a place called Paardeberg.

Cronje had had no need to be caught at Paardeberg. He could have abandoned his cumbersome, twelve-miles-a-day bullock wagons and high-tailed it to Bloemfontein before the claws of the pincer grabbed him, there to regroup and fight another day, as was indeed the Boers' usual tactic. But for some inexplicable reason he elected to fight. All night the burghers spent entrenching themselves in the steep sandy banks of the Modder.

Bobs had caught a chill and was confined to his bed twenty-five miles back at Jacobsdal, with a fuming Jack and his men guarding his wagon. In his place, he appointed Kitchener as battle commander, which created an immediate clash between him and General Kelly-Kenny. Kelly-Kenny had planned to encircle the Boers and bombard them into submission with his heavy artillery, but now found himself overruled. Kitchener had not been at Modder River, or Colenso, or Magersfontein. And he had certainly not experienced the task of attacking trenches manned by superb marksmen armed with modern smokeless long-range rifles in the Sudan. His tactics were to prove disastrous. He threw battalion after battalion into an inferno of Mauser bullets and thud-thudding pom-poms; the East Kents, the Welch, the King's Own Scottish Borderers, Hannay's Mounted Infantry, the West Ridings, the Gloucesters, the Seaforths, the Oxfordshire Light Infantry, the Shropshires, the Argylls, the Black Watch and the Royal Canadians all suffered heavy losses as they advanced. Then

73

an unexpected turn of events occurred. Cronje was thrown a life-line by none other than Christiaan de Wet.

De Wet, now the proud owner of 140,000 tins of British biscuit, meat and milk, had followed his ears towards the thunder of big guns. With only three hundred burghers, and unnoticed, he had taken a kopje commanding the whole south-east ridge to the flank of the British during the late afternoon. With de Wet blazing away at the British lines below, Cronje had an easy escape hatch via this position, if only he had chosen to use it. But still the old fox stayed in his sandy lair, looking sad and, according to a Boer prisoner, holding the hand of Mrs Cronje, "a thin decrepit old woman in a rough straw hat and a dirty old black dress, without a cloak or shawl".

It was the British artillery barrage which finally decided the battle. Kelly-Kenny had had his way in the end. Hour after hour, for days on end, they had been steadily pounding the Boer baggage wagons. Curls of oily green smoke from the Navy's 4.7 inch lyddite shells signified a terrible destruction. Just before dawn on 27 February, at 3 a.m., the Gordon Highlanders made the final infantry advance, with their bagpipes wailing like banshees, as they exchanged murderous fusillades with the defenders. By daybreak Cronje at last realized that all was lost. His men, with their personal belongings now being picked over by British troops miles away in the Magersfontein trenches, were starving and clamouring for him to surrender, fearful of the terrible bayonet assault that they knew would soon be upon them. His supplies and his horses had been destroyed. De Wet had melted away, having failed to relieve him. He was completely surrounded.

White flags now fluttered from among the warren-like trench-works in the banks of the Modder. It was 6 am on 27 February 1900. 27 February! The anniversary of Majuba! And away to the east, later that same day, there would be still more cause for cele-bration. Buller's troops were in Ladysmith!

Bobs, now recovered from his chill, had brought his Headquarters up to Paardeberg the previous evening and was watching events from the little lean-to tent which was fixed to the side of the travelling wagon in which he worked and slept. "Splice the Mainbrace!" he commanded like an Admiral, as Jack stood

74

beside him, beaming widely. Cheer after throaty cheer rippled through the British lines, and Jack had won another medal.

The first indication of Cronje's surrender was brought in by two Boers, mounted on sorry horses which displayed some wounds. Message was sent back requesting the Boer General to make his surrender in person. Some critics argued that in this Roberts had been cruel and ungenerous. But it has always been customary in war for surrenders to be made in person by a vanquished commander. And in any case, faced by a clever enemy, Roberts was prudent to be on guard against possible trickery. In fact, he proved his magnanimity when Cronje finally arrived, a heavy, unkempt bearded bundle of a man wearing a loose brown overcoat and veldt boots, topped by a wide-brimmed grey felt hat, escorted by General Pretyman. "I am glad to see you," said the pint-sized Field-Marshal. "I am glad to meet so brave a man."

Jack was standing at Roberts' right shoulder, towering over him, wearing his forage cap and high-necked tunic with its two shoulder pips. Bobs turned to him and asked him to arrange for a table and two chairs to be brought out and placed in the shade of a tree on the riverbank. Then he saluted his fallen enemy and handed him towards a chair. When the formalities of the surrender had been completed Roberts rose from his chair, bowed and retired to his wagon, leaving Cronje in the care of his staff. Evidently the Boer General was hungry, because for his breakfast he ate their last piece of ham, which Jack had had his eye on, and smoked their last cigar.

After Spion Kop Paardeberg was the most bloody battle of the Second Boer War. When the fighting had stopped, the battlefield scene was horrific. The dead, dying and wounded of both sides lay among the burnt-out wagons and heaps of charred supplies spread over an area of half a mile. British military doctors searched among the scattered clothing, harness, empty shell-cases, bloated corpses of horses and bullocks, broken boxes, mattresses, Bibles and cooking pots in the Boer laager to render any humane assistance they could, but the stench was so sickening that even their hardened stomachs were turned.

The Boers had polluted the waters of the Modder with the bodies of dozens of dead horses and mules, and the sweet stink of their decomposing carcasses soon became overpowering in the windless late summer heat.

In urgent need of potable water, Roberts moved his forces upstream, which meant, fortunately, advancing nearer to Bloemfontein. But his way was not open. His scouts reported that those Boers who had escaped capture at Paardeberg had now joined with de Wet, who had a force of 6,000 behind a ready-prepared line of defences in the kopjes before the Orange Free State capital, on a front of about ten miles, at a place called Poplar Grove.

On 7 March the Battle of Poplar Grove, if it could be called a battle, was a disappointment for the now cock-a-hoop British. Almost at the first exchange of shots, it seemed, the Boers took flight. Why on earth had they not defended Poplar Grove as stubbornly as they had Paardeberg? The reason for this was not clear to Roberts until the next day, when his Intelligence told him something else that was to deepen his disappointment still further. And his fury with the erratic French knew no bounds when he learned of the most sensational, undreamed-of opportunity that had been missed thanks to his (Roberts') orders not being followed correctly.

Roberts had ordered French to take his makeshift cavalry, with forty-two mobile artillery pieces, on a seventeen-mile detour to outflank the Boer trenches, take up position on the Modder to their rear and so cut off de Wet's retreat to Bloemfontein. Once they were in position, and he had the Boers tight in a noose, he planned to throw in his infantry. But French had (a) proceeded at walking pace, with some cavalrymen even dismounted and (b) made a 'detour' so narrow that his movements were well within the sight of the Boer lookouts. Christiaan de Wet was no fool. He could almost feel the first cold touch of the pincers that were about to bite into him as they had done to Cronje. And so he fled before their jaws could close around him, to melt among the kopjes in his own backyard, from where he would continue to tease the British for the rest of the war.

But the escape of de Wet, although he would have made a handsome prize, was not the only reason for Bobs' towering displeasure with French. For among the 4,000 burghers who had so very nearly been surrounded were two other very important person-

76

ages. They were none other than President Paul Kruger himself, accompanied by President Steyn of the Orange Free State! The two Presidents had arrived on the scene in Kruger's state carriage, drawn by four smart horses and escorted by a detachment of Zarps, to try to boost the flagging spirits of their army after Paardeberg by dint of a mixture of soft soap cajolery and hard-edged tongue-lashing. Kruger in particular, sporting a silk top-hat for the occasion, was said to have worked himself into a state of such high dudgeon that he laid about him with his *sjambok*.

Roberts, while scathingly critical of French, did not reserve any words of praise for Kelly-Kenny either, whom he considered had been far too slow in sending in his infantry. In turn, they both blamed Bobs for losing the baggage at Waterval Drift, which meant that the stand-in Diamond Fields Artillery horses were on rations of only eight pounds of oats a day and were virtually starving. The men, too, were hungry and there were only enough water carts to provide each man with half a water-bottle full.

Whoever was to blame, the fact remained that if the British had captured the two Presidents the war would very likely have ended there and then. As it was, their failure at Poplar Grove was to have painful and long-lasting effects.

Roberts' entry into Bloemfontein was a strange affair. As he and his staff breasted a rise to gain their first view of the town, a deputation from the municipal authorities, clad in knicker-bockers and shooting suits, was seen approaching to make a formal surrender and to present the town keys. Jack , by the Field-Marshal's side as usual, loosened his revolver in its holster in case of a trick. But this was no trick. The Orange Free Staters had never been as anti-British as their cousins in the Transvaal. For example, the use of English in official circles had never been banned, and its population of Uitlanders had enjoyed a com-paratively trouble-free existence. In fact, the Free Staters had only been cajoled into the war at all by Kruger's subtle politicking. And now it seemed almost as if the British had liberated the town. Most of the 4,000 inhabitants seemed to have turned out to welcome Tommy Atkins, who was showing distinct signs of travel wear and tear after his long foot slog. Surgeon Jeans, of HMS *Monarch*, now ashore with the Navy's guns, wrote in his diary: "Their clothes in rags and their boots worn out, the soles tied on with string, and some even walking with their puttees wrapped round their feet, they went limping by. Their faces were black with the sun and sand, bearded and parched; their lips were swollen, cracked and bleeding; their eyes were bloodshot, but their heads were held high, and they had that grim determined expression which success, and the knowledge of their power and strength, alone could bring, and carry them, with empty stomachs, through the terrible marches under the burning sun by day, and those as terrible bivouacs in the rain and cold by night."

Nevertheless, a triumphal procession into town began. Several ladies were handing out sandwiches to soldiers as they passed, and a big muscular African yelled out repeatedly "Thank you. Thank you". And a silk Union Flag (with a tiny shamrock that had been embroidered discreetly in the corner by Lady Roberts) was hoisted on a pole in the grounds of the President's residence.

To War Office, London   Bloemfontein, March 13, 8 pm.
By the help of God, and by the bravery of her Majesty's soldiers, the troops under my command have taken possession of Bloemfontein.

The British flag now flies over the Presidency, vacated last evening by Mr Steyn, late President of the Orange Free State.

Mr Fraser, member of the late executive government, the Mayor, the Secretary to the late government, the Landrost and other officials met me two miles from the town and presented me with the keys to the public office.

The enemy have withdrawn from the neighbourhood and all seems quiet. The inhabitants of Bloemfontein gave the troops a cordial welcome.

Roberts.

The Times correspondent wired his report to London:

The Free State, in spite of urgent representations from the Transvaal, decided yesterday to surrender the capital, Mr Steyn leaving secretly at 6.30 for Kroonstad, the new seat of Government, without replying to Lord Roberts' demands for surrender within twenty-four hours. The keys were given up four miles out at 11 o'clock today. Lord Roberts headed a cavalcade a mile in length, descended the southern slopes beside the railway and entered the city at 1 o'clock, meeting with an enthusiastic reception. There were renewed cheers as the procession passed into the market square. A great reception was given to the British commander by the members of the Club. Going to the Government buildings, Lord Roberts took possession of Bloemfontein in the name of the Queen. After inspecting President Brand's statue, Lord Roberts turned to the left, crossed the river and entered the grounds of the Presidency amid great cheering and singing of 'God save the Queen'. A Union Jack, specially made by Lady Roberts, was hoisted at 1.30 in the grounds. The Boers and their sympathizers have fled. Mr Steyn's brother entertained General French at his farm yesterday, and Lord Roberts had breakfast there today.

President Steyn had clambered aboard the last train to leave north before the British blew up the line both to the north and south of the town, which was short-sighted in view of the fact that they would soon be depending on that very track for delivery of their own supplies. But now it was time to rest, take stock and beef up with men and supplies, ready to make the next 'tiger-spring' towards the Transvaal, which would surely be stoutly defended.

Jack spent convivial off-duty evenings at the Club, sitting down to dine at a table with a snowy-white tablecloth, clean plates and plenty of good food, smoking afterwards outside on the cool moonlit veranda, listening to the nightly tattoo of the pipes and drums of the Highland Brigade as they played in the town square.

But although the stay in pretty Bloemfontein was pleasant after the gruelling 100-mile slog through rocky deserts and muddy waters, it was not entirely free of problems. Enteric fever and dysentery took a heavy toll among the visitors. Surgeon Jeans wrote: "Few are likely to forget the long string of stretchers which passed through the camp, morning after morning, and wended their way down to the field hospitals with their burdens of fever." It was the same at Ladysmith and the other fronts in the war. Indeed, when the cost of life came to be totted up at the end of the fighting, it was found that enteric (typhoid) fever had claimed far more men than the Boers.

Bobs waited at Bloemfontein until he had amassed an army of

30,000 before he struck out again, north-east. Most of his forces had departed by 2 May. Brandfort, Lindley and Kroonstad were all taken almost bloodlessly. They saw barely a single Boer as they advanced, cutting a fifty-mile-wide swathe that straddled the railway all the way across the Orange Free State. Even the scouts ahead saw little more of the enemy than the occasional smoke of a retreating train rising above the kopjes, or sometimes caught a fleeting glimpse in their binoculars of some distant galloping horsemen. Everyone had expected the Boers to defend the border of Transvaal, but as Roberts' troops splashed through Viljoen's Drift and into their country, there was still not a burgher to be seen. It was at Doornkop, on the fringes of Johannesburg, that the last set-piece battle of the war took place and the commandos of Viljoen and de la Rey made their last stand. Somehow, it was fitting that it should be so, because it was on the exact spot where the pathetic champagne-sodden figure of Doctor Leander Starr Jameson had raised the old *tanta*'s white apron of surrender four years before. Bruce Hamilton's Gordon Highlanders advanced in open order, with all their traditional swagger, and displaying cast-iron discipline as a deluge of Mauser bullets zipped past their ears, plucked at their kilts and punched fatally into ninety-seven of their bodies. As they gained the crest, the order was given "Fix bayonets!" That was enough. The battle was won. Within Johannesburg itself, chaos reigned as the street-fighting started. Bullets flew in every direction as people huddled in shop door-ways and under railway platforms. Women were screaming and men were falling dead among the giant heaps of spoil, but the tall chimneys continued smoking and the winding gear of the mines carried on turning as if oblivious to the battle that was being fought about their ears. In the end the civic authorities emerged under a flag of truce and promised Roberts that provided the Boer army were allowed to retire intact the Golden City would be surrendered. He gave them twenty-four hours to do this, on the understanding that the gold mines would remain undamaged. This place, of course, was a second home for Jack, although on this visit there would be no Zarps to escort him to the border. No doubt he took the chance to look round some of the haunts that he had not seen for four years and to check whether those in his circle of Uitlander friends had survived the street fighting.

By 15 October Roberts was in Pretoria. Oom Paul Kruger, now in deep despair, said farewell to his ailing wife in their house in Church Street (they were never to meet again), took as much gold as he could lay his hands on and transferred his seat of government to a railway carriage, which, amid some desultory fighting gradually retreated down the line to Komati Poort, on the border with Mozambique, leaving behind him a trail of burnt-out railway trucks containing ruined materials and equipment, forage and foodstuffs contaminated with paraffin. One eight-mile stretch of line was thick with the bloated bodies of horses, oxen and mules, upon which fed squabbling families of vultures and great buzzing swarms of fat bluebottle flies. Finally, he fled to Lourenço Marques, to be borne away into exile by a Dutch warship.

But that was not the end of the war. Guerrilla fighting was to continue for another two years, until an uneasy peace was achieved. Bobs, however, considered that he had little further part to play after Pretoria fell. A few months later he handed over to Kitchener to mop up and he and Jack both went home, Roberts via Colenso to visit Freddie's grave. It was November 1900.

10

A MARRIAGE, A MINE
AND A RAILWAY

Jack had spent but a few months in England over the previous twelve years and when he arrived home this time he found himself to be more than somewhat of a 'square peg'. This time, of course, he had come from a war and it is common for returning veterans to need some time to 'fit back in' with their domestic circles. But his problems were magnified by the cold behaviour towards him of Gwladys' brothers.

A guerrilla war, of course, was still rumbling on among the South African kopjes, with the persistent de Wet, and the likes of Hertzog, Jan Smuts, Denys Reitz and Kritzinger all tormenting the British forces. General Sir Herbert Kitchener was resorting to some pretty stern measures, with his usual eye to economy and expediency at the cost of any sense of humanity. The first concentration camps, a Kitchener invention, were crammed with Boer women and children on starvation rations – a sure recipe for disease – thus earning bitter criticism worldwide. At home the liberal anti-Kitchener, anti-Unionist, anti-war, anti-everything lobby was growing ever more strident, especially having discovered that Colonial Secretary Joseph Chamberlain had made capital out of the war by feeding armaments contracts to a firm in which his family held a major interest.

The situation was all very much to Jack's disgust, and he infuriated Gwladys by going to the lengths of advertising in the morning papers for medical students to come with pipes and whistles to break up the anti-war meetings that were being held in Queen's Hall. It seemed to her foolish to expose himself to this type of publicity when his main objective was to be seen as a serious businessman and so improve his financial predicament. She felt that she was on the verge of losing her faith in him. The little Rhodesian Mining and Development Company had finally disappeared into thin air, marriage seemed to be as far away as ever and her brothers had not relented in their attitude towards Jack. Her mother may have succumbed to Jack's charms, but they certainly had not. In the absence of a father, who had died during Gwladys' childhood, they had taken it upon themselves to see that their sister was 'walking out' with a suitor of whom they were able to give their approval. And they had grave misgivings about the wild colonial Jack Griffiths.

Before long, however, Jack's fortunes were to take a distinct turn for the better. Exactly how this happened has been lost to history, but by some means or other he came into contact with a wealthy financier by the name of Herbert Stoneham. Nothing of note seems to have survived regarding the background of this gentleman. And strangely, although he was probably the most important catalyst in setting Jack on the road to future fame, he does not appear to feature at all in his subsequent life. Stoneham had received news on the grapevine that there was a quantity of placer gold on the Ivory Coast. He wanted Jack to go to America to look for a dredging plant and set it up on the Ivory Coast. At last the big break had arrived! The salary was to be huge. With £5,000 a year plus £1,000 in expenses for the trip to the States, Jack and Gwladys could live like Royalty. With his usual impetuous excitement, Jack barged into Mrs Wood's house at 6, Woburn Square, Bloomsbury, swept the five foot one inch Gwladys up into his arms and waltzed her round and round the drawing-room, singing and laughing as he told her the good news.

He had booked a state room on the *Umbria*, which was to sail from Liverpool for New York on Saturday 7 September. And of course she must accompany him. There must be no more tedious separations to test her resolve. It gave Gwladys and her mother barely a week to arrange the wedding. But the brothers were still uneasy. "What if he goes out to West Africa and dies?" thundered the mean-minded Guy. "Where will you be then? Thrown back on us, penniless, and probably with a baby." Silently, Gwladys had to agree with that point. West Africa was well known as the 'white man's grave'. But, as she confessed in her memoirs many years later, she told herself that even if the marriage were to last only a year it would have been worth it.

The wedding was fixed for 8 o'clock on the morning of Saturday, 7 September 1901, at St Nicholas Cole Abbey, so as to give them time to hurry to Euston for the boat train to Liverpool. Only a few close family and friends were invited. Aunt Chris came up on the early morning milk train from Teddington. To her mother's horror, Gwladys insisted on wearing a duck's egg blue dress with a little silk coat and a white wide-brimmed hat, eschewing the white chiffon gown that she had worn at her own wedding. She walked up the aisle on Guy's arm, but he would not give her away. Mrs Wood did that, although it was clear from her tears that she found it painful to part with her only daughter. Then it was a quick photograph, a hurried breakfast of bacon and eggs, cold partridge and ham, and a tumble into a cab for the station.

The *Umbria* was an ancient tub making her last Atlantic crossing. She rolled unmercifully and, having booked so late, Jack had been only able to secure a cabin right for'ard. After a terrific battle, he persuaded Gwladys to sleep in the saloon for better comfort. So that was their honeymoon, fighting sea-sickness in separate rooms in the middle of the ocean. In New York they stayed at one of the best hotels in town – the Holland House. Then it was Chicago, Milwaukee, Denver and San Francisco, where their house had geraniums climbing all over it, and finally to an alluvial mining camp at Featherville, in the beautiful Rocky Mountain wilds of Idaho, where Jack found the machinery he was looking for and where they sat round a huge camp fire, eating hot Mexican food and drinking whisky and coffee with 'the boys' until 2 am. Gwladys suddenly realized what a sheltered life she had led until now. Now it was set to change forever.

In 1902 the Ivory Coast was practically *terra incognita*, a French colony in its embryonic state. The only Administration was in the chief town, then Grand Bassam, a typical little colonial port with a sandy street that ended on the beach and wooden bungalows with wide verandahs. A few District Commissioners were in scattered settlements along the coastline, but there were no connecting roads or railways. Native paths were the only means of access from the landing-stage to any part of the interior. To start up a mining operation under these conditions was nothing short of pure exploration of the unknown, and every piece of machinery would have to be carried by porters. There was no sensible alternative for Gwladys but to stay at home. Indeed, there were almost no white women at all on the Ivory Coast at that time. Jack would be away for six months, but this time she had a flat at 10 Hyde Park Mansions, an income of £5,000 a year and her wedding photograph to comfort her.

The only descriptive report we have of Jack's adventures on the Ivory Coast is an eloquent account of the journey to a place called Mafere, written by an anonymous member of his party. Whoever he was, he had the Joseph Conrad touch:

The choosing of the foodstuffs for the prospecting party, the packing of cases and tools in that corrugated-iron-roofed store have taken more time than we thought. The loading of the steam-launch has been slow and when she was ready to start the supply of firewood for the engine proved insufficient. We shall never reach Mafere tonight as planned.

This is a hastily chartered, dirty little steam-launch; we lost our own in the surf two days ago. Five hours of a bumpy crossing on a rough lagoon, seven of us cramped in the cabin, nine by five, crammed full with cases of every description and tugging two native canoes overloaded with carriers.

We land at Etoué at 9 pm. Pitch dark. No moon. A strong smell of drying fish and swampy water. Myriads of mosquitoes. Voices shout in the night. Two or three hurricane lamps seem to dance of their own accord in the darkness. The hissing steam of the engine is deafening. Somebody stumbles over a case and goes sprawling in the sand, swearing. The unloading goes on. Where can we sleep in this place? Only a few bamboo huts, probably already packed to suffocation. In the open? Experience forbids. Better pace up and down the sandy beach, inhaling ad nauseam the fish and swampy smells.

"Kouakou!"

"Yassah!"

"All men here?"

"Yassah!"

"One man, one load. We go!" The sound of scurrying feet, bumping cases, altercations.

"Suh! Some men say he no be fit." A thud; a form flitting past; some more voices; the tramping of bare feet.

"Get some torches Kouakou!"

The night becomes lighter; a dozen native-made torches flare all around. The procession of natives, their heads disappearing under all sorts of packages, goes forth. Laughter; shouts in the distance . . . The dislike of the black man for the night and its imaginary terrors has disappeared; the white men do not fear fetishes . . . that walk in the dark is new for them. It is also new for some of us. Ten minutes and we are walking upon what feels like spongy ground, then like some thick mud and now like some soft noiseless liquid. It is a stream, the only path and a very uneven path at that, water to our thighs.

The night is like an oven, not a breath of air, the water is tepid and fetid. Bats, disturbed by the torches, turn wildly round our heads with noises of clapping velvet. A halt. We leave the stream. Some carriers have difficulties in getting onto the bank. What a path! We are hemmed in by bush but the night seems to have lost some of its stuffiness. Some old plantations; the trees are smaller. Now the darkness, dense again. Now we are puffing, climbing a stiff hill; bumping against roots across the path. It seems hours since we started. The relief of getting rid of gumboots is forgotten, replaced by the disagreeable sensation of wet garments, clinging to our limbs and hampering our movements. Nobody talks. Even the carriers have become silent. The torches have died out. What time can it be?

A dog barking in the distance. Some farm probably. Are we nearing Mafere? The stars have lost their brightness; a cool breeze springs up, the forms in front acquire a more distinct shape. Some more barking of dogs . . . and a cockerel, somewhere on the left. Surely, there must be a village not far away. The leaves take shape and tree trunks appear grey in a white steamy mist. We reach Mafere at daybreak , to see the first arrows of the sun strike the tops of the false cottonwood trees.

"Cook! Get chop ready. Two hours time, we start for Aboulié!"

"Kouakou! Tell the men to get their rice!"

The first few months were spent in pegging out claims and obtaining the necessary permits from the French administration.

Jack had very little time for leisure. He was always the first to rise at dawn, shouting to the carriers to get a move on, and last to take to his camp bed at night, after spending time poring over some technical problem with the moths dancing in the light of the hurricane lamp in front of his tent. Quick-tempered and impulsive, although always ready to sympathize where a genuine problem beset a colleague, he had no time for laggards.

When the prospecting was done and the machinery in place, he prepared to hurry home to his wife. There was staff to hire, Britishers, Frenchmen, Germans and Americans, all hard-bitten men, hand-picked, who had already experienced life under the blazing suns of every corner of the tropics. But she forestalled his plans. She arrived at Grand Bassam to meet him, disembarking from a little ship, the *Akabo*, by sitting on a plank like a chil-drens' swing, to be lowered down into a canoe pitching crazily in the surf.

They went home to Hyde Park Mansions, but Jack soon had to return to the Ivory Coast to oversee the new operation. It was on 4 March 1903 that a runner arrived with news for him. He had become a father. His daughter Ursula had been born on 27 February. 27 February! Majuba, Paardeberg, Ladysmith and now Ursula! At home, Gwladys rewarded herself by buying their first motor car, a Gladiator, and issued firm instructions to the chauffeur not to run down any dogs.

As the job was drawing to a close in the spring of 1904 a serious problem arose which prevented Jack from going home. A yellow fever epidemic broke out on the Ivory Coast. The whole colony was placed under quarantine and ships were diverted to ports in neighbouring countries. With his usual impulsiveness, Jack packed a few essentials into a bag and set off on a four-day tramp, quite alone, along the beach to Axim, in the Gold Coast, to catch a homeward bound British ship. There were black sentries with loaded rifles guarding his exit from Grand Bassam, but somehow he ghosted his way past them. He did the same when he got to the boundary between Ivory Coast and Gold Coast. These exploits, and the many other feats of seemingly impossible journeys in incredibly short times through the wild inhospitable jungle, later earned him the name of *Griffittee* among the natives. To them he was different from other white men, something like

87

a magician, an awesome being who could pass anywhere, through trackless regions, to be seen at one place when his presence was known to be at some other. The French administration had a different opinion of him, however. If ever he returned to French territory, he stood to be heavily fined and imprisoned.

Jack had left his indelible mark on the Ivory Coast and in doing so proved he was a natural leader of men. By the time he returned to London his name was well known in the colonial world as the galvanizing spirit who had brought an almost unknown country to the forefront of gold mining. It put him in automatic touch with the financial world. Now he was set for the big time.

The family moved to an ivy-covered flintstone house, Mole Cottage, at West Humble, Sussex. The rent was 5 guineas a week. Jack set up a firm of consulting mining engineers with an acquaintance, Bruce Marriott, and among his new circle of dinner party friends were three financiers: Frank Hilder, Temple Patterson and Athol Thorne. Through them opportunity came in the form of a scheme to build a railway in Portuguese West Africa, to run from Benguela on the Angolan coast, 400 miles inland to access the Katanga Copper Mines in which the financiers were interested, under a concession from the Portuguese Government. It had first been offered to the old railway construction entrepreneur Sir George Pauling, who had made a start from the village of Benguela, but then abandoned the project when he discovered its appalling difficulties, the main one being that the harbour at Benguela was completely unsuitable for landing heavy construction materials, much of which had been lost in the surf.

It was an immensely risky business. There were only eighteen months left on the concession to build the first 100 miles. It had to rise over several thousand feet, over mountains and across rivers, gorges and ever-rising undulations until the tableland was reached. The country was rife with malaria, had little water and only a scant population from which to draw labour.

"You're a mining engineer, not a contractor," pleaded a terrified Gwladys.

"I know, but I've watched," came the terse reply.

In November 1904 Jack sailed for Africa again. We do not know how he had come to hear about Lobito Bay, just to the north of Benguela, but we do know that he bribed the captain of his ship £100 to put in there. It was a superb natural harbour. It had a long spit of sand across its entrance to protect it from the endless scrubbing of the Atlantic surf and the bay itself was large enough to accommodate a navy. A 10,000-ton ship could find four fathoms a mere eighteen feet from the water's edge. His first job was to build a wooden jetty to land the railway construction materials. His main problem had been solved in one fell swoop, and he had founded the Port of Lobito. There is a commemorative plaque, dedicated to his memory, on the very spot where his jetty stood.

In no time he was filing his first report to the Agent of the Benguela Railway Co. 25 November 1904:

> I take the first opportunity of writing to tell you that in accordance with our contract for the first section, from here to Catumbella, that the construction work commenced on 22 inst. The first three kilometres of earthworks are almost ready for the platelayers . . . At present we have only 111 boys but we are anxiously awaiting the arrival of more natives . . .
> Yours truly, J. Norton Griffiths.

Typically, there was no mention of the difficulties in hiring labour. At full swing, the project would eventually employ 200 whites, 20,000 labourers and 3,000 Senegalese platelayers. But first they had to be found. And this was where Gwladys was to prove her mettle. She was determined to be part of her husband's enterprise. There was to be no more moping around in London for her, waiting for him to come home from some far-flung colony, only to see him dashing off again on the next boat. She left her baby son, Peter, who had arrived on 3 May 1905, in charge of a nanny at the house of his Godmother, Mrs Somers-Clarke, hired a nurse for Ursula, and they all set sail for Africa. She met her brother Ralph, an accountant in Johannesburg whom she had not seen for nine years, and together they went to see Mohandas Gandhi. Gandhi, a barrister with a law practice in Johannesburg, had already become somewhat of a revolutionary, devoted to guarding the interests of the thousands of indentured labourers who for years had been swarming into South Africa from the Indian sub-continent on five- or ten-year contracts. "He was a sort of revolutionary labour leader with whom we had to negotiate for labour for the railway. Such a nice little man," she wrote. "It's a pity he gave us so much trouble later!" Gandhi, of course, was the gentlest of men. During the Boer War, with many of his compatriots, he had acted as a stretcher-bearer with Buller's army. Now he was only too pleased to steer his people towards an employer who would treat them well and pay them well. But first there was a fly in the ointment to overcome. It was the Natal Government, which said it was owed much tax by out-of-work, ex-contract labourers and would not give permits for them to travel outside Natal until it was paid. Gwladys, with Gandhi's assistance, negotiated a deal whereby Griffiths & Co would deduct £3 from each of their wages and account for it to the Government. So 2,274 Indian men, together with their families, set sail from Durban for Lobito Bay.

Gwladys stopped off in Cape Town to buy four horses, sixteen mules, four cows, masses of poultry and a donkey for Ursula, and loaded them all on deck. The sailors dubbed it 'Mrs G's menagerie'. Lobito, by now, had grown to something more than just a simple jetty. It boasted a village of tents on the sand, from which there was a ten-mile dirt track, without a single green leaf of any description in sight, along the coast to Catambela. It was another fourteen miles to Benguela, where Jack had built a large cement house in a big sandy garden. Everywhere was sand. Nothing but sand. Baking hot sand. The chickens and turkeys started dying right away, the cows dried up almost at once and on only the second day they were just in time to stop Ursula trying to pick up a snake in what was called the garden. And the mosquitoes! After a week Ursula succumbed to a fever and had terrible convulsions. Jack cabled for the next Union Castle ship to call in for her and the nurse and telegrammed his mother-in-law to meet it at Tenerife.

Life was harsh. Malaria was rife, even Jack had fearful attacks, although he would never give in except for a few hours of un-controllable shivering and nausea. One day there was a big load due at Catambela when one boy, Johnny, was the only one not sick. Gwladys, just over five feet tall, found herself driving a wagon with a box under her feet, hauled by a team of eight mules for the first time in her life, with Johnny beside her holding the whip. She had to learn to be a nurse. One common injury to the plate-laying gangs was severed toes, caused by dropping rails on them. Jack insisted on being always at the railhead and therefore their bedroom was a box-truck, sleeping on camp-beds with a small enamel basin for washing and a piece of tin for a mirror. Jack was no typist, nor was Gwladys, but he delegated the report-writing to her in another truck which they used as an office. The mind conjures up a picture of a wonderfully typical character of the times, one that Katherine Hepburn, of *The African Queen*, might have played well. An Edwardian lady, long skirts trailing the dusty floorboards, in a high-necked blouse, bending laboriously over a great clacking typewriter as she sweated, or rather perspired, in insufferable heat in some as yet uncivilized part of the dark continent.

The first thirty miles of line were over a flat sandy plain, but then there was a steep rocky ridge to negotiate. Jack decided on a two-mile-long rack and pinion section through Lengue Gorge. It cost £20,000 a mile, which was way above the estimated cost of £4,000 a mile for the whole project. But it saved the £135,000 which a detour would have cost. And the ability to point back at a successful rack and pinion railway construction would earn Jack a fortune later in South America.

Soon after Christmas Jack decided that they should go up country to check the survey work being done by a Mr Alexander and a Mr Jones. With two of the engineers, they set off on horse with Ursula's donkey laden with pots and pans, and about 100 boys carrying the supplies. The countryside was impressive, with huge clumps of cactus up to 100 feet high, great termite mounds like Cleopatra's Needle and baobab trees with trunks like lumps of granite. One day they were unable to find any water at all until 3 a.m., and then it was thick with mud. The boys brought them buckets of the stuff, which was full of tadpoles, laid some big green leaves on the ground for them to stand on behind their tent, and they gave each other a welcome shower. There were signs of plentiful game, with lion, leopard and hyena spoor all around. At night they would retire to their tent and listen to the roars, the squawks, the barks and all the other night time noises of the jungle, with a gigantic fire outside as a safeguard against attack.

It was amazing that none of their tethered horses or mules was taken.

Jack decided that it was best to trek by night to avoid the worst of the heat, with water being so scarce. They breakfasted on porridge, tinned kippers and fruit at 4.30 in the afternoon and set off at six o'clock. Here there was jungle and in places it was so dense that they often lost sight altogether of the person in front, only a horse's length away. And when coming into a clearing, perhaps one full of dazzling flowers, it was terrifying to find that they had been following the edge of an unseen precipice with a drop of several dozen feet right beside them.

By 10 February, the eleventh day, they had trekked 160 kilometres and came to Hauha Fort, a two-roomed wattle and daub hut with about twenty grass huts around it. The Portuguese commandant was a nice little chap, with a native wife and child, who insisted on killing an ox for them, a local custom to welcome honoured guests. That night they sat in thin dressing gowns, dining on the choicest cuts from the smoking carcass.

Two days later they reached their destination, Caconda, to find that Alexander and Jones had completed their work and that the way was clear for the first 100 miles of the Benguela railway to be laid. It was done by the end of July 1906, to be acclaimed in the English-speaking press as a triumph of British engineering.

11

'EMPIRE JACK'

At home in England, Mrs Wood had spoiled Ursula dreadfully, and Peter, now one-and-a-half, was a shrieking wreck. A sepia photograph shows him peering sadly at the camera, clad in a sailor-suit. Perhaps, a century later, many a child psychologist would have a perfectly logical explanation for such things. But another baby was due. Phoebe was born in November just after Gwladys had recovered from a bad bout of cerebral malaria. Jack had taken a house in Oxford Square for the confinement. Cousin Ethel paid a visit, dressed in pale mauve velvet, draped in vast white fox furs and a gigantic hat. "How are the children?" she enquired. It was to be a long time before the woman understood that Gwladys's world had expanded, taking her interests far beyond the limits set by her children.

From the turn of the century up to the First World War, the whole world seemed to be building its infrastructure. Railways, dams, skyscrapers, bridges and ports were springing up every-where. It was a contractor's paradise. Almost anyone who had the courage and the flair for risk-taking could compete. A contractor did not have to be an engineer. He had only to know where to find the best engineers. Likewise with money. He did not need to be rich, merely to know where to find the finance.

South America was a rich source of contracts and Canada was just opening up. But Governments were not as rich as they are today. The British Government kept a certain distance, contenting itself with a paternalistic view and slightly pompous statements such as the following letter, buried deep in Foreign Office files: "Mr Griffiths seems to be a keen and enterprising man and in conversation seems disposed to regard himself as a

93

pioneer if not a sort of discoverer of possibilities in the matter of engineering construction in Chile." When things went wrong, there would be a little flurry of correspondence, couched in the cagey language of diplomats which leaves the ordinary reader none the wiser - "I beg your Excellency to deal with it in the ordinary way."

The contracting fever had taken a strong hold of Jack. The golden pot at the end of the rainbow beckoned, and there were rainbows everywhere. The eternal problem was the finance. In one sense all through his life so far Jack had had it too easy. He had always managed to be in the right place at the right time to meet the right people, relying on his natural magnetic charm to win the day. It had all left him with very little fear of what the future might bring. He had reserved very little in the way of financial resources from his successes on the Ivory Coast or the Benguela Railway. It was one of his ongoing shortcomings, without which he might not have found himself in such a mess later in life. But now he met Lord Howard de Walden, the wealthy poet and philanthropist, who saw the promise in this large eager man with the sleeked back black hair and penetrating eyes, who had pulled off such spectacular pioneering projects in the wilds of Africa. His Lordship was prepared to back him.

Jack took a prestigious City of London office, in London Wall, which he named Griffiths House, and in no time the big names clustered around. It made no difference to Jack whether a man was a duke or a dustman, he treated everyone the same. But in 1908 it was the 'Dukes' who had the money. Denbigh, Bute, and several more: they all had eldest sons who fell over each other to invest in Jack's operations. He called them his 'House of Lords'.

He formed a Canadian company, the Norton Griffiths Steel Construction Company, with a paid-up capital of £1 million, and in that year, 1908, signed a contract to build one of the most famous buildings in Vancouver, the Dominion Trust Building. For a while it was the tallest building in the Empire, with fourteen storeys, which was two more than the building permit allowed. He threw a sumptuous lunch party on the roof when it was finished. He never did anything by halves. Today, it is a national monument, an imposing red triangular edifice, occupying the corner of West Hastings and Granville Streets. The top floor, where Jack had his offices, is where a womens' self-improvement group now meets.

Between 1908 and 1913 Vancouver was considered the gateway between the West and the Orient. It was in full bloom, driven by the logging and coal-mining industries. The Dominions Trust Building was quickly followed by another of Vancouver's historical buildings, the Vancouver Block, which was described in architectural guides as a terra cotta wedding cake. Jack's companies carried out $3 million of building contracts in Canada during this time. His payroll was $12,000 a week and he was the largest single employer of labour in British Columbia. The 'Dukes' had tripled their money in five years.

On 30 September 1908 Jack and Gwladys had their fourth and last child, Michael. Jack was in London at the time, supervising the building of the Battersea to Deptford main drainage system – a nine-mile-long tunnel which starts at Limburg Road on the corner of Wandsworth Common and ends at Greenwich pumping station. Together with Manchester's main sewers, this would provide the tunnelling know-how he would need one day for one of the two most hair-raising exploits of his life.

Dudley Docker was the Chairman of the Patent Shaft, Axletree & Metropolitan Railway Carriage Company in Birmingham. Jack had given him large orders for bridges and rails on the Benguela Railway job. They met again in 1909 and Docker promptly suggested that he should stand as the Conservative and Unionist candidate for Wednesbury at the January 1910 election. Gwladys was appalled, but she should have known him better by then. Although he knew absolutely nothing about politics, he jumped at the idea with characteristic impetuosity, was adopted at once and dashed off to campaign. The two main Parties stood on platforms which might be thought strange in the light of what we would expect today. The Liberals were in power. According to the newspapers, they stood for Free Trade, Home Rule for Ireland and destruction of the Constitution. The Conservative Unionist Opposition Party were the social reformers of the day. Their programme was Poor Law Reform, (health and un-employment benefits, housing reform, universal education), proportional representation, reform of the House of Lords and

95

an increased defence budget in the face of widespread concern over the growing German Navy. "We want eight [new battleships], and we won't wait!" was the cry on the stump.

Jack fought the election on tariff reform and Empire versus free trade. Cheap food imports were undermining the British farmer and cheap imported manufactured goods were causing unemployment. He toured the Black Country in mid-winter, wearing a trilby, pin-striped suits, shirts with stiff rounded collars and smoking a pipe, climbing telegraph poles to cry: "Tariff Reform and the British Empire for the British race!" He made thundering speeches on the unity of Empire. The walls of buildings were strung with slogans: "Empire is not a matter for party politics" – "Let's fight for something worth fighting for" and "The Day of Empire has Come". And once, when a heckler made his temper boil over, he strode from the platform, punched the man on the jaw, climbed back up again and continued his speech as if nothing had happened, all to tumultuous cheering of the crowd. He held forth, in a voice like thunder, in favour of Imperial Preference, and advocated an Imperial Senate, where the Empire's needs would always be heard instead of being ignored as he felt they were at that time. His fellow Conservatives began calling him Empire Jack, his Liberal opponents dubbed him The Monkey Man after the time he had admitted being hungry enough in Africa to have eaten monkey. One commentator described him as "a man of large physique and gigantic personality, a swashbuckling, trail-blazing, loyalist demagogue of the old school".

"VOTE FOR EMPIRE JACK AND PROTECT ENGLISH TRADE" screamed the banner headlines. It was an enormous tribute to his personality that the voters listened and he won the seat, arch-Tory that he was, in such a poor working-class constituency. "Go to Canada, where big men are bred!" he cried to the struggling coal miners of Wednesbury, Tipton and Darlaston. And he put up the money to pay for their emigration to British Columbia. Thousands sailed for a better life in the Far West thanks to Jack's munificence, and thousands were therefore 'taken off the rates' at home. He made his maiden speech in the House on 9 February 1910, on Canadian preferences. Quite unmindful of the etiquette, where 'new boys' traditionally maintain a demure manner when first rising to their feet, he roared at the assembly, "Do you want to lose Canada the same way you lost the U.S.A.?"

In that same year he signed two contracts to build railways in South America. Chile would be celebrating its centenary of Independence very shortly and Chileans had long dreamed of a railway stretching the length of their long lanky country. It would be wonderful for them to mark the event with such a development. But there were teething problems. Lord Cowdray of Pearsons had been almost at the point of signing up to do the work, back in 1907, but had pulled out for various reasons. The Arica–La Paz contract was then offered to a German firm, Holzmann of Frankfurt, but they had difficulties with their bankers. A little-known entrepreneur named Williams then tried to muscle in on the action, but was exposed at the last minute by the London press as an ex-convict and his contract was annulled in June 1908. Chile's railway seemed doomed to be a non-starter.

Then, on 18 May 1910, the Chilean Government suddenly invited tenders again via a notice in *Financial News*. Leaving their children in the charge of Mrs Stapleton-Smith at Mole Cottage and making arrangements for parliamentary telegrams and reports to be forwarded to them at various ports of call, Jack and Gwladys left immediately for South America. In Rio they were joined by Sir John Jackson, who was tendering for the Arica–La Paz railway jointly with Jack. It would be the highest railway line in the world.

In Buenos Aires they were fêted like royalty – the National Military Parade with the President's party, the races and a motor launch party on the Tigre. But it was June, mid-winter, and they had to get over the Andes to Chile before the passes snowed up and access by land would be impossible for five or six months. Otherwise it would mean a hellish sea voyage around Cape Horn. Jack sent two men ahead to report on the condition of the passes and whether they could get through by mule. The message came back that it was possible if they hurried.

It started to snow as soon as the train left Mendoza for Las Cuevas, which was the railhead for the Andean tunnel under construction. By the time they arrived there it was dark, with a howling blizzard. They spent the night in a hut, at 12,000 feet above sea-level, with nine blankets on their bed and a huge fire blazing. Gwladys, the only woman in a party of nine men, kept a heavy fur coat, woollen gaiters and two hats on. But still they shivered. It was all very different from Angola or the Ivory Coast.

The only mules at Las Cuevas had been taken by another firm, Grace & Co. who were racing them to Santiago to try to obtain the contract. And the last train for six months was about to leave and go back down the mountain. It looked as if it would be Cape Horn after all. But not Jack. He commandeered the last two mules and set off with a guide for the next village. Setting his mule's head towards the mountain, which seemed like a white curtain, he vanished within seconds. Then came a nail-biting six-hour wait before a telegram arrived to say that he had bought twenty mules and to be ready to start first thing in the morning. Next day there was brilliant sunshine and a blue sky. All the same Gwladys was now wearing a pair of men's boots and six pairs of long woollen socks. Jack had tied a fresh sheep's fleece around his legs and feet. The mule train, with Jack leading, set off. Their luggage, piled high on the mules, took up the rear. One animal bore Gwladys's gigantic hatbox, wobbling precariously on top. It was like climbing up a wall. "Look up!" Jack shouted back. "Don't look down! For God's sake don't look down!"

It was a two-hour climb to the plateau where the Argentina–Chile border was marked with a giant statue of Christ Triumphant, arms outstretched, embracing the world. There were shining snow peaks all around, dominated by Aconagua glistening in the sun. They dismounted to rest before tackling the much more difficult descent into Chile. There was much more snow on this side of the Andes, with deep dangerous drifts like quicksand. At times only the mules' bellies stopped them from disappearing altogether. But they made it. In a few hours the ordeal was over and the next day they were in a train speeding towards Santiago.

In Santiago, where the men wore colourful ponchos and rode horses with huge elaborate saddles and silver stirrups like ice buckets and the women draped their heads in black *manta* veils, the press were overawed by *los intrepidos y corragiosos* who had braved the Andes at this time of year, and the party dined with the American Chargé d'Affaires.

They sailed from Valparaiso, the port for Santiago, to go to

Arica, 700 miles up the coast, in a funny little coastal steamer the SS *Loa*. From there Gwladys was going home, but Jack and the others had to go up to La Paz, in Bolivia, to sound out some more facts about that end of the scheme. He was leaving nothing to chance, which was perhaps a little out of character.

The contract was finally awarded to Howard Associates, the financiers of Griffiths & Co. on 10 August 1910. The 400-mile line was to run from Cabildo, passing through Limahuida, Illapel, San Marcos, La Serena and Copiapo. It would be the most difficult railway in the world to construct, as well as the highest, at 13,650 feet. There were three miles of tunnels, two miles of bridges and 14,000,000 cubic metres of spoil to be moved. The cost was £4 million, to include the rolling stock, and Jack immediately placed some very lucrative orders with Wednesbury firms. It was a marvellous contract and it was to make a lot of money, but conditions were horribly harsh for the construction workers, many of whom came from the South American underworld and turned out to be vicious killers. There were never less than two murders a week all the time the work was going on.

In November it was time to fight the next General Election. Jack's campaign speeches, made with an enormous map of the Empire at his back, were full of colour and sincerity. His meetings were always packed and a good-natured atmosphere prevailed, except in Darlaston, which was the hard kernel of the constituency, where tempers sometimes overboiled and things could get a little rough. He rode through the streets driving a four-in-hand, with Gwladys clad all in red and perched on the box beside him. Sometimes he took off in a hot-air balloon, trailing a banner proclaiming "Prosperity, Imperialism, Tariff Reform" beneath it. He was returned with an increased majority and carried through the streets of Wednesbury on the shoulders of his supporters in a torchlight procession. He waved a big white hat to the loudly cheering crowd as bugles blew and the eulogies flowed. Prime Minister Balfour wired his congratulations, and Empire Jack took his wife skiing in Switzerland for Christmas.

1911 was the year of King George V's Coronation. Jack had been presented to the new King at his second levee on 28 February at St James's Palace. All through the spring Commonwealth dignitaries were pouring into London and it was suggested that Jack, who had made such a name for himself as the Defender of Empire, keep open house for the Coronation to receive these important visitors. He rented a magnificent riverside mansion, Temple House, Marlow, from Mrs Hwfa Williams for 100 guineas a week, where he entertained several thousand guests. Each weekend there were never less than 500 of them. The guest book is a thick tome full of illustrious names of the day.

A week or so beforehand, Gwladys fell ill with a virulent form of jaundice. She grew thinner and thinner, yellower and yellower. Jack was beside himself with worry. He sent for specialist after specialist, but nothing, it seemed, could be done for her. And so, while hundreds of guests circulated on the lawns, she lay in a bath-chair under a tree, where the likes of Prime Minister Balfour, Austen Chamberlain, Alfred Lyttelton and Lord Charles Beresford came to her with their commiserations. Then they all disappeared to go up to London for the Coronation, leaving her under her tree. It was a year before she was fully well again.

In ten years Jack had developed from an unknown, penniless colonial soldier into a prominent figure – an MP, a philanthropist and an international businessman. He was forty years old, still slim and handsome with piercing blue-green eyes, not a grey hair on his head and at the height of his career. His order books were full. In Great Britain alone his contracts included Yarmouth Pier, Southsea Promenade, a pier at Weston-super-Mare, a jetty at Heysham, Battersea Power Station and the City to South London Underground. Early in 1911 he secured a £1,200,000 contract for a waterworks at Baku, on the Caspian Sea, and was back and forth to Canada and Mexico, where he had £27 million of work to look after, as though the Atlantic did not exist. Indeed, it is astonishing that he was able to flit around the world so easily, all the time maintaining contact with his vast connections, in the days before air travel, e-mails or mobile phones. On 11 August he arrived in La Paz for the inauguration of his railway from Arica on the anniversary of Bolivia's independence. Apart from passengers, it would be used to haul copper, tin and silver, plus sulphur from Tacora volcano. How the conquistadors would have marvelled at it.

In 1912 Jack and Gwladys began to have their first anxieties. She was particularly worried because she felt that he delegated responsibility too freely to his subordinates and that they were not fully tried and efficient. Consequently, he began to find things going wrong and, to make things worse, getting money out of the 'House of Lords' now seemed like getting blood from a stone. Financiers, of course, are no fools when it comes to parting with their capital. They keep their ears very close to the ground, and they could hear the distant rumblings. Canada's boom was beginning to dry up, and the likelihood of a major war was being discussed in ever louder whispers.

Jack went out to Baku to look at his waterworks project. It was a £1.2 million job, to build a concrete conduit bringing water to the town from the Shollar springs in the Caucasian mountains. Well into the contract it was decided, and it is not clear by whom, to try a special kind of pipe instead of the concrete conduit. If it had worked it would have saved the town a million roubles. Thousands of these pipes were made and tested at pressures far in excess of what Jack maintained would be necessary for them to withstand, but they were found wanting. It all degenerated into an unholy mess. The lawsuits took off, with Jack suing the town (1) for breach of contract by their Consulting Engineers having changed the design and (2) demanding an extension of time on the ground that it was not fair to debit him with eighteen months' time lost in testing the pipes. By then it had become impossible to complete the work in the remaining nineteen months.

The town's response was to send armed men to seize the works and the plant belonging to the company. One of the engineers was badly roughed up and one of the town men was tipped head-first into a trench, amid much waving of rifles and revolvers. Jack wrote to the Foreign Office, asking for British intervention:

15 August 1913. It is quite possible that bloodshed may be caused at any time if the considerable number of Englishmen employed upon the contract take any steps to protect their employer's property, or even appear to do so. We would therefore beg that the British Ambassador at St Petersburg be notified by cable to request the Russian High Authorities to look into the matter at the earliest possible moment. You will understand that in a matter of this nature every hour is of importance.
Your obedient servant, &c

But it went against him. The consulting engineer, Sir William Lindsay, sided with the town of Baku, calling Jack's organization defective and unsatisfactory. The Russians succeeded in taking over the plant and Jack was kicked out. Baku seems to have been his first big mistake and, to make matters worse, he had abandoned an $11,500,000 contract to build a new docks for the eastern terminus of the Canadian Pacific Railway at St. John, New Brunswick, in order to pursue what he thought would be a straightforward water-pipe project in Russia. Gwladys said it broke his heart.

In the spring of 1914 Jack and Gwladys were invited to Egypt by Lord Kitchener, the *enfant terrible* of the Boer War and now the Consul-General in Cairo. Kitchener and Jack were of course old acquaintances, having been in close contact with each other when soldiering with Roberts in South Africa. It was a holiday trip, rather than a business tour, although it was possible that discussions took place about the Aswan Dam, which was to figure so prominently in Jack's post-war future. Kitchener entertained them lavishly, proudly showing them around his magnificent residence, which housed his valuable collection of Rhodian china. They had a wonderful time and the *Wednesbury Herald* ran a picture of their MP and his wife perched high on camels with the Sphinx in the background.

Next stop was Melbourne, Australia. This time business was very much on the agenda. It was an entire development programme, including railways and ports for New South Wales, amounting to £10,000,000. But the 'House of Lords' fought shy of it, even to the extent of writing to *The Times* saying that they had no connection with the company which had obtained the contract, i.e., Griffiths & Co. Looking back on it, ninety years later, it might be assumed that Jack had simply blotted his copybook in Baku. In big business you are only as good as your last job. What you may have achieved before that does not always enter into the equation. On the other hand, with war clouds gathering, financiers everywhere were pulling in their horns. None wanted to be burdened with fresh liabilities. It may have been a simple question of cold feet on their part. During the general strike of 1913 Jack had asked questions in the House about relief to workers whose families were in distress. When nothing was forthcoming, he gave money to the strike fund in his constituency out of his own pocket. This, plus the loss of the Australian contract, cost him £1 million. His morale was at an all-time low. Those who knew him said they had never seen him in such dismal spirits. But war was in the offing. Soon he would be a hero again.

12

WHEN DUTY CALLS

Jack had foreseen war as early as 1908. Indeed, he always said that that was his main reason for going into politics. Each year since, he had watched in dismay as Germany grew stronger and the Kaiser more belligerent, while flustered European diplomats performed antics which filled him with trepidation. In Parliament he accused the Government of being 'dummies and waxworks walking through the lobby'.

The origins of the First World War are complex and difficult to understand. The connection between the assassination of an Austrian Archduke and his wife by a skinny nineteen-year-old Serbian anarchist, Gavrilo Princip, in the streets of Sarajevo, the capital of Bosnia, on 28 June 1914 and Great Britain's declaration of war on Germany five weeks later, baffles the mind. It is even argued by some that the fine point of the real tap-root to the First World War was the Kaiser's telegram to Kruger after the Jameson Raid in 1896. Queen Victoria, his beloved Grandmama, had taken this as an unbearable insult and had administered such an imperious tongue-lashing that poor Willie's ears rang and he was soon sending her fawning letters begging forgiveness. Nevertheless, it was the start of an internecine squabble between conflicting egos which was set on a spiral of crescendo to rise from an exchange of peevish whispers to a clash of almighty roars.

It was the Naval Arms Race which played centre stage in the simmering drama. Hence Jack's General Election battle-cry in 1908 – "We want eight and we won't wait". Indeed, the British Admiralty had complied with such demands and ordered eight new dreadnoughts the following year. But the Germans ordered four. And so it continued, tit for tat, but Britain gradually built up a commanding superiority. In 1913 five super-dreadnoughts of the Revenge class were ordered, against the Germans' three, and on the eve of war the Royal Navy possessed thirty-four against the High Seas Fleet's eighteen. It was almost a two to one advantage. Britain was alone among the major European Powers in relying to such a high degree on the strength of her Navy. She had no conscript army, as had the others. Her land forces were comparatively small, but highly trained.

Superficially, there was an atmosphere of *bonhomie* between Britain and Germany. Both seemed anxious to display an innocent face as the rest of the world looked on with baited breath. A 'goodwill' visit to Baltic ports by the British Fleet took place a mere five days before Archduke Franz Ferdinand was killed in Sarajevo. At dawn on the morning of 23 June 1914 the grey shapes of the Second Battle Squadron, under Admiral Sir George Warrender, materialised through the mist shrouding the Kieler Bucht. As they entered Kiel Harbour the summer sun burst through. Launches and yachts, each crammed with sightseers, circled the great ships and the shoreline was packed with hordes of spectators. Twenty-one-gun salutes thundered out as the Kaiser arrived in his Royal Yacht, the *Hohenzollern*, and aeroplanes and zeppelins droned overhead. As the *Hohenzollern* passed the mighty *King George V*, hundreds of white duck-suited British sailors and red-jacketed Royal Marines lined the battleship's rails.

For the rest of the week there was to be a yacht regatta. On Friday the twenty-sixth the Kaiser invited Admiral Warrender and the British Ambassador, Sir Edward Goschen, aboard his racing yacht *Meteor*, while German officers sat in the wardrooms of the British ships drinking convivial whisky and sodas, and young British officers went ashore to flirt with the local girls. And every day hundreds of free railway passes were available to allow the British 'lower deck' to visit Berlin. But under the surface there was mistrust. "Be on your guard against the English!" hissed the German Naval Attaché, von Müller, to any German officers who seemed to be overcome by the spirit of fellowship which prevailed. "England is ready to strike; war is imminent and the object of this visit is only spying. Whatever you do, tell them nothing about our U-boats!"

It was half past two in the afternoon of Sunday the twenty-eighth when a telegram arrived in Kiel informing von Müller of the Archduke's assassination. He quickly ordered a fast launch and set out to find the Kaiser, who was racing again aboard the *Meteor*. Wilhelm was standing in the stern with his guests as the yacht was overhauled. Müller called out that he was the bearer of grave news and would throw the telegram across, but the Kaiser insisted on knowing at once by word of mouth. He kept very calm, merely saying, "I think we should abandon the race".

Kiel Week ended in anti-climax. Flags were lowered to half mast and receptions and dinners cancelled. Early the next day Wilhelm departed to Vienna for the funeral and Admiral Warrender addressed a massed hall, full of sailors from both Navies, speaking of their friendship and calling for Three Cheers for the German Navy to which a German Admiral responded calling for Three Cheers for the British Navy. On the morning of 30 June the Second Battle Squadron weighed anchor and sailed from Kiel. The yards of the German ships flew signals of "Pleasant Journey" and Warrender sent back a wireless message "Friends in past and friends forever".

They were wasted words. The fateful die had already been cast.

What would have been a local squabble in the Balkans was expanded when Germany encouraged Austria-Hungary to attack Serbia to avenge the Archduke's life, telling them, "Go ahead, we'll back you." This made Russia's hackles rise. Serbia was her ally. The mighty Russian Bear immediately mobilized. Unsuccessfully, France tried to restrain Russia, but, faced with a combined German/Austro-Hungarian axis, she did eventually back down and left Serbia to its fate. The issues became obfuscated on a bewildering chequer-board made up of dual monarchies and triple alliances, with a cast of waffling, fear-driven Heads of State acting the pawns to a megalomaniac King named Wilhelm.

If you want to pick a fight, serve an impossible ultimatum. Paul Kruger had done just that fifteen years before. In July Austria-Hungary served such an ultimatum on Serbia. Germany did the same to Russia and France. Throughout July everybody seemed to be issuing warnings to each other; mobilizing their reservists and moving troops towards frontiers. On the thirty-first, three days after Austria had declared war on Serbia, *The Times*, which was read throughout Europe, carried a prescient editorial to the effect that a German advance through Belgium to the north of France was quite possible, acquiring Antwerp in the process, and might even result in Dunkirk and Calais becoming German naval ports. "That is a contingency," it growled, "that no Englishman can look on with indifference."

The London *Daily News* sent its famous reporter H.W. Nevinson to cover the growing war hysteria in Berlin. He sailed from Dover four days before the British ultimatum to Germany to respect Belgian neutrality would expire, and war would be declared.

On the evening of July 31 I started for Berlin. Down the midnight Channel the searchlights were turning and streaming in long white wedges. Passing into Germany we met trains full of working men in horse-trucks decked with flowers and scribbled over with chalk inscriptions *Nach Paris* (to Paris), *Nach Petersburg*, but none so far *Nach London*. They were cheering and singing as people always sing when war is coming. We were only six hours late in Berlin and my luggage was lost in the chaos of crowds rushing home from their summer holidays. For two days I watched as up and down the wide Unter den Linden crowds paced incessantly by day and night singing the German war songs – *Was blasen die Trompeten? Deutschland über Alles* and *Die Wacht am Rhein*, which was the most popular. As I walked to and fro among the patriot crowd, I came to know many of the milling faces by sight and I still have clearly in mind the face of one young woman who, with mouth that opened like a cavern, and with the rapt devotion of an ecstatic saint was continuously chanting

Lieb Vaterland kann ruhig sein!
Fest steht und treu die Wacht,
Die Wacht am Rhein.

So the interminable crowds went past, agog for war, because they had never known it. Sometimes a company of infantry, sometimes a squadron of horse went down the road westward, wearing their new grey uniforms. They passed to probable death amid cheering, hand-shaking and gifts of flowers and food. Sometimes the Kaiser himself swept along in his fine motor-car, the chauffeur clearing the way by perpetually sounding his horn.

107

Every hour a new rumour surged through the city. Every hour a new edition of the papers appeared. Nevinson went backwards and forwards to the telegraph office, all day long and far into the night, trying to send his report to London, but telegrams had already ceased to run. On the morning of 4 August he tried to enter the *Schloss* to hear the Kaiser's address, but was refused permission. In the afternoon he heard that the British Ambassador, Sir Edward Goschen, had demanded his papers and that war was declared. Without ceremony, he was thrown out of his hotel, the Bristol, as a dangerous foreigner, and later, over dinner at the Adlon, he listened to the sounds of breaking glass as crowds stoned the British Embassy in the next street. He was grabbed by two armed policemen and dragged out with a revolver held to each of his ears. They flung him to the mob, who set upon him with sticks, fists and umbrellas. He was taken in a taxi to the Central Police Court to produce his passport, and afterwards back to his hotel, where he found the chambermaid "to be much moved, and refusing to be comforted because her three brothers and her lover were already on the march". In the evening he received a kindly invitation from the British Ambassador to come into the Embassy, which had been barricaded. Before dawn on 6 August a convoy of motor-cars drew up outside the Embassy, sent by order of the Kaiser to convey the British staff away to a railway station a few miles outside Berlin. Nevinson and some other correspondents were invited to join it. For twenty-four hours their train trundled in fits and starts across the North German plain towards the Dutch frontier:

On our way we passed or were impeded by uncounted vans decorated with boughs of trees and crammed with reservists going to the Belgian front. The men had now chalked *Nach Bruxelles* or *Nach London* as well as *Nach Paris* on the vans, and we were met at every station by bands of Red Cross girls bringing coffee, wine and food. At all the larger stations news of our train's approach had been signalled and to cheer us on our way all the old men and women of the place came down with their musical instruments, and standing thick on the platforms they played the German national tunes with *Deutschland über Alles* predominating. Sometimes, to impress their patriotism more distinctly upon us, they brought their instruments so close to our window that the shifting tubes of the trombones came right into the carriage. Sir Edward Goschen sat with his hands on his knees, making as though no sight or sound of this had reached his sense.

In Westminster Parliament had been pre-occupied with the Irish problem. What Lloyd George called the "muddy tracks of Fermanagh and Tyrone" seemed far more important than what had happened at Sarajevo. The Liberal cabinet was sharply split on its attitude towards the growing turmoil on the Continent. The critical day was 1 August, when King George V announced that "public opinion here is dead against our joining in the war". That was certainly true in the City, where there were fears of wholesale bankruptcy. "Money," wrote Lloyd George, "is a frightened trembling thing." But the issue turned increasingly on Belgian neutrality. Foreign Secretary Sir Edward Grey sent for the German Ambassador and warned him formally that failure to respect Belgium would result in difficulty to restrain public opinion in England. On 3 August, while the rest of the country was taking a Bank Holiday in blazing sunshine, he told the divided House of Commons that if Britain did not stand by France and stand up for Belgium "we should be isolated, discredited and hated". On the same day King Albert of the Belgians sent a telegram to King George V, making a 'supreme appeal' to Great Britain, which Grey read out to the House. As if by magic, this won immediate support from all sides, not least from the Irish. Arthur Nicholson, Permanent Under Secretary at the Foreign Office, waited anxiously in his office while Grey was addressing the packed Commons. At last a secretary came in with a strip of paper from the tape-machine. "They have cheered him, sir," he said. "He has had a tremendous reception." "Thank God," breathed Nicholson, "at last the way is clear, but it will be a terrible business." It was an accurate forecast.

The British ultimatum was issued, and duly ignored by the Germans. The 11pm 4 August deadline came and went, and a euphoric British nation took to the streets. The flag-waving crowds were so dense that motor-cars could not get through, and a massed throng gathered outside Buckingham Palace to cheer the Royal Family on the balcony and sing repeatedly *God Save the King*. At the other end of the Mall, another mob was smashing the windows of the German Embassy. In Trafalgar Square and in every town square across the country there was a mass of straw-boaters, bowlers, trilbies and cloth-caps, queuing to take the King's shilling while avuncular (for the time being) sergeant-majors looked on benignly.

Jack Griffiths had had no patience for any of the shilly-shallying. From where he stood the choice had always been a simple one. Four days before, on 31 July, not being able to contain himself any longer, he had placed an advertisement in the *Pall Mall Gazette*:

> MP's INVITATION TO OLD FIGHTERS.
> With a view to working in unity if duty calls, all Africans, Australians, Canadians or other Britishers who served in either the Matabeleland, Mashonaland or South African War and are not connected with any existing military or naval organisation and would be desirous of serving their Empire again are requested to forward their names and addresses with particulars of service to Mr John Norton Griffiths, M.P., at 3, Central Buildings, Westminster.

They came by the thousand. Tough leathery men, many wearing medals from the old campaigns in Africa, surged into Jack's office, leaving a queue which stretched into the street. Some were annoyed not to be signed up on the spot, and Jack was obliged to run another advertisement in the *Star* of 6 August begging for patience. "All applications are being dealt with," he promised.

When he had his regiment together, Jack called on Lord Kitchener, recently appointed Secretary of State for War. But Kitchener refused point blank to commission it. "Is this another one of your twopenny tricks?" he bawled, referring to a party trick Jack had shown him in Cairo, where he made two coins appear to be three. They argued for hours. And days. In the end Kitchener relented, and on 24 August the Colonial Corps was formally authorized and named the Second King Edward's Horse. They were inspected on Horse Guards Parade by General Bethune, who himself had had a regiment of irregular mounted infantry, Bethune's Buccaneers, in the Boer War. All were in

110

civilian clothes, with one trooper resplendent in a top hat and morning coat. But by September, with help from his friend Lord Lonsdale, who put up £1,000, Jack had equipped the Second King Edward's Horse with horses, equipment and uniforms by digging into his own pocket to the tune of £40,000. Lieutenant-Colonel Montagu Craddock took command, and Jack was 2 i/c with the rank of Major. They were headquartered at Langley Park, near Slough.

At about this time a man named Benjamin Excell was looking to sign up as a driver. He had worked for the Lanchester Motor Company in County Durham, which was known for its high quality automobiles. In those days the number of ordinary people who knew how to drive a motor-car was still relatively small. It was a comparatively new art, reserved for the rich man and his chauffeur, and had not yet percolated through to the masses. He was told by a friend to go down to the War Office and ask for Major Norton Griffiths. At 10.15 on the dot next morning he arrived for his interview. Jack stood by his desk, booted and spurred, tall and fierce-faced. Excell told him he had come from the Lanchester Company.

"You have, have you?" barked Jack. "And you're going to drive me, are you?"

"If I suit."

"That's right. If you suit."

He took Excell out onto the steps of the War Office and said, "Right, there you are. There's your car," pointing to a magnificent Rolls-Royce landaulette with a Rothschild body. It was chocolate-coloured, picked out with black lines. The dashboard was engine-turned aluminium, the radiator nickel-silver. It had silk blinds all around, and a table in the back.

"Oh, I thought it would be a Lanchester."

"No, it's a Rolls. Get on with it. I want to go to Langley Park quickly. You'll have to drive like hell!"

Jack was staying overnight at Langley Park.

"Where will I sleep?" queried Excell.

"Couldn't you sleep in the car?"

"No." He thought it was time he showed he had a bit of spirit.

"Right then, I'm sleeping at the farmhouse opposite the pub. You can have my tent."

In the morning, Jack asked, "How did you sleep?"

"Not very well. I had to sleep in my trousers. Look at me. I look a right mess."

"Don't worry about that." And he took out his cheque-book and wrote him out a cheque for £5 to buy another suit. Then he said, "You'll suit."

A great relationship had been born. Each respected the other, as master and servant, but each became the other's friend, too. Excell let Jack's snorts and bellows wash over him, but everywhere they went, he had to drive like hell. If anybody impeded their progress by getting in the way, a red-faced Jack would lower the window and roar, "COWSON!!" at them.

"They were a desperate lot of blighters, the colonials," said Excell, years later. "They didn't care tuppence."

The war produced many good contracts for Griffiths & Co. – camps, hospitals, aerodromes, a jetty at Hartlepool, a dry-dock at Queenstown and a naval base at Haverhill. But it was wartime and everyone was looking for economy, even those who were accustomed to dealing in millions of pounds. Jack and Gwladys moved to Brighton, where houses were cheaper. They kept £20 in gold sovereigns hidden behind one of the fire-places and bought a whole side of bacon. That was their idea of making provision for a rainy day. Gwladys started a day clinic for the men of the regiment and took them in for their typhoid inoculations.

One night in late September Jack said to Excell, "You can think yourself highly honoured. Tomorrow I want you to drive Lord Roberts down to Salisbury Plain. We are going to review the first contingent of Canadians. Pick us up at 8.45 a.m. You'll have an escort in the front with you." Excell was getting the car ready in the morning when a man came marching out with a rifle. This was the escort who was supposed to sit in front with the chauffeur. When Jack saw him he shouted, "What are you doing with that rifle, you cowson?" And with that he snatched the weapon from the astonished man's grasp and chucked it over the hedge.

Lord Roberts got in. He had aged considerably since Jack had last seen him after Paardeberg nearly fifteen years before. Surprisingly, it was a big German Mercedes which cleared their way down to Salisbury and behind them were four more big cars from the War Office. The convoy made 60 mph or more all the

112

way, skidding round corners with the tiny Roberts, white-faced, clinging to the edge of his seat. At Basingstoke, we are told, a tyre blew out. In Salisbury it was pouring with rain, but he refused to wear a raincoat while he inspected the troops. When the time came to return to London, Roberts came up to Excell, and said, "Now chauffeur, I want you to drive very, very slowly. It's a long time since I've been here, and I want to see it all again." The years had not deprived the old man of the skilful tact for which he was famous. It seems that the mishap at Basingstoke was probably a little more than just a burst tyre, judging by the note he wrote to Jack. Or perhaps he may have been referring to another incident, the details of which are not recorded more fully.

Englemere, Ascot, Berks.
26. 10. 14.
Dear Norton Griffiths,
    I am much concerned that – after your kindness to me on Saturday – you should have returned home with a battered head and an injured car. I do trust that the wound is not serious, and that Mrs Norton Griffiths will not be long without being able to use her car. Please give her my best thanks for lending the car.
    Yours sincerely, Roberts.

It would have been one of the last personal notes that the Field Marshal was to write. Less than three weeks later, on 14 November 1914, he died whilst inspecting his beloved Indian troops at St Omer in France.

The men of the Second King Edward's Horse began to grow restless through the long winter. Overtraining and their impatience to get to the front affected them as it has so many other bodies of men who find themselves inactive after being honed to fighting pitch ready for the fray. Early in the New Year one of the squadrons mutinied at Hounslow Barracks where they were then quartered. The exact circumstances of their discontent have faded with history, but Jack went down there, threw his hat on the ground and offered to fight any one of them. That quietened them for the time being, but it was clear that they were straining at the leash to get at the Germans, and it was doing no good to their morale by keeping them cooped up in Hounslow. Kitchener said that they could leave immediately for France if they left their horses behind. In other words, he required them, a trained mounted infantry regiment, to fight as foot-soldiers. Little realizing what this meant, they agreed.

"God bless you, my dear boys," whispered Gwladys to herself as they boarded the train to leave for a Channel port on the night of 3 May 1915, "and may Good Luck go with you wherever you go."

The first few days of the war had been fast and furious. The Germans swept through Luxembourg, crashed through the Belgian defences and struck southwards for Paris. The French, having quickly lost more than 300,000 men to the invaders, were forced into headlong retreat. The main British Expeditionary Force, 86,000 strong under Field Marshal Sir John French, crossed the Channel on the 12 and 13 August and took up position on a twenty-mile front near Mons, a Belgian mining town. Nothing much happened for days. The great slag-heaps around the mines made ideal lookout posts, but all seemed quiet, although they knew the Germans would eventually come. The citizens of Mons went about their daily business as if nothing at all were amiss. Many of them were in church on the morning of Sunday, 23 August when the Germans finally appeared at 10 am. It was a close-up, hand-to-hand fight which went on all day, with the British, vastly outnumbered, getting the worst of it. And then, in the late afternoon, a messenger arrived to give French some hair-raising news. The French Army had disappeared from the scene. His little BEF had been standing all alone, facing a huge German Army, without even knowing it. Without more ado, the British joined the French in retreat.

The Allies retreated for over 100 miles until making a stand a few miles north of Paris. It became the turn of the Germans to retreat. They took up a line on the River Aisne. Trench warfare began and would continue for four more years. Sir John French's cavalry had been already outdated when it relieved Kimberley in 1900. He seemed always to be fighting the last war: a military anachronism. So too, in many respects, were the likes of Kitchener, Haig and a dozen other top-brass who had been in the Redcoat Army since long before it switched to khaki. The futile tactics of some of them were to become famous to history.

114

The King Edward's Horse were hurried into the trenches just before the Battle of Festubert on 15 May 1915. The British, having just fought the inconclusive Battle of Aubers Ridge, which achieved nothing whatsoever except to lose many young mens' lives, planned an offensive push against a bulge in the German line to their south. The British bombardment opened with a total of 433 guns firing over 100,000 shells on a 5,000-yard front. The main objective was to destroy the enemy's breastworks and barbed wire, leaving gaps through which the infantry could pour. But they had no high explosive, only shrapnel shells, which were ineffective for the task, and many of them failed to explode. And to make matters even worse, many of the artillery pieces were antiquated, with badly worn bores, with the result that many shells fell short of the target – even killing many of their own advancing infantry.

The battle raged for ten days. It was reported in the press as 'the Festubert setback', in which their ranks were 'sadly thinned'. In reality, two-thirds of the Colonials had been wiped out. Many had died with their Boer War ribbons on their tunics. A beautiful testimony to their valour survives, engraved like an invitation to a ball. It bears witness that the regiment was Mentioned in Despatches by Field-Marshal Sir John French, and DSOs were liberally awarded to surviving officers, including Jack.

Those of them that remained spent the rest of the war in the mud-filled trenches of Flanders, and Gwladys threw herself in war work, making plaster casts for the legs of the wounded 'Blighty cases' at the Pavilion Hospital, Brighton. What became of the Second King Edward's Horse mounts, left behind at Woodbridge, we do not know.

Jack had had an idea in his mind since very early in the War. It sprang from his contract for the Manchester sewers. In France, two lines of belligerent trenches now faced each other, in places less than 100 yards apart, stretching from the English Channel to Switzerland, with colossal support – men, ammunition dumps, mules, horses, ambulance wagons, great piles of hay and forage, motor-lorries, stacks of food, flimsy kite-like aeroplanes, field hospitals and kitchens, and on the British side even London omnibuses, all littering the countryside for miles behind them. Neither was likely to give way, nor did they all that much, for four years, despite the efforts of the other to shift it. He went to inspect the lie of the land on the front between Ypres in the north and Vimy. It was clear to him that what had been a political stand-off in July 1914 had undergone a metamorphosis. It was indeed now a military stalemate.

It was open, almost flat, countryside, with patches of wood. Nowhere were there any hills to speak of, but the Germans had dug in on such high ground as there was on Vimy and Messines Ridges, leaving the British to wallow in the lower wet dyke-drained mud before them. There they sat, with both sides making sporadic 'offensives', which gained or lost a few yards. And winter was on the way.

Already the miserable waterlogged clay-clogged existence that was the lot of the British infantry was becoming famous. But Jack knew that it would be 'home from home' to his Manchester sewer tunnellers, or 'moles' as he called them. The soil he had seen in France was very similar to what they had burrowed through in Lancashire. And on a raw day towards the end of December 1914 he arrived in Kitchener's office clad in a mixture of uniform and hunting togs with his idea. Underground attack, that was the answer. Tunnel under the German lines, plant high explosives and blow the 'cowsons' sky high. In fact, he believed that the Germans had cottoned on to the idea themselves and were already digging. There was no time to be lost, but if he could be allowed to take a few of his 'moles' to France they would show how they could tunnel at speed using their 'clay-kicking' technique.

With that, he seized the fire-shovel from the grate, threw himself on his back in front of an amazed Kitchener and began flaying his arms and legs. "This is clay-kicking," he panted between strokes. "It's how my moles make tunnels." Clay-kicking was also called 'work on the cross'. The tunneller lay on his back, at 45 degrees to the floor of the tunnel, and facing the work-face, supported by a wooden back-rest shaped like a crucifix. He dug away at the wall of clay before him, using a special long-bladed light spade between his feet. The clay was hauled out by the digger's mate, who worked behind him with another man who helped him load it into gunny sacks to be dragged to the rear. A second team lined the tunnel with wooden

116

props to prevent it from collapsing. It was a very rapid method of constructing a narrow tunnel.

But Kitchener was not impressed. Nor, apparently, was Sir John French. Like so many of the British High Command, they were still fighting the Boer War. For once, Jack's powers of persuasion had failed to work. His suggestion was filed away, probably under M for moling, and forgotten. "He was frantic for action," wrote Gwladys in her memoirs, "nearly like a lunatic." But there was nothing he could do. And his proposal would probably have yellowed on a shelf until the end of the war. It could well have been gathering dust in the labyrinthine vaults of some archive even until today but for a sudden turn of events.

The Indian Sirhind Brigade was holding the line on a front of ten miles, not far from Festubert, where the Second King Edward's Horse were to have their baptism of fire the following spring. Fresh from their more accustomed surroundings in the hot and dry Uttar Pradesh, the Punjabis were finding this cold, wet and generally dismal European winter to be somewhat of a trial in its own right, regardless of what other unpleasantness the Germans were throwing at them. At half-past ten on the evening of 20 December all was quiet when a clutch of flares soared skywards from the German lines. Next minute there was a tremendous roar. It rolled, like a crash of thunder, along half a mile of the Indians' trenches. The mud shook beneath their boots. Suddenly an enormous rift appeared in the ground and an invisible, insuperable force drove upwards from below, throwing men, tons of earth and cart-wheeling bits of duck-board high into the air. Those who could still move scrambled from the trench and ran to the rear, dazed and disorientated by what had happened. And waves of German infantry poured over no-man's-land to take the position without losing a single man. In the dug-outs they found many corpses, still sitting relaxed. They had not been disturbed by what killed them, or known what it was.

Sir John French, now pressed by some of his Corps commanders to set up a special mining battalion, continued to procrastinate. Mentally, he was still in Kimberley. And anyway, was not mining the job of the Royal Engineers, who had recently shown so little aptitude for it? It was true. At the turn of the year

117

the 20 Fortress Company of the RE had tried to drive a tunnel under the German Line at Rue du Bois, near Armentières, but it filled with water faster than their ancient pumps could clear it, no matter how hard they strove to keep at it. Their morale, already low, was dealt a severe blow when a notice was hauled up above the German trenches saying in perfect English, "No good mining. Can't be done. We've tried." The mining operation was cancelled forthwith.

But the Germans, having seen success once, did it again. This time it was further north, near Saint Eloi, where the 3 East Yorks were mined from their trenches on 3 February and then hurled back in disarray under heavy mortar fire. And again, at almost the same spot a week later, when the 11th Hussars and 16th Lancers sustained heavy losses. By now there were pressing demands from all along the front for protection against this type of attack. The harmful effects even of bullets, bayonets, shells, grenades, lice, rats, filth and fearful weather conditions could all be guarded against to some extent, but there was no answer to sudden explosions from mines laid silently beneath the ground, and there was no way of knowing when enemy diggers were at work below. There was to be no warning. The tenterhooks were impossible to bear. The London Rifle Brigade did come up with a crude listening device. They took the petrol tank from a shell-wrecked vehicle, cut the top off, filled it with water and sank it into the mud. The 'operator' then knelt in the slush, and often it was a foot deep, to dip an ear into the icy water and hold it there for as long as his will-power held out.

On Friday 12 February Jack received a telegram ordering him to report to Lord Kitchener. The Secretary of State, by now in the process of waking up to the modern tools of war, was finding himself more and more at odds with the dilatory Sir John French. He sat at his desk, gazing dejectedly at some papers. He seemed to have aged years in a matter of weeks and was hardly the picture of a great and famous fighting man in his old, well-worn blue undress tunic. He looked up at Jack through a pair of heavy horn-rimmed spectacles and shoved the papers over the desk towards him, motioning to him to read them. They were all signals from French, reporting on the drastic effects of the German mines.

118

1. Commissioner Street, Johannesburg, in 1891.

2. T. H. Slater's "Dr Jim's March" was published shortly after the Jameson Raid.

3. Officers of the Mashonaland Field Force, 1896. Norton Griffiths is third from the right in the back row.

4. Jack's sketch of Fort Martin, 1897.

5. Cronje surrenders to Roberts at Paardeberg, 27 February 1900. Jack is on the far right.

6. The Wedding Day.

7. Landing at Lobito.

8. Garden Party at Temple House, Marlow, for the Coronation of King George V, 1910.

9. Gwladys typing on the Benguela Railway contract in 1906. The temperature was about 40°C.

10. Crossing the Lengué Gorge on the Benguela Railway, 1906.

11. Jack the Politician, September 1909.

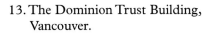

12. Crossing the Andes, 1909.

13. The Dominion Trust Building,
Vancouver.

14. Jack in spats. Photograph
by 'Pip'.

15. Sewer tunnelling in London.

16. The Family at home at Wonham, c.1920.

17. Jack the Businessman.

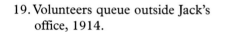

18. Colours of the 2nd Battalion, King Edward's Horse.

19. Volunteers queue outside Jack's office, 1914.

20. The Last Portrait.

21. In the Trenches.

22. Burying the Dead.

23. Rest and
    Relaxation.

24. La Boisselle
    Crater.

25. Jack rides Hero.

26. Jack and the Rolls.

27. About to sail for France with the Stanley Heading Machine.

XMAS 1915

WE'LL SEE YOU BLOWED FIRST

WISHING YOU THE COMPLAINTS
OF THE SEASON
FROM 173ʳᵈ Coy. R.E

28. 173 Mining
Company
Christmas Card,
1915.

29. 184 Mining Company Christmas Card, 1916.

30. Destroyed oil tanks at Ploesti.

31. Braila.

32. Jack with Queen Marie and other members of the Romanian Royal Family.

33. and 34. Working on the Aswan Dam.

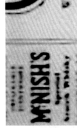

35. *Evening Standard*, 27 September 1930.

"The only thing I can suggest, sir," ventured Jack, "is that we use moles."

"What on earth do you mean?" came a tetchy response. Obviously, he had forgotten.

"Clay-kickers, sir. Workers on the cross."

And for the second time Jack grabbed the fire-shovel and sat on the floor to demonstrate. Instantly, Kitchener recalled their earlier meeting. He cleared his throat and the horn-rimmed glasses swung to look out of the window for a few seconds. His decision was instantaneous. Anything was worth a try and he knew Jack well for his ability to make things work.

"Get me 10,000 of these moles," he ordered curtly, "And I mean immediately!"

Jack hastened to point out that he did not think there were that many in the country. And in any case he would need to check that the ground where they would be put to work was suitable for their methods. But Kitchener, who was prone, normally, to let an idea mull in his mind before deciding on it, had been spurred into immediate action this time by the fraught situation in the trenches and by Jack's enthusiasm.

"Right," he rejoined. "Then leave for France at once. Tonight."

After braving a night crossing of the gale-swept Channel, Jack breezed into the Engineer-in-Chief's office at GHQ in St. Omer next day, to be greeted by an array of the Royal Engineers senior brass. The Engineer-in-Chief, Brigadier-General Henry Fowke, took an immediate liking to Jack, whose well-practised charm rarely failed to work. But here it was more than just charm. They were both engineers, and of course Jack was able to point to a formidable track record of success on major projects all over the world. There was a mutual professional respect. Fowke, for his part, was in many ways a very similar character to Jack, who was six years his junior. A big man, and still boyishly ebullient with a loud bellow of a laugh, he was an amusing raconteur. He played, or tried to play, most sports that his younger brother officers indulged in, none very well, but with the "exuberbant energy of a bull". And he was a superb engineer.

Fowkes' 2i/c, Colonel Harvey, who was to become Jack's friend and special confidant, wrote later:

On Saturday 13 February 1915 Major John Norton Griffiths walked into the Engineer-in-Chief's office at St Omer. I was assistant to the Engineer-in-Chief at the time, and I think that both he and I were relieved to find that the man in question really possessed practical knowledge of his subject, and was one to whom the word 'impossible' was unknown, and whose forceful character and enthusiasm swept away all opposition to his proposals, and at the same time was a most interesting and amusing companion.

Jack went straight into his explanation of moling. He was convinced that clay kickers could quickly burrow their way, in narrow tunnels not much wider than a coffin and undetected by the enemy, under the German lines. They could then "blow the cowsons sky high" and also intercept the Germans' own tunnels driving towards them. The mining initiative was there to be seized, he concluded.

The Royal Engineers brass were doubtful. They had all been through the School of Military Engineering and had encyclopaedic knowledge of all kinds of practical field work. It was amazing that none of them had ever heard of clay kicking. They would have to have a private discussion about it, they informed him.

Jack was well accustomed, by now, to the almost traditional reluctance to adopt innovations by British High Commands. The tragedy, on many occasions certainly since 1899, was that the enemy had so often capitalized on such lethargy. And so when he set out after breakfast the following day with a couple of his civilian engineers from Griffiths & Co. into a blustery sleet which swept down across the open tracts of Flanders to take a close look at the sub-soil along the front line at Givenchy about a mile from where the Indians had been blown up, there was a sense of foreboding gnawing at his spirits. In the trenches at this spot uneasy British troops had been constantly hearing faint noises from beneath the mud. It could have been some rats scratching around. They were crawling everywhere among the filth: a perpetual menace. On the other hand, it could equally have been German tunnellers at work. No wonder they were on edge.

One of the Griffiths & Co. engineers knelt down and took up a handful of clay.

"Just the ticket, isn't it?" asked Jack. It was more of a statement than a question.

"It makes my mouth water," replied the man, looking up with an evil smile.

They made their way back to St Omer, arriving just before midnight. Colonel Harvey was still up. Over nightcaps, he made it plain that he was now convinced that Jack's idea made sense. The brass had been discussing it behind closed doors all day. And he was pretty sure that Fowke himself, now fast asleep, was of a like mind. The Brigadier-General had actually been 'sold' on the proposal more or less as soon as Jack had first demonstrated it, but had wisely kept it to himself until his subordinates had had their say. His 'all clear' came over breakfast. But the way forward was still barred by the final and what could prove to be the most difficult hurdle to jump - the stubborn and erratic Sir John French, who sent for Jack to give him a first-hand explanation. But French, who probably felt sandwiched between Kitchener and his own staff officers, appeared to have already acquiesced. Most of their meeting was spent in discussion of how the new Mining Corps should be structured, and a telegram winged its way to the War Office formally requesting permission to set it up.

Jack had already despatched one of his engineers home to close down the Manchester sewer contract and to sign on volunteers from among those men consequentially laid off. He followed on behind, with his heart much lighter than it had been a day or so before. Urgent action and exciting times were ahead. It was the very stuff to bring out the best in him.

Another advertisement appeared in the national press the next day:

All those who have worked for the Metropolitan Tunnel and Public Works Company or in similar works who want to serve their country should apply to John Norton Griffiths, 3 Central Buildings, Westminster.

Over two hundred replies came in by return, mostly from his own former employees or sub-contractors. Many of the men were middle-aged, small and sinewy, typical miners. One of these men,

John McCreesh, an Ulsterman who had settled in the North-East of England to become a coal-miner, was a forty-year-old married man with a family. At the outbreak of war he had immediately volunteered to join the Durham Light Infantry, but had been refused owing to the fact that he was too old, had only one eye, was only just over five feet tall and was barely nine and a half stone in weight. Undeterred, he replied to Jack's advertisement, was signed up at the Westminster office and was on his way to France within days. Quite a few applicants had silver hair and must have been in their sixties, who when they were informed they had been passed fit for duty broke into gummy smiles. The doctor was worried that they would have difficulty in chewing hard tack emergency rations. Jack gave the first batch a pep-talk in his office. He explained what their job would be and promised that when the plunger was pressed they were to be privileged with a front-seat view of the Germans 'going up'. They were in uniform by Thursday, in Dover by Friday, France by Saturday and digging tunnels on the Sunday morning. None of them had admitted to being over thirty-five. Colonel Harvey said later that he thought this was probably the quickest *intentional* move of the war!

In London Jack was soon back in Kitchener's office demanding more and more urgency. The Secretary of State, now war-weary, suffered this harassment with solemn politeness. He was with Jack, but he knew that his Army chiefs were decidedly uneasy about the sudden arrival of swarms of rough ex-miners and civilian labourers, traditionally strong-minded, with no experience of military discipline, or indeed training of any kind, in the front-line trenches. And they would have to be employed *en masse*. There was a real danger that they could turn out to be an unruly mob.

French had at first agreed that a batch of two hundred coal miners should be sent out as an experiment, but he impressed upon the War Office that he wanted only reliable men and, as far as he was concerned, that meant definitely no Scotsmen. But he came under persistent pressure from his senior officers in the line, who were clamouring for still more speed. Most of them had warmed to Jack. Fowke himself was supremely confident, and so the Commander-in-Chief soon withdrew his limitations. It seemed as if he was, at last, possibly on his way into the twentieth century.

The War Office despatched their formal approval to Fowke without delay. There were to be nine Tunnelling Companies, RE, numbered 170–178, each with five officers and about 250 men, under the command of a senior Royal Engineer. They were to be supported by temporarily attached infantrymen, drawn *ad hoc* from various units to act as labourers, which was to be the cause of considerable friction between their own baffled officers and Jack, who was to act as Liaison Officer between the tunnellers and the HQ brass in St. Omer.

"I wonder," wrote one officer in his private diary, "how many rules and regulations he has broken, or worse still, has promised his recruits that their commanding officers will break for them," after watching Jack ride roughshod over all manner of military etiquette, stealing men from infantry regiments wherever he could, and all the time keeping up a lively commentary on progress in spicy unconventional language.

In order to carry out his allotted function Jack needed reliable transport. He would need to cover many miles through the shell-pocked mud and over the slippery cobblestones of Flanders. He decided that he was entitled to do this in a reasonable amount of comfort, so he persuaded the War Office to buy the Rolls from Gwladys, who was its official owner. A cheque for £750 was sent to her in Brighton and within a couple of days, the luxurious chocolate coloured beast was swung aboard a boat and delivered to him in France, together with his two favourite horses, Hero and Mint. For the most part the horses were kept safely behind the lines, out of harm's way, but Jack would send frequent instructions back to "give Hero a jump, he does love it so". Hero survived the War, by which time he had been ridden by so many people that Jack had had a special browband made for him, with the names Tom, Dick and Harry embossed on it in copper. The Rolls was soon to be a familiar sight, as it rocked and slithered its stately way among the shell-holes, with its driver's eyes glued steadfastly to the track, Jack in the back and a boot full of vintage port, Scotch and champagne with which to bribe commanding officers, recalcitrant at the prospect of having their men spirited away to haul clay out of Jack's holes in the ground. He was very disappointed, however, that Excell had refused to accompany him to the front, despite assurances of instant fame, heroism and medals.

There were, however, a few early problems with the ex-miners. Some had arrived in France with the idea that they were going to be digging only coal from mines far behind the lines, while some thought that they were going to be conveyed to and from work by Rolls-Royce! And as for parade drill, that was out of the question as far as 173 Tunnelling Company was concerned. Their CO, Major Guy Williams, received a deputation from them. (A more 'correct', less tactful, disciplinarian might even have considered them to be mutinous.) Their spokesman stepped forward to announce that "drill, or any form of military training, was not in their 'contract', which was to mine only." Williams listened politely, and suggested that it was in the interests of their own safety that they should know a little about soldiering as they were going to be working in dangerous surroundings. Quite what stamping their feet, sloping arms and 'about turning' was supposed to do with their safety is not clear, but they went away to confer among themselves and came back agreeing to be drilled. And they did so with gusto. Eventually, a year later, one senior officer saw them marching and honestly mistook them for a unit of the Guards!

Another *contretemps* arose over pay. And this time an out-played Jack found himself holding the wrong cards. Many regiments, especially those from Yorkshire, South Wales, Lancashire, Tyneside and the Black Country, contained a large number of ex-miners. These were just the sort of men the Tunnelling Companies needed. The 8th South Wales Borderers were one such unit. They were stationed at Hastings, awaiting shipment to France, when the War Office request for volunteers arrived. A parade was called, the notice read out and volunteers for special front line duty ordered to step forward one pace. The response was embarrassingly scant. The men were dismissed and sent for their tea.

One private, a youngster named Morgan, was sitting with his nose thoughtfully buried in his mug when the quartermaster-sergeant strode up to him and re-opened the subject. A juicy carrot was dangled. Six shillings and sixpence a day! That was *treble* what he was drawing as an ordinary squaddie! It was too good to refuse. The sergeant asked him if he could organize a group of eleven other volunteers and report to him in his office. For 6/6d a day, that was easy. They were to be marched to the Palace Hotel to be interviewed by an officer, but, before they left, the sergeant explained that the 6/6d rate was only payable to men who knew something about a special method of tunnelling called 'clay kicking'. At this, they all looked nonplussed and exchanged head-shakes and shoulder-shrugs with each other. "Take a look at this," said the sergeant, holding up a light spade with a long blade. "This is called a 'grafting tool'. If anybody asks you, remember to give the right answer. A grafting tool."

At the Palace Hotel Morgan snapped to attention in front of the officer, saluted and was stood easy. Various questions about mining were asked of him, which, as a Welshman, he was able to answer with ease. Then came the spade. Answer – grafting tool. And he was in. Next day he and his group found themselves on a train to London to be interviewed by Jack. The Sergeant-Major in charge of the party turned out to be a fatherly 'old sweat'. Over the years he had had a countless number of young recruits like these pass through his hands, and was the sort for whom most of them, after a couple of weeks in his tender care, would have fixed bayonets and charged into the jaws of hell itself. He warned them not to sign up for anything less than 6/6d a day. If they were asked to accept the standard rate of 2/2d, don't fall for it. Stick out for what had been promised.

They lined up at 3, Central Buildings. The first man was called into the office, where a bristly Major thrust a slip of paper towards him, saying, "Sign here". But the man hesitated, remembering the Sergeant-Major's words of advice.

"What's the rate, sir?"

"Two and tuppence."

"Sorry, sir, but I won't sign."

Jack, overhearing the exchange, interrupted angrily.

"Then get out!" he yelled.

The man quickly got out, and told his mates outside what had happened. They were all called in, one by one, and all received the same short shrift from a furious Jack.

Outside in the drizzle they formed up again into a squad to be marched back to the station. So it was going to be back to Hastings, back to the South Wales Borderers, and back on 2/2d a day after all. Never mind, they had had a day out. "By the left, quick march!" Then "Left . . . left . . . left" chanted the Sergeant-Major. They had only gone a few yards when a powerful voice rang out above the clatter of the London traffic. "Halt the men, Sergeant-Major! About turn and bring them back."

In the doorway of Central Buildings stood a large officer, trying hard not to appear too contrite. It was Jack, of course. He needed these men badly, and had decided to swallow his anger and relent. Six and six a day it would be, with one and ninepence on top as a ration allowance for the day they had spent in London.

Morgan's party lugged their kitbags down the ship's gangway at Boulogne. It was in the middle of the night and heavy snow was falling. A train stood alongside the jetty. Shivering beneath the upturned collars of their greatcoats, they boarded it. It snorted off to Bethune, where they climbed into the backs of a couple of open-topped, solid-tyred juddering lorries, to jolt and jar their way towards Ypres, sixty miles of badly rutted road away, with the rumbling sounds from thousands of guns growing louder in their ears with every mile. It was early afternoon when they arrived, stiff with cold, and by which time some of the older men were suffering badly from the effects of exposure. And still the snow fell.

They were billeted in a shell-damaged building that six months or so before had been a convent. But there was little time to thaw out or rest. That very evening, in pitch darkness that was regularly speared by the flashes of big guns and coloured flares, they were marched in single file up to the front line, facing a large steep hummock that their sergeant guide referred to in highly irreverent terms as 'ill 60. The famous Hill 60, an absurd pimple on the face of the planet, was in fact a giant heap of spoil from a nearby railway cutting. It was nearly 200 feet above sea-level, (in fact 60 metres, hence its name) and whichever side possessed it was afforded a magnificent view of the flat Flanders landscape all around. For that reason, it was a jewel to be coveted by any military commander. A whimsical advertisement appeared in the *Wipers Times*, a periodic publication for the troops:

PROPERTY
Building Land for sale on Hill 60.
Bright, breezy and invigorating. Commands an excellent view
of the historic town of Ypres.
For Particulars of Sale, apply: **Boche & Co. Menin.**

Hordes of young and healthy men would gasp their last breath
in the struggle to own Hill 60. The sergeant guide was to become
one of them. Suddenly, and without a word or a sound, he
toppled sideways in the muddy slush. Anxiously, they bent to
look at him, but he was quite dead, shot clean through the head.
Now they did not know what to do or where to go. They were
quite lost. So they simply crouched down, as low as they could.
But then, in the momentary light of a bright green flare, they
made out the shape of something big looming a few yards away.
It was a haystack that had somehow miraculously escaped
destruction. They dived deep into it, grateful for the little warmth
it offered, but even more thankful that at least they were out of
sight to any more eagle-eyed snipers. They stayed there until
dawn, when their officer, Lieutenant Hill, was able to lead them
to the rear.

Back in their convent they spent the rest of the day stretched
fast asleep on the floor, but when dusk fell they were mustered.
Again they found themselves facing the ugly lump that was Hill
60. There was just enough light for them to pick out the putrid
bloated corpses, each clad in khaki, blue or *feldgrau,* that were
liberally scattered in no-man's-land like so much debris left
behind on the terraces of a football stadium after the crowd
has departed. Many of them were sprawled in stiff grotesque
attitudes.

The staccato noise of gunfire grew until it had reached a
ferocious pitch. The Germans were coming! Men shouted and
ran to grab rifles. Morgan grabbed one and leapt onto the fire-
step. There were men in grey running towards him. They were
close enough for him to see the hate on their faces. His guts began
to tremble. They were coming to kill him. It was as if a huge fist
was clawing at his stomach as he squeezed the trigger of the Lee-
Enfield again and again, shoved in another clip of ammo as fast
as he could, slammed the bolt and squeezed and squeezed again.
Suddenly it was all over, finished as quickly as it had started. The

Germans had fallen back. Morgan had never killed a man before, and now he looked, horrified at what he had done, straight into the dead, open eyes of a youth who was somebody's son from Aachen, Bremen or Cologne. Given another five strides, he would have killed Morgan.

Morgan, of course, was a fully trained South Wales Borderer, but many other members of the special tunnelling intake had come almost straight from their civilian jobs in mines or sewers. They had had no weapons-training and, even at the height of the battle, had not been trusted to handle a rifle. Now they sat, many of them trembling visibly, in a slit trench, well out of the way, waiting for the order to retire. Frightened they were, any man alive would have been, but none had panicked. Quite what they were doing there, pressed into the front line, unarmed and without any apparent purpose, is mystifying.

Two days later eighty ex-miner volunteers joined, all transferred from the Monmouthshire Regiment, and it was announced that the mining party was now up to company strength. 171 Tunnelling Company, Royal Engineers, was fully-fledged, and could now go about its business.

13

HILL 60 GOES UP

By early 1915 the British had nearly a million men under arms. The British sector of the 400-mile front line trench work was concentrated in the north, where their line ballooned forward to embrace the ancient Flemish weaving town of Ypres. It was a narrow sector, by comparison with the French, but it was here that the fighting was most intense and brutal. The line moved constantly back and forth, waving before the gales of repeated attack and counter-attack. Ypres itself had no particular qualities that made it a natural strategic strongpoint, other than it was close beside what the Allies called the Messines Ridge. Whoever commanded this high ground commanded Ypres. But it was the Germans who held the ridge, whilst the British held the town. It was a recipe for much bloody battle.

With the war barely a couple of months old, the fiercely fought First Battle of Ypres had been a near disaster for the British. The Germans broke through their line and looked set to swarm into the town, which was saved only by some desperate fighting. In November 1914 the Germans tried again, with an all-out offensive involving twelve divisions of the Kaiser's best infantry. But again they were repelled by the British, aided by gallant French reinforcements, at a cost of 50,000 Allied lives. Since that time the spires and roof-tops of Ypres had been subjected to incessant shell-fire from the German heavy artillery perched three miles away on the Messines Ridge. Many citizens refused to evacuate their homes at first, and shops and cafés stayed open for business. There were evening concerts given on the bandstand in the marketplace and British Tommies crowded in to dance and flirt with the local girls. The besieged town had become a world-famous symbol of defiance, and the Ypres Salient was rarely absent from the daily war reports in the British national press.

Messines Ridge was about fifteen miles long. It was a crescent-shaped line of hummocks, extending from the hamlet of Hooge, due east of Ypres, southwards towards Messines past a copse of shattered willows and snapped off poplars somewhat ironically named Sanctuary Wood. Then it curved back south-westwards, through Hill 60, then skirted the Ypres-Comines canal before ending at a sorry pile of ruins that had once been a quiet rural village named St Eloi. Sir John French and his generals had long since come to the conclusion that they had to conquer this sliver of shell-churned Flanders at all costs. The German defences were known to be exceptionally strong, 'abnormally' so in the words of Sir William Robertson, the British Chief of General Staff. But somehow this only served to increase the obsession to take it.

An attack by mining seemed to bear distinct possibilities and orders were issued from GHQ for digging to begin at St Eloi and Hill 60. Major David Griffith, Royal Engineers, was put in charge of the planning, and ex-South Wales Borderer Garfield Morgan and his mates, together with 173 Tunnelling Company, were sent up the line. Their equipment – air pumps, water pumps, digging tools, wooden shuttering and other paraphernalia arrived by train at Estaires, a dozen miles to the south, and was dumped in a huge pile. One ex-miner from Yorkshire, a man named Mosley, was told off to guard it. He was astonished at what he saw, especially the essential air pumps. All seemed crude and ancient to his knowledgeable eye. And he was right. It was sheepishly admitted later that the stuff had lain in army stores since the Crimean War of 1854! In the event, it turned out that these antiques were extremely noisy when working, and silence was imperative if the Germans were not to have their suspicions raised. The diggers even took to swearing under their breath to avoid being heard by the enemy. At best, this would destroy the element of surprise and render the operation pointless. At worst, the enemy could explode a mine nearby which would collapse the tunnel and bury the tunnellers alive. The Crimean War machinery was discarded at an early juncture, to be replaced by a simple blacksmith's bellows-type arrangement, which carried a continual supply of hisses of fresh air via a hosepipe directly to the workface. The drawbacks with this were that it affected the sight and hearing of the diggers, and as the tunnel grew longer it was unable to deliver a sufficient supply of oxygen.

Although the local soil had made the Griffiths & Co. engineer's 'mouth water', the choice of a starting point and path for each tunnel was very much a matter of trial and error. It was winter time and the water-table was high. Generally, the method was to dig a narrow vertical shaft, sixteen or so feet deep, from the bottom of which would lead the tunnel proper on the desired path to the target. The first attempt to 'get started' under Hill 60 was abandoned when it was only a few feet deep. Every spadeful of soggy clay that was squelched away from the workface was instantly replaced by water and more gooey slurry. And even when a tunnel did get underway, the earth was so saturated and the pressure so great at over sixteen feet down, that squirts of porridge-like mud shot through any chinks left between the wooden shuttering preventing the walls from collapsing.

At last, by 8 March, three sound 'jumping-off' spots had been selected, named M1, M2 and M3. Morgan was put to work on M3, together with another Welsh ex-miner, Albert Rees. M3 started in Trench 38, in a very dangerous position, only fifty yards from the German line and perilously exposed. They started on their sixteen-foot shaft into the heavy waterlogged clay. Only a few spadesful of surface soil had been removed when they came across a body. It was that of a French soldier, highly decomposed and crawling with maggots. They tried to lift it out of the hole, but as they did so it fell into pieces under its own weight. They were told to put it into sandbags, and to do the same with any more bodies they might find. Within the first couple of hours they turned up three more, all in the same state of decay. Gagging with nausea, they loaded all of them into bags and, when darkness fell, dragged them to the rear of the trench to be buried in quicklime. There were many more to come, so many that the acrid fumes of quicklime soon came to hang over the whole sector. Half a century later men who were there said that they had never, since that day, been able to get a whiff of quicklime in their nostrils without being reminded of Hill 60.

The shafts crept forward, at about ten feet a day as the men

131

dug, all around the clock in three shifts of eight hours apiece. The digger hacked out sodden chunks of clay and shoved each one back to his mate behind him. The mate heaved it into a sandbag, which when full was hauled back to the tunnel entrance on a rope by labourers. In some of the larger tunnels, as work progressed, they introduced trolleys on which the spoil could be transported. Each shift would end with the tunnel-men soaked in sweat and mud, and with nowhere to dry their clothes. Then it was a tot of rum 'to ward off the chill' and then to sleep, usually fully dressed in dugouts in slip trenches. After each sopping-wet week in the tunnel, they had three days' leave to let off steam in town. This they did with vigour. Every other private house seemed to have opened in business as an *estaminet*, where Tommies could buy wine and cognac, flirt with Mam'selle under the watchful eyes of her mother, bounce toddlers on their knees and sing 'Tipperary' to their hearts' content. But Ypres had in effect become a garrison town, and as with all garrison towns relations between the civilian and service populations were not always as cordial as one might have hoped. But Ypres was no ordinary garrison town. It was in a theatre of war. A group of British soldiers were stretching their legs in a small village a couple of miles behind the lines, which they had assumed, quite reasonably, that it was safe to do. A shot cracked out from a sniper and one of the men fell. Luckily, the bullet had only grazed him. But the sniper had been spotted by some other soldiers, who hauled him down from a tree. He was a seventeen-year-old Belgian youth, who, when searched was found to have no fewer than a dozen British identity tag 'trophies' round his neck. He showed absolutely no remorse, even under the threat of severe punishment, when questioned on the spot by a British officer. In fact, he remained vehemently and fearlessly pro-Kaiser. The officer called for a spade, handed it to the boy and ordered him to dig. Now he began to show signs of fear, but he kept digging. Finally, a pair of soldiers held him over the hole while the officer drew his pistol, walked up to him and shot him through the head. They used the spade to bury him. The other squaddies looked on, apparently unflustered. It had been swift justice, even too swift for many. But these men had watched more men die and seen more dead bodies in one hour than most people back in Blighty

132

would see in a dozen lifetimes. They had become inured to such sights. They turned to resume their walk.

At St Eloi the Germans were putting down such a deluge of fire that it was hardly possible to move from cover for a minute. The casualty rate was consistently high and 171 Company had a tunnel to dig there. They tried to get started the first night, but the German gunners had pinpointed the range. All they had to do from their eyrie on Messines Ridge was to keep heaving their shells in, slamming shut the breeches and pulling the lanyards. Digging at surface level was impossible in such conditions, and when dawn broke not a spade had been turned. They tried again the next night, only to spend the entire shift crouched in dugouts as the earth above them trembled under the onslaught. On top of all that, the subsoil there was of the worst kind for tunnelling. Water and loose sand rapidly back-filled each hole the spades made. The officer-in-charge decided that St Eloi was not a suitable place for mining after all and retired them to the rear.

Jack was informed of this and the reasons for it when he arrived, as usual like a human tornado, at Ypres on Sunday 7 March. Typically, he could not accept this at all, but was told by Lieutenant-Colonel Lock of the Divisional Staff that the decision had been taken amid much anxiety about the St Eloi situation, and that it had the blessing of the Fifth Corps commanders. From now on all efforts were to be concentrated on Hill 60. At around midnight Jack arrived at St Eloi to see for himself. A horrific scene presented itself to him in the light of gun-flashes and flares, and the shells rained down as usual. But he was still convinced that mining was possible and spoke his mind to Fowke. Spurred by reports that there were suspicions of German mining opposite St Eloi, they did try again, but with no success. The running sand and water were as persistent as ever. If the Germans were indeed tunnelling there, it had to be in a different kind of soil. One or two 'listeners' were placed in a couple of abandoned tunnel works. One man, Lance-Corporal Leonard, spent hours doubled up in one of them holding one end of a piece of stick in his teeth, with the other end pushed into the earth. The idea was that, if the Germans were tunnelling, he would feel the vibrations as they worked. The problem was that his teeth were jarred continually as the ground shook under the relentless shelling. Nobody had explained to him how to distinguish between that and the vibrations from men digging. Jack was overruled and his St Eloi men were re-assigned to the M1 tunnel at Hill 60. For them it was a fortunate decision.

It was at precisely five o'clock in the afternoon of 10 March that it happened. The rain had ceased, but the ground was still ankle deep in churned mud and a chilly wind tugged at the soldiers' clothes. The German barrage had lifted for a minute. Normally that was a sure sign that something was about to happen. Anxious lookouts all along the British parapets peered through binoculars and the tangled barbed wire before them for signs of a German infantry attack. But it did not come.

Seconds later came an almighty roar from underground. Three giant fountains of mud rose from the British trenches, carrying men, rifles, duck-boards, sandbags and great clods of clay spinning high into the sky. So high, in fact, that the cascade of debris was still falling as the advancing Germans charged through it. One of them, a young *feldwebel* in the 23 Bavarian Regiment named Michael Schneider, had stood nearby with nerves taut, watching the German sappers as they waited for the order to press their plunger. The wait had seemed to last for hours. At last, the order came – "*Fertig machen!*" (Get ready!) and then came the rumbling crash from the British lines and the sky filled with earth and men. "*Heraus! Heraus!*" (Get out of here!) screamed a frantic *hauptmann,* wildly running up and down behind his troops to hurry them 'over the top'. Schneider gripped his Mauser Gewehr 98 tightly, gritted his teeth and scrambled out of the trench, followed by his platoon. The sight he saw would be forever imprinted on his memory; that of British soldiers in mid-air, as he put it "bursting like fat toads". They charged over the hellish landscape of no-man's-land. The British were still dazed and the Germans were quickly upon them. The shots, shouts, and screams of hand-to-hand fighting rent the air. One young German went to throw a stick grenade but it slipped from his grasp to explode only feet away and he fell backwards with blood gushing from his head. A lanky bolt-eyed Englishman clad in a torn woolly jumper leapt up and was promptly felled by a bullet in his belly. Another Tommy popped up and shot a young Bavarian straight through the forehead barely two seconds before

134

Schneider shot him too. Soon the British were in retreat, and, as they ran towards their support trench, the triumphant Germans dropped to one knee and picked them off as if it was target practice, killing dozens of them. Schneider, euphoric with victory and with the adrenalin now pumping wildly, started to pursue them. But after a few steps he too was hit. Lying in the mud on the very edge of the huge crater that had been torn by the explosion, he was relieved to hear the order being shouted to dig in where they were. Their objective had been achieved.

The British made a half-hearted counter-attack that night, but it came to nothing. St Eloi, for now at least, was German. News of the debâcle reached Hill 60 within minutes. The Germans were clearly ahead in the war underground. And here the muffled sounds of their diggers at work could be heard quite clearly. 171 Tunnelling Company began to double and redouble their efforts. It would be a very clear-cut thing. The simple fact was that the winners would be whichever side pressed their plunger first. The terrible race for life, or death, was on. And the losers would have been digging their own tombs.

The British sappers, already exhausted, now found unrealized reserves of energy. With earth in their mouths and ears, and sweat running into their eyes, they hacked away at the clay desperately, knowing that their lives depended on speed. Ten feet a day had once been considered to be a reasonable rate of progress, but now they were achieving twelve or fourteen. And as they burrowed deeper, so the sounds of the Germans on the other side became louder and more distinct. One day Morgan and his mate Albert Rees were grafting away when Rees's spade went into the clay-face, right up to the handle as he thrust it in. He had dug into thin air. They both stared in frozen silence at the sinister black opening, the size of a rabbit hole before them. It could mean only one thing – they had met the German tunnel head-on. And they were left in no doubt about that when there were sounds of men moving – voices, a cough, and a splash as a foot trod in water. Rees blew out their candle and they scrambled back to the shaft, never more thankful to see the sky. Given the general urgency under which every man was labouring, it is surprising that it took Second Lieutenant Black, on duty in the officers' dugout, over an hour to decide that he must take a look. They groped their way back in complete darkness, guided by the wooden sides of the tunnel, until Morgan whispered to Black that he thought they had arrived at the spot. The Second Lieutenant snapped on his flashlight, to be greeted instantly by a loud crack as a bullet ripped through the sleeve of his tunic. The three fled back to the shaft, where Black sat for another hour, pondering on what to do next. "We'll go back now," he announced with boyish bravado (he would have been only nineteen or twenty years old), "and don't forget the Boches are as scared as we are." They crept back into the blackness, dragging a hundredweight of guncotton apiece, to find no Germans but a canister of explosive with wires running from it. They cut the wires, reconnected them to their guncotton and retired. Obviously there was no more digging to do in that particular tunnel, but later the guncotton was doubled and left to assist in the really big bang which came later. For once the Germans seem to have been slow on the uptake, because they do not appear to have investigated the reason for their canister failing to explode.

Jack had been charging around the front in his brown Rolls and on Hero's back like a man possessed. For seven weeks he had kept up this frantic pace, despite many sleepless nights and a debilitating attack of 'the trots'. He was far from happy with the speed of progress and arrived in Ypres on the evening of Saturday, 3 April, in a hurry as usual, intending to inspect the Hill 60 tunnels. He charged into the office of Major David Griffith, the commander of 171 Company, who refused to be bombarded by his questioning and stated that he could not arrange for Jack to visit the tunnels until the Monday. Jack (who of course was his equal in rank) and Griffith plainly did not like each other. Griffith had been in the army for twenty-six years and was himself the son of a Royal Engineers officer. The long-accepted etiquettes of military behaviour were instilled in him. Everything he did and said was 'as per the book' and he took severe exception to the other's breezy attitude which cut right across the grain of what he had been accustomed to accept. And it still rankled with him that Jack had disagreed with his opinion that St Eloi had been unsuitable for mining. Furious at being treated with such disdain, Jack left. He was not at all sure of the weight of his authority and had hesitated to try to bulldoze this 'cowson', which was what he probably muttered under his breath as he climbed back into the Rolls. The truth was that no senior officer knew quite where his authority lay in connection with the new Tunnelling Companies. It was a problem that festered for much longer than it should have, especially in time of war, when it is absolutely essential to have a clearly defined chain of command. He tossed and turned in his bed through the night at Poperinghe, which was at that time seven miles behind the lines, and blew back into Griffith's office next morning. He stated, baldly, that he thought that two sections of 171 were under-employed, and that moreover some unskilled labourers had slipped through the net and were working as skilled tunnellers. But again he was stiffly stonewalled. Griffith refused point-blank to discuss any of the matters on Jack's agenda. Jack, now boiling, went straight to the Chief Engineer of Fifth Corps, Brigadier-General Petrie, and sought advice. The senior man knew Jack's civilian reputation, both as an engineer and as a man-manager, and he respected him for it. The telephone wires hummed and Griffith was persuaded to climb down. Their next meeting was coolly polite. Griffith showed him the Hill 60 plans, now displaying a willingness to discuss them up to a point, and explained that work had been impeded by lack of air pumps and lighting equipment. The man's stiff-backed military ego had achieved nothing but waste twenty-four hours of Jack's time.

Tunnels M1 and M2 ran straight for about 100 yards into no-man's-land, then each formed a two-pronged fork just short of the German trench. The tips of these prongs would make four explosion chambers. M3, and its off-shoot M3a, now packed with Second Lieutenant Black's guncotton, was already prepared. Digging was finished at Hill 60 on 10 April and Major David Griffith sat down with the Manual of Military Engineering, which was never far from his side in any event, to calculate the required charges. A crucial factor was the depth of the mine, and nobody seemed to know what the depths were, because the constant heavy fire had prevented a calm and collected survey of Hill 60 from being carried out. He could but guess, and decided on twenty feet for M1, fifteen for M2 and twelve for M3. The formula in the 'book' was based on the use of old-fashioned gunpowder and, to blow a crater sixty feet across, Griffith found that he would need to pack no less than half a ton of powder into each of the M1 chambers and in M2 about a quarter of a ton. Lieutenant Hill was given the order to proceed with the charging. This was the same Lieutenant Hill who had led his green intake of shaken diggers back from their warm haystack on their very first morning in the line. It had been his first morning too. But he was now a fully seasoned officer with seven weeks' experience.

Handling gunpowder in 100 lb bags is a ticklish business. Here, ninety-four of them had to be delicately manhandled up through the support trenches, lowered on pulleys down the shafts and carried gingerly on a man's back along the tunnel to the chamber. If a machine-gun bullet or a piece of hot shrapnel were to ignite one of them in the process, the result could only be imagined.

The charges, in special waterproof boxes, double fused and wired back to their three plungers, with a massive thirty-foot-thick wall of sandbags, the 'tamping', blocking each tunnel behind them to ensure an upward and forward blast, were all in place by 15 April. The chocolate Rolls skidded into Ypres again. At 27 Division H.Q. an excited Jack gave all the credit for the preparation work to Lieutenant Hill. Major David Griffith would get no kudos from him, that was sure. And he outlined his views on how the planned infantry assault should proceed following the blast. He wanted them to charge into no-man's-land before the flying debris had fallen back to the ground, just as the Germans had done at St Eloi. It would be far better, he suggested in his habitual spicy language, to have a couple of men killed by falling German bodies than a lot of men killed by machine-gun bullets.

Two days of mind-chilling suspense followed. The infantry assault was to be carried out by troops of 13 Brigade, who were not due in the line until the following night. Zero hour for the blast was set at seven o'clock on the evening of 17 April 1915. Hill ordered repeated checks of the fuses and wiring. His sappers, nervous as actors before curtain rise, squelched down the tunnels with their flashlights, inspecting every inch of wire. They could hear clearly the sounds of the German tunnellers, now working directly overhead. If they were to press their plungers first . . .

17 April turned out to be a bright spring day. The routine sporadic firing from both sides went on all day, but died away

towards the evening. It was the lull before a storm. Griffith, Hill and one or two more officers stood in the command dugout beside the bank of three plungers. At five past seven he nodded to the others and each slammed a plunger handle hard into its box. The violence inside the guts of Hill 60 erupted with a roll of thunder that went on for a good ten seconds. A huge cloud of assorted debris and bodies soared into the air for hundreds of feet to fall back over a radius of 300 yards. One British soldier peeped above his trench and was killed by a chunk of it which hit him squarely in the face. A ferocious artillery barrage began from three British artillery brigades, joined by French and Belgian batteries. And to the sound of their regimental bugles, units of Royal West Kents and Home Counties Field Company, Royal Engineers, fixed bayonets and charged 'over the top' towards the hill, which now had a hole the size of a football pitch in it.

A prisoner, lucky to be alive, told them that the Germans had planned to blow their own mines just two days later.

But what appeared at first to be a major triumph had all been for nothing. The break-through on Hill 60 had been deep and narrow which meant that the British, as they advanced, had left themselves exposed on both flanks. The German gunners seized their opportunity and began a vicious enfilading fire as a counter-attack. The British put up a stubborn defence and rushed seven more battalions up to support the West Kents. They were still fighting three days later when the Germans switched their attack to the town of Ypres itself. Huge 17-inch shells, bigger than were fired by most naval guns of the period, landed in the market square, killing several civilians. At last the population had suffered enough. They began to trudge out of town with push-carts, perambulators and wheelbarrows piled high with bundles of belongings. Some of the shopkeepers did not even pause to empty their tills.

At five o'clock that afternoon the Germans made military history. Five miles to the north-east of Ypres some French Algerian troops had just arrived in the line to see a greenish layer of mist rolling downwind towards them. Chlorine! With streaming eyes and burning lungs, they ran from their trenches, but the gas was drifting quicker than they could run and it soon spread to Hill 60. By then it had thinned and was no longer disabling, but it was enough to make the conditions there infinitely worse. Came the dawn of 5 May and the British were still on top of the hill. They had won four VCs, but were dead-beat after battling non-stop for days on end. At 0845 there was a shout from a lookout, "Gas! Gas!" This time it was coming directly for them, swirling, dense and green. They had no gasmasks but cotton pads hurriedly issued by the stores as rudimentary protection against this new evil of war. This time the British retreated from their hard-won hill and Morgan staggered into the clearing station at Ypres clutching his throat and coughing up bright green puke. He was in hospital for eleven weeks.

About two thousand Tommies lay dead on Hill 60. The British army had not experienced such concentrated carnage since Spion Kop. But Jack and 171 Tunnelling Company had their own private, more mundane problem – money. British miners have never felt adequately paid for the work they do and the dangers they face. Many would agree they have a point. In consequence they have become among the most bloody-minded of all work-forces. They have even brought down Governments. The six and sixpence versus two and tuppence daily rate still rankled with the tunnellers. Jack was determined that there should be a pay differential between those actually working at the face and their mates behind them, and he was sure there was a wangle going on, where men inexperienced in clay-kicking were wrongly being paid the higher rate. This was one of the things about which he had fallen out with the officious Griffith. Even as the battle for Hill 60 was raging, the muttering grew in the ranks of the miners, culminating in a strike notice being thrust before the Commanding Officer. Six bob a day, all round, was the demand, or no more digging would be done. It was wartime and this was mutiny. It could mean the death penalty for those who had signed the notice.

The men were paraded in a barn nearby to be scathingly lectured by an agitated red-faced lieutenant. Their ringleader, if found, would be shot, he shouted, and stormed out. That brought them to their senses. Finally it had been hammered into their heads that they were in the army. But Jack, tactful for once, had been quietly making his own enquiries and he suspected that the unhappiness arose because more or less all of them had probably been promised the higher pay. This led to an altercation with the Royal Engineer Lieutenant who was organizing recruiting back at 3 Central Buildings in Jack's absence at the front. A hundred men a week were passing through his hands, he asserted testily. It was not only impracticable, but physically impossible, for him to ascertain the level of skill of each of them. In the end the War Office came to the rescue. Every man was to start at two and tuppence, they decreed, and once he had demonstrated his proficiency could apply to be upgraded. Jack remained adamant that wherever he could find fair proof that a man lacked the necessary skill he would be removed, and, to show his resolve, he did return a few men back to their regiments within the next week, after which he arrived to address 171 Company's clay-kickers, about fifty men in all, in their barn. He told them how proud he was of the good work they had done and then sat in a corner with Lieutenant Hill to interview each of the six bobbers singly. Only two of them failed to come up to scratch and were told to pack their kit. Then he went outside to the boot of the mud-splattered Rolls and hauled out a case of whisky for the rest of them.

171 Tunnelling Company re-discovered itself that night.

14

BRING UP THE AMMONAL

Away to the British left of the salient stood the hamlet of Hooge. It was really little more than a large ruined château and its outbuildings, stables and suchlike. The front line ran right through the middle of it, so that the Germans held the house and the British the stables. Brigadier-General Hoskins, commanding 8 Brigade, had been ordered to remove the Germans, and called the officers of 175 Tunnelling Company to see him. Jack was not 100% happy with some of the 175 Company officers. In his habitual manner, he wrote in his diary for Monday 10 May 1915 – "Proceeded to 175 Coy. Cowan rec'd no news to proceed 2 Div, but ready. Don't think much of Birkett. Gas bag. Suggested to Cowan to push his nose into the first job and keep him there. Rest of officers appear equal to anything yet received. Mostly Royal School of Mines. The pucker article is the best. Think wise to stipulate RSM qualifications sine qua non. Not one, I think, of the RSM men has disappointed."

Nevertheless, he needed some assistance by mining and 175 were the nearest tunnellers to hand. Over generous glasses of the Brigadier-General's apricot brandy, Lieutenant Geoffrey Cassels found himself volunteering to lead a mining party to achieve the objective.

With a starting point from the inside of a stable, unseen by the enemy, he had expected a straightforward job, but then he encountered the usual problems with running sand and water-logged earth. His tunnel was running off-target and it had gone too far to be corrected. It then occurred to him that he now had a better target than the château in his sights –a pair of brand-new concrete redoubts, or large pillboxes. He took the idea to his CO, Major Cowan. The Germans had almost abandoned the house, leaving only a couple of snipers inside, and moved the main body of the defenders into the redoubts. Cassels' plan was a sensible switch and Brigade gave it the go-ahead.

But again his tunnel ran off course. Only slightly, but it was veering away from the desired midpoint between the two 'semi-detached' pillboxes. He cursed the quality of Government-issue surveying instruments and stood deep in thought. Another plan struck him. If he could blow up the right-hand redoubt, it should throw enough material into the sky to bury the other when it came down. But how to calculate the necessary charge? He had no idea of the weight of concrete his explosion would have to heave up. He consulted Cowan. Together, they decided to err on the safe side. Better to use too much explosive than not enough. Then Cowan recalled hearing about an explosive which had three and a half times the power of gunpowder. It had been around for years, but as far as they knew it had never been used before in anger. It was called ammonal

Ammonal is composed of 75% ammonium nitrate, plus aluminium, spiced up with TNT. Its rate of detonation is something like three and a half miles *per second*.

Fifth Corps agreed to its use and Cowan requisitioned the ammonal from the Quartermaster-General at GHQ. This created a fluster, because nobody there had heard of the stuff. A message arrived on the desk of the quartermaster at Fifth Corps. "Can you please say if you have made any use of ammonal, and if so, were the results satisfactory?"

The Fifth Corps quartermaster was equally nonplussed and replied, "This is not understood. For what purpose is ammonal used please? Is it a drug or an explosive?"

"Perhaps the Medical Officer attached to your Corps HQ will be able to give you the required information."

"In accordance with your Minute 4, I have consulted the MO. He informs me that ammonal is a compound drug used extensively in America as a sensual sedative in cases of abnormal sexual excitement. So far as I am able to ascertain this drug is not a medical issue to Corps HQ. At the present time, the MO states that no cases have occurred among the Corps personnel indicating the necessity for it."

Meantime, Cassels was growing impatient. He rushed around, scrounging whatever explosives he could from neighbouring units, but only managed to get his hands on an amount woefully short of what was needed. At last a wagon appeared, loaded with ammonal, dangerously driven up in broad daylight in full view of the Germans, and Cassels got to work. By 2.30 pm on 19 July the biggest mine yet laid in the war was ready, soundly tamped and with wiring fully tested. Barely minutes before zero hour – seven o'clock – Cassels was waiting, ready to depress the plunger, when he was horrified to see a German shell explode near the wiring. He ran with a corporal to see if any damage had been caused. It had. The corporal found that the wiring had been cut clean through. They hurriedly re-joined the ends, ran back to their dugout and re-tested the circuit. All was well. They had just made it. There were still a couple of minutes to go.

All was quiet now. Somewhere, among the desolation of ruined buildings, blackened dead bodies with their swarms of flies, barbed wire and smashed trees, a bird sang. And an orphaned black kitten which Cassels had befriended jumped onto his knee. Then the minute hand on his watch clicked upright to seven o'clock and he slammed the two handles down.

The sudden violence was almost beyond description. Among the spiralling material in the sky he saw a complete tree 'gyrating like a match-stick', and bits of bodies fell around him. It was time to leave. Back in the comparative safety of his dugout in Sanctuary Wood he looked at the still smoking spot where the redoubts had been, which was now a crater 120 yards across. But he could see no British troops. The planned infantry assault to take the crater was to have been made by the 4th Middlesex and the 1st Gordon Highlanders, who were, of course, well forward. He was appalled to learn later that, although several hundred Germans had been killed in their redoubts, ten men of the Middlesex had also been buried and lost.

The Hooge mine had been a case of an enormous 'overkill'. 3,500 lbs of ammonal had been needed to do the job, but Cassels had used 4,500 lbs. He feared he would be in serious trouble for what had happened to the Middlesex men, but instead he was taken to lunch with Lieutenant-General Sir Edmund Allenby and the C-in-C, Sir John French, and was later awarded the Military Cross.

This innovative use of ammonal, and its awesome results, gave fresh impetus to an idea that Jack had been nursing for months.

15

CODE NAME – DEEP WATER

One day in the spring of 1915 Jack had stood in the drizzle gazing thoughtfully across no-man's-land, letting his eyes sweep to and fro across the Ypres Salient. He was convinced that a mining operation could be carried out on a large enough scale to make a real difference to the outcome of the war. The breakthrough at Hill 60 had been on far too narrow a front and had met with consequent disaster. Therefore, why not blow the whole of the Ridge away? As he saw it, it could be done on the crescent running from St Eloi, through Wytschaete to Messines itself. It was a distance of three and a half miles and the explosion would be immense, so immense that such a job would probably need an officer much senior to himself with the necessary authority to pull its various threads together. For one thing there would be the question of having enough men available to tackle such a job. But there were more immediately pressing things to do, so the thought remained at the back of his mind.

He continued to charge around with boundless energy, stealing men from their units, handing out endless bottles of champagne or whisky to mend whatever fences he trod down in the process, dealing outrageously with 'difficult' officers senior to himself, inspecting various tunnels in hand, handing out advice left, right and centre, and hurtling up and down the twenty-eight miles between the front line and St Omer. A young Canadian Corporal named Basil Sawers was sitting in a tent somewhere south of Ypres one evening when a soldier poked his head through the flap. "There's a bloody general outside looking for you, Corp," he announced. An astonished Sawers stood up, stuck his arms into his tunic, made sure that all his buttons were fastened and

146

hurried outside. There stood a brown two and a half ton 1911 Rolls-Royce Silver Ghost with a large officer alongside it. Somehow Jack had come to know that Sawers was a mining engineering undergraduate from McGill University in civilian life. Never one to beat about the bush, Jack asked him straight out if he would like to transfer to a tunnelling company, and if so there would be a commission in it for him. They chatted for a few minutes and, as the Rolls purred away, Jack called back to say he would hear in a day or so. Three days later, a chit arrived – "Second-Lieutenant Sawers to report to R.T.O. Steenvoorde for transportation to 177 Tunnelling Company, RE." Sawers' commanding officer was furious. He had been told nothing of this and had never seen such irregular behaviour. It took him six days to check on the authenticity of the chit, during which time he told Sawers nothing of it. The corporal must have thought that he had been the subject of a hoax. Eventually, his commanding officer had no option but to release him, and another bottle of Scotch changed hands. That swoop was a typical one of Jack's many raids for a useful recruit.

Soon the tunnelling from both sides left no-man's-land like a veritable rabbit warren, with countless shafts, listening posts, galleries, saps and explosive chambers combing it at various depths. To many non-tunnelling officers they were a dangerous ploy. Even Jack's friend, Major the Hon Arthur Murray, who had helped him form the 2 King Edward's Horse, now in the line at Messines, bristled angrily when told that tunnelling was about to start in his sector. "To Dante's Inferno with your accursed tunnels!" he shouted. "The Germans will see you and they'll blow us all to Timbuktu!"

Murray certainly had a point. The infantry had grown jumpy. And who could blame them after they had seen the dreadful damage under Hill 60 and heard the enormous blast at Hooge? Every little sound, to them, was a German tunnelling team at work. But tunnelling officers sent to investigate found, more often than not, that it was rats, or somebody hammering or chopping wood in a dugout along the trench. Jack had arranged for medical stethoscopes to be issued for the purpose, but Cassels, of ammonal fame, acquired a wooden box, stuck a few lengths of impressive wire to it and, with a pair of headphones, made a bogus 'listening apparatus' with which to soothe the troops. 177 Company went even further. They appointed two elderly ex-coal miners, a pair of barrack-room comedians named Laughton and Bickley, to be official visiting listeners. They would listen intently at the clay-face and then, with solemn faces turn to the anxious waiting infantrymen and say "Yes, they're there all right. We can hear them. Sounds like they're f*****g."

"What the Germans?"

"No, the rats."

Apparently the joke even found its way across to the German lines.

But sometimes it became clear that the sounds *had* been German tunnellers. And, what was more, they were achieving the better results. In the mid-afternoon of 20 May a young lieutenant of the 5th Lincolnshires, Eric Dyson, was on the telephone in his dugout. Suddenly all became dark and every puff of breath was involuntarily expelled from his body by some overwhelming weight. The Germans had blown a mine and Dyson had become buried under tons of debris. He had been hurled several yards and had been saved from certain death only by a sheet of corrugated iron that had become wedged a few inches above his head. He was doubled up, with his head on his knees, and jammed under the wreckage. One arm was the only limb he could move. As his head cleared he looked at his hand. It still held the telephone. It was the 'phone that brought his rescuers to him, fourteen hours later, by the sound of him hitting it onto the corrugated iron like a drumstick. He was maimed for life, and fifteen of his men had been killed. They never found four of them.

In the meantime there were high-level squabbles going on between the British and French Field Marshals which were to impinge indirectly on Jack and his efforts. In a fit of pique, the erratic Sir John French fired his senior commander, General Sir Horace Smith-Dorrien and then got himself involved in a fracas with his French opposite number, Joffre. The French argument was that the British were not manning their fair share of the line, whilst the British pointed to the fact that their sector had seen disproportionately heavy losses. Indeed, there was much concern at home, both in the Commons and in the parlours and pubs, as the casualties crept well into the tens of thousands, and with precious little advantage to show for such blood. Sir John French, in the end, caved in to Joffre and the British Second Army stretched itself northwards to cover an extra two miles of the line. Jack, already with a lengthy beat to patrol for one man, now began to feel that he had really too much on his plate. But there was far worse to come. Joffre, not satisfied with the deal he had struck with French, then began to heckle the War Office in London for them to take over a twenty-one-mile stretch some sixty miles south of Ypres, along the Somme. Amazingly, the War Office gave him his way, with the result that the British Third Army was formed and was on the Somme by August. It meant, of course, that the Third Army was to be completely isolated from the rest of the British forces by a section of line manned by the French Tenth Army and that the mileometer on the Rolls-Royce would be working at double the rate. Then there was the problem of language. Jack had no French, except for *n'est-ce-pas?* and would have to rely on charm to talk his way through their sector each time he travelled.

Recruiting continued to be a bugbear. Some of Jack's reports to St Omer and messages to colleagues, the pungent language of which earned them the sobriquet of 'Punch', are indications of his frustration. It is clear he was keeping a very close eye on certain individuals and that did not exclude one or two generals! No wonder some of them despised him.

> "This officer collapsed on his first visit and had to be hauled up the shaft by ropes. Hyland states that on physical grounds alone, leaving out the spiritual side, this OC if he does his duty he will die in the attempt, or he cannot efficiently carry out his work . . . during the visit a flask was constantly resorted to. On enquiry said it was tea. It has been obvious from the start that this officer is absolutely incapable to command . . . another example is Bliss, who never goes near his trenches.
> "Lts Palmer and Bill not any use to us, so please block way. Don't let anyone slip through."

Sunday 29/8/15. To see Capt Prothero. I do not think this officer will make a successful OC. He possesses neither push nor go necessary. Fat and round, will probably go off himself in a small tunnel. Had not received his transport or his NCOs – arranged that he should ring me up directly he has collected his regular NCOs.

The hapless Prothero was soon on his way.

2 Oct 1915.   Sometime ago, CE suggested that Capt Prothero should be allowed to go home to get material for a Tunnelling Coy from men he originally enlisted. I think CE would like this arranged with a view to getting Prothero away.

But Jack was equally generous with praise, where due. In one report to HQ, he wrote:

1 April.   . . . gave them Easter eggs [he was probably referring to a party recruited from the 5 South Lancs] . . . Bombs effective and useful little chaps . . . proceeded to E1 to see new shifts start work . . . good kicker going well . . . wanted technical advice so I went and put them right and got sopping wet into the bargain by a slip [this probably refers to the time when, in his usual rush, he slipped from a board and fell into a shell-crater that had been used as a latrine]. Four of our fellows knocked out. Generally, I think it is little short of a wonder that in a short month so much has been done . . . Another thing, they can't get it away fast enough [the spoil] for the kickers when they kick!
     New heads sent out from England are a washout . . . Johnston doing more work than he can or should do . . . at Hill 60 last night . . . lot of men gassed . . . enemy could have walked in . . . nothing to stop them. Something must be done.

The situation at 3 Central Buildings, or the Depôt as it had become known, still continued to bother him. The Royal Engineer lieutenant who ran the show had been transferred and Jack had appointed in his place a civilian named Miles Bailey. It was not one of his more successful appointments and the two were soon at daggers drawn. It was the same old story of the six shilling rate, with too many men arriving at the front who were allegedly skilled and were being paid accordingly, but soon turned out to be only fit for labouring or mates' duties. Jack took Bailey to task over this, considering that he had been too free and easy with his recruiting technique. After a considerable amount of tactical sparring between them, Bailey wrote to the War Office demanding to know whether he reported to Jack or to them. Jack, he complained, had threatened to annul the trade certificates of some of the men who had been passed by himself. With surprising alacrity for a bureaucrat, an R.Curtis of the War Office wrote to Fowke in St Omer accusing Jack of causing 'complications', having no credentials and irregular behaviour, insisting that he return to France immediately. Then he wrote to Jack, in obvious ignorance of his Authority to Recruit, informing him bluntly that his brief was to liaise between the front and St Omer and that the writer had been directed to inform him that "the administration of the Tunnelling Depot, 3 Central Buildings is now under the control of Mr Miles Bailey".

To say that Jack was thunderstruck by these developments is to understate the case. "Dear Harvey," he wrote to a sympathetic Brigadier-General Harvey, Fowke's No.2 at St Omer, "I am hustling all I know how to get back as I positively hate being on this side with WO 'frills' . . . makes one want to tear one's hair out."

And a day or so later:

My Dear Harvey, Swollen Head has prevailed and a childish letter like the enclosed was written behind my back, lodged and action taken before my return. I don't want to worry you with domestic politics . . . but Swollen Head is a dangerous complaint for us to rely on. When I suggested Miles Bailey it was owing to no technical man being available at that moment, and I thought, of course, that he would be alright – so he would have been if he had been under my thumb. However, my only consideration is not to let the Chief [Fowke] down and see that he gets the right type of men. If they have not stopped the seventeen men which Miles Bailey has passed as experts we shall have to send them straight back. Would you be so kind as to send the car to Boulogne to meet me.

Miles Bailey had let seventeen men through, at the six shilling rate, who were plainly no good. Three, in fact, turned out to be hopeless drunks.

Jack replied to the WO to the effect that he understood their

151

because in certain cases [it/point] to be [placed]
in this locality being favourable for
mining. Such a scheme would want
some to make to complete & it should
be possible for mines to break the line at
say 6 given points. To do this however
a close examination of the area should
be made by me first for the personal
information of the C-in-C to discuss then
with the C.E.'s otherwise the most
suitable points may not be selected
from a mining point of view & these would
have to be combined with the tactical
points as far as mining will permit –

Lt ELoi

✗✗

Wytschaete

✗ Messines

As there is much else to do do not
propose to examine all this area unless
the C-in-C considers there is something
in the idea –

Shortage of men – O.C.'s are calling for
the return of men attached to 174th.
too – at a bunch leaving recently.

152

instructions and suggested that a Doctor Cadman, Professor of Mining at Birmingham University (an old friend who had good connections with all the major mine owners), should be appointed as supervisor over Bailey's head, "failing which I suggest that Chatham [the Royal Engineers base] take over from my office."

It was a thinly veiled threat to wash his hands of recruiting altogether. Nothing more was heard on the subject of Miles Bailey.

The over-kill success of Geoffrey Cassels' ammonal mine at Hooge rekindled the idea of a major blast along the Messines Ridge in Jack's mind. After studying the trench maps, he put his plan to his friend Harvey for consideration by Fowke. It should be possible, he thought, to do the job with six big mines, laid deep, provided that they were sited at points chosen with professional skill. Tactfully, he suggested that the selection of these points should not be made by local R.E. officers in the first instance, but that they should be consulted after he had looked closely at various possibilities himself and handed his recommendations to Fowke. Thus in reality it would be a top-down decision, although having the appearance of a bottom-up one. He attached a crude thumb-nail sketch of the area in question.

To his surprise, the normally warm-humoured Engineer-in-Chief not only rejected his proposal out of hand, but reacted with fury. The man was enormously over-worked, as they were all. But his good nature had brought him everyone else's problems to solve as well as his own and they were not just engineering ones. Indeed, his administrative skills would eventually be recognized more than his prowess as an engineer and mathematician. In less than a year he would be knighted and appointed Adjutant-General of the Forces. At St Omer Fowke was 'uncle' to a good many of his enormous circle of friends in the mess and they tended to confide in him. Such a project as Jack now put to him was probably just one too many items for his plate. And besides, the British tunnellers could barely keep pace with the Germans now and had been assigned a much more defensive role. Therefore, how could they ever achieve what Jack proposed?

It seemed as if the plan had been nipped in the bud, but Jack, dogged as ever, continued to discuss it with Harvey who although powerless, showed much enthusiasm.

Meanwhile, to the south, 174, together with the newly formed 178 and 179 Tunnelling Companies, had been assigned to that part of the line on the Somme vacated by the French as per General Joffre's overtures to the War Office. By now the Tunnelling Companies were beginning to develop an *esprit de corps* all of their own. Their trademark was a cheerful informality, which in turn led to complete disregard for stiff military protocols. They took an immense pride in their work.

They found the trenchwork left by the French to be full of rotting bodies and far too shallow for comfort, with the Germans only thirty yards away. The French tunnels seemed to be a masterpiece of absurdity. They went at varying depths, in illogical directions, stopped in illogical places and many had already been blown. And, more often than not, they did not coincide with the plans the French had provided. The first job, therefore, was to overhaul them wherever possible.

Twenty-one-year-old Lieutenant Edmund Pryor had been a student mining engineer in Civvy Street. He had volunteered when war broke out and was gazetted in the 8th Norfolk Regiment, with 53 Brigade. Shipped to France, he found that his own HQ and that of 178 Tunnelling Company were neighbours in the same small village, Meaulte, on the Somme. Whether Jack stole him we do not know, but it would have been typical of him to have done so. In any event Pryor transferred from the infantry to 178, where he found that his CO was a Captain Edward Wellesley, grandson of none other than the Duke of Wellington, who seemed to run his Company like a civilian firm. Nobody saluted anybody else, the word 'sir' was unheard of and nobody held parades. It was a strange metamorphosis for an infantryman, but Pryor soon found himself running around in a scruffy old cricket sweater and a pair of tennis shoes with a canary in a cage dangling from his hand for gas detection.

Jack had seen an experiment on the use of canaries for gas detection carried out by his friend Professor Cadman on his visit to the Midlands, although these particular experiments involved the use of a 'new' gas, sulphurated hydrogen (H_2S), rather than carbon monoxide (CO). Fortunately, the new discovery was never used.

22 May 1915. Visited with Prof Cadman Chance & Hunt's works. Experiment was made on top of a waste heap in a fresh breeze which veered slightly. Breeze estimated at 12 miles per hour. Gas containing 30% H_2S turned on at 11.47 am. Pressure was said to be 40lb per sq inch. Birds in cages were placed to leeward at distances up to 100 yards.

At 11.55 bird fell dead at a distance of 25 yards.

At 12.01 bird fell dead 40 yards from gas pipe.

Prof Cadman and three men, wearing oxygen rescue apparatus, entered the gassed zone and observed the birds, signalling when they were dead.

Further tests are being made tomorrow, Sunday. If successful will have matter brought to the attention of Prof Haldane.

Such precautions had added importance in the more chalky soil along the Somme, which tended to trap pockets of carbon monoxide gas from blown mines more easily than the heavier clay around Ypres. Gas was a persistent menace to the tunnellers on this section of the line, where they were subjected to endless small doses of it, which led to nausea, vomiting and dizziness. But if they were caught by a significant amount an early death was almost always the result, sometimes even before they had been able to reach fresh air. Several victims, hurrying up the shaft ladder to escape the insidious odourless fumes, suddenly became paralysed and fell to the bottom to die there. The irony was that the action of the gas on their blood gave them an appearance, in death, of being in the pink of health.

An extract from a 172 Company report describes one of these incidents:

28. 4. 15. German work so close that difference between noise made by different shifts could be distinctly noticed. Time of blowing, noisy shift on. Camouflet fired at 3.25 pm 27th. Enemy sap estimated 4 ft distant from head of right Y. Charge of 25 lbs ammonal. Crater approx x5ft diameter.

Orders sent up 4.15 pm to start work on ventilation. Shaft entered at 7.45. Sgt Harper leading. Lt Daniel second – Lt Williamson third. Map.

First two gassed at Y. Williamson following short interval heard snoring guessed what had happened, made for shaft.

155

Collapsed at bottom after shouting "help". Lt Severn at once descended, had Williamson hauled up then went in, grabbed Daniel, got him halfway back and collapsed on top of Daniel. Pvt Hayes, Sap Hattersley, Bennett and Cpl Day all attached to tunnelling Co. did most courageous work bringing out between them both Lt Severn and Lt Daniel. After first rescue, Hayes and Hattersley collapsed in effort. Day and Bennett then proceeded to head of Y to rescue Harper. With difficulty Harper was brought out. Every effort to restore failed. Lts Daniel and Severn ultimately recovered after 15 mins hard work.

On the odd occasion a canary would escape from its cage, which always caused some panic. If seen flying around by the Germans, a canary would immediately indicate the presence nearby of a mine. A mass canary-escape occurred when the 178 Company cook accidentally set fire to a wooden aviary near his kitchen. About a hundred little yellow birds flew out into no-man's-land and settled on the barbed wire. It was a bright sunny day, rendering any attempt at recapture highly dangerous, even suicidal. Nevertheless, a young officer and party of men crawled on their stomachs to the wire and managed to trap the birds under their hats, one by one. By the time the Germans realized that there were British soldiers to be fired on, most, if not all, of the birds were safely back in custody and the last of the party was wriggling back into his trench.

Another time a single bird flew out and sat in what was left of a shell-shattered bush in no-man's-land. It began to sing its heart out, happy with its new-found freedom. If the Germans did not see it, they would certainly soon hear it. It was nearer to the German trenches than the British, which made retrieval impossible. Some infantry riflemen were ordered to kill it, but, despite several crashing volleys, the bird continued to sing cheerfully on its perch, with not a feather out of place. Somebody suggested a hand-grenade, but none were to hand, so a mortar was ordered to range on the bush. At last a well-placed shell dispatched bird and bush together.

One clever bird became as crafty as any human 'old sweat'. On being taken into a tunnel it would immediately fall off its perch and feign death in the bottom of the cage, only to recover

156

miraculously when brought out again and resume hopping about, chirruping merrily.

The six-foot-two Pryor was always more comfortable below ground. Down there he still could not quite stand upright, but on the surface, at this hot-spot, to be seen was to die. He also found it exhausting, and back-aching, to spend his time in the shallow French-dug trench doubled up to avoid being bagged by a sniper.

178 took over a section of the line at a place called Tambour du Clos, near Fricourt. It was a very exposed and dangerous position, on highish ground, with the spires of Amiens in clear view to the rear. Their neighbours, a few yards away, were 174 Company. The French seemed very pleased to be vacating this embattled section. One young British officer was being shown around by a *poilu* who was about to depart. Several times the Frenchman pointed at the ground and exclaimed *"Très dangereux. Boche mine. Poof!"* with a huge upward sweep of his arms and a wide grin on his face.

Wellesley had been given three objectives: first to hold the high ground at Tambour du Clos; second to intercept and destroy the German tunnels opposite, and third to mine and destroy the German trenches opposite to enable an infantry advance to be made. On the face of it it seemed straightforward.

The tunnel plan took the shape of a giant garden rake. Entering horizontally via the front wall of a trench, the five-foot-high by three-feet-wide tunnels stopped after a few feet and from there a shaft would descend vertically for about thirty feet. Sometimes there was a ladder, otherwise you shinned down a rope. At the bottom there was a lateral gallery, lit by candles, parallel to the surface trench. From that, at intervals, little fighting tunnels, like the teeth of the rake, jutted out towards the Germans. These could be used for listening posts or primed with a small amount of explosive, known as a *camouflet*, to be fired if the enemy came too near, so as to collapse his tunnel and fill it with gas. The Germans, of course, were doing the same thing from their side, so an atmosphere of suspense always developed when the sound of enemy activity stopped. Usually that meant they were about to blow. Quite simply, it was a game of blind man's bluff.

One young subaltern in 174 Company had just charged his mine with 1,000 lbs of ammonal. It was fully tamped and wired.

All was ready to blow. Then he realized that all was silent on the German side, guessed that they had interpreted his own silence as being ominous and had retired to safety. He rigged up his exploder just outside the tunnel entrance, crept back down the shaft to his tunnel, all alone, with a couple of tin-cans and began banging them together, talking to himself all the while in a loud voice. Very soon he heard noises again from the German side. They had come back and had resumed digging. He raced back along the gallery and up the shaft as fast as he could go, to fall on the exploder as he made his exit. There was an enormous upheaval as the mine blew, which dislodged a couple of sandbags from a parapet, showering with sand the immaculate Corps Commander, Lieutenant-General Sir Thomas Morland, who happened to be passing along the trench, on an inspection with his highly-polished entourage. The Germans immediately opened up with an artillery barrage. That was the normal routine after a British mine had blown. The General's aides fussed about him, hastily brushing him down as shells fell all around and the ground shook. Then they hurried the distinguished personage to a slip trench, out of harm's way, where a proud subaltern, clad in the usual tunneller's jumble sale garb, covered from head to toe in chalk dust, still sweating and panting, was standing by his exploder box. At great risk to his chances of promotion, he bowed grandly and said, "All my own work, gentlemen". The General's comments are not recorded.

Pryor was a good Trench Officer. He was known for his uncanny knack of guessing correctly what the Germans were up to, although underground combat was highly demanding, and sometimes he found himself shaking with fatigue. On one occasion his listeners at a forward post reported noises. Pryor went to listen for himself and decided that the Germans were ramming some tamping into place, which meant that their mine might be blown at any time. He sent a runner to Wellesley, requesting permission to drive an emergency tunnel towards the noises. Permission granted, the work began. His diggers understood the rules of the game. Speed was of the essence. They responded magnificently by driving a two-foot square untimbered tunnel through the chalk at about nine feet an hour. They went as far as Pryor dared – about forty-five feet. He went down himself, shuffling along feet first on his back with the chalk about a foot above his face, dragging a 50lb bag of gelignite behind him. He heaved it over his head and down his body, kicked it into place at the end of the tunnel and called for more. He spent a couple of hours doing this, after which he had rammed nearly a quarter of a ton of the stuff into place and tamped it with bags of spoil. He hauled himself back on his elbows, with his body aching all over and covered in chalk. Leaping on his motorcycle, which was parked in a communication trench, he sped to Company HQ to get permission to blow the charge, but to his dismay Wellesley would not hear of it. Pryor was sure that the Germans were about to blow their mine and pleaded with Wellesley so forcefully and at such length to change his mind that the CO felt fit to tell him to pull himself together. He left, to sit in his dugout tense with suspense all evening. By ten o'clock he was beside himself with worry. If the Germans blew their mine, it would seal the fate of the British shift working below. He telephoned Wellesley, who this time was uncharacteristically formal. If Pryor pestered him any more or interfered in any way, he stated stiffly, he would be court-martialled.

By three o'clock in the morning Pryor could not stand the suspense any longer. His bones told him that the Germans would blow soon. And a court-martial would be preferable to seeing a couple of dozen of his men killed. He clambered down the nearest shaft, shouting for everybody to leave the gallery immediately. They began to appear one by one, to be hustled out of the shaft by a hectic Pryor. All but three had emerged safely when there was a cr-rump and the ground seemed to sink then rise under their feet. When he went down to look for the missing three, all he found was a pile of debris with a hand sticking out of it. His admiration for Wellesley, who in the informal atmosphere of 178 Tunnelling Company was seen more like the captain of a cricket team than an army officer fighting a war, did not suffer because of this incident. Pryor knew that Commanding Officers had more than one cross to bear and more than one ball to juggle in the air at any given time. It had been a simple case where one man had guessed right – Pryor, and the other wrong – Wellesley.

Pryor's final adventure in the front line tunnels happened when he was in the act of rescuing some men who had been affected by gas following a German 'blow'. He was down a long sloping shaft, using a Proto ventilator, the control of which he had almost no knowledge. He had just reached an unconscious tunneller and was trying to get a bowline round him when he collapsed himself and fell down the steep shaft a good forty feet, bouncing off its sides and still strapped to the 32 lb Proto apparatus. When they pulled him back and outside into the open air, he was still unconscious. In fact he appeared to be dead. Later that day he recovered his senses enough to know where he was, but his heartbeat, which had been thudding rapidly into his ears now slowed alarmingly. He resigned himself to death, and slipped away again into oblivion. That afternoon his men came to look at him and saw that he was lifeless. In freezing weather – it was 21 December 1915 – they tossed him over the back of the trench, clad only in one gumboot and a pair of trousers to join a number of other corpses for burial. Some time later a German shell burst in the middle of this heap of stiff bodies and a piece of hot shrapnel punched into his half-naked body. By some mysterious stroke of good fortune, Pryor's batman came to look at him to see if he had anything in his pockets that could be sent home to his family by way of a memento, only to see that his master's eyelids were flickering. He had been extremely lucky not to have been buried alive, but had caught a 'Blighty one' for sure. He was to spend the next two years on crutches, but he had been luckier than the 300 of his comrades in 178 who had died during the five months he had spent at the front.

Many sappers were killed underground by collapsing tunnels. As the tunnels went deeper so did the risk of accidents. Some went down seventy feet. A few went down a hundred, although 'fighting' tunnels seem to have been restricted to about thirty feet in order to act as 'cover' for the deeper ones which were being prepared for the 'big blow'. This work was code named Operation Deepwater. Most men who died underground were killed by enemy *camouflets*. Either they were crushed by the collapse of their tunnel or found themselves trapped in a pocket of carbon monoxide. The chalky soil of the Somme section had been fined down into small particles by the continual vibration from exploding shells. The resulting craters became giant sumps when filled with surface water, which would percolate through the porous chalk, often causing a gluey drip to fall on the heads of the labouring tunnellers many feet below. Frequently the grey glue was tinged red with blood.

After one German *camouflet* blew, tapping sounds were heard coming from behind the spot where the British tunnel had caved in. This time there seemed to have been some survivors. But the chalk was so waterlogged that it had the consistency of plasticine, and therefore highly prone to further collapse. Any rescue attempt would have been very dangerous to the rescue party. Nevertheless, the officer in charge of the rescuers, Second-Lieutenant Robert Mackilligin, whose recently wounded brother Alfred was also a member of the Tunnelling Company, decided that they must try to get the men out. Gingerly, using stout timber shuttering, they edged their way through the pile of debris for about thirty feet. They could now hear the shouts for help quite plainly. But did those men have enough air to survive the wait for rescue? How much gas was trapped with them in their pocket? Mackilligin ordered a narrow hole to be made, barely large enough for a man to wriggle through and with absolutely no timber supports. They took it in turns to slither forward on their stomachs clawing back the grey 'plasticine' with their bare hands. It was treacherous work and could have meant instant death to the rescuer at any second. The mole-hole had gone about twenty feet when the digger called back that he could see two men about ten feet ahead of him. They were lying face down, pinned to the spot by boulders and broken shuttering. Mackilligin called the man back and went to see for himself. The men had been badly stunned and were, in fact, being kept alive by the shattered timbers above their heads, which were preventing some large wedges of chalk from falling. But there was an ominous sound of water splashing down. It was creating a large pool just behind the trapped men, which was held back from their faces purely by some debris on the floor of the tunnel. It was plain that it would soon overflow.

Mackilligin stared in horror. There was absolutely no way that he could shift the timbers that held the men down: even if he had been able to do so, it would have created another instant fall of debris. As it was, he could feel his own tunnel starting to 'give'. In fact, its putty-like chalk was actually beginning to tighten

161

around his body. It was time to get out. He started off backwards, but he had left it too long and soon became unable to move under his own strength. It was only the quick thinking of his men behind him that saved his life. With literally two or three seconds to spare before the mole-hole finally closed in they snatched his feet and hauled him out. His last sight of the doomed men was when the pool of water overflowed to swirl around their heads. As his own men grabbed his heels to drag him to safety he saw them choke on their last breaths as their lungs filled with water.

On 13 August 1915 175 Company was ordered to start work on four heavy mines about twenty-five miles north of Loos, a typically sombre little northern French town between La Bassée and Lens, where a big autumn offensive was planned as a diversionary tactic. This initiative came officially from Major-General Glubb, Chief Engineer of the Second Army, who had almost certainly been persuaded to take it up by Jack during a discussion which seems to have taken a somewhat odd course. Glubb had entered the conversation by stating that the present arrangements were for all mining activity to be on a defensive basis only, and therefore the Tunnelling Companies should lie quiet for the time being. But barely minutes later he appears to have undergone a major change of mind, almost certainly infected by Jack's powerful enthusiasm for action. He wanted Fowke to suggest the plan to General Sir Herbert Plumer, the Second Army Commander, but Jack, behaving for a change with the utmost formality, advised an approach not from 'the Chief' but from Glubb himself. In other words from the Second Army's own Chief Engineer. Plumer, who could not stand the sight of Jack, agreed to a four-mine 'blow', but stipulated a point a couple of miles to the north of Hill 60.

175 were less than enchanted at these prospects, which gave them a heavy extra workload. There were to be two tunnels, of 220 and 320 feet respectively, each with the traditional Y-shaped ends to create four explosion chambers. On the night of 25 August Lieutenant Arthur Firebrace telephoned his CO Major Hunter Cowan to report noises coming from below his tunnel. Cowan ordered him to bore a hole eight inches or so wide ten feet down immediately above the noises and hurried over to take

control himself. He planned to pack it with explosive and collapse the German tunnel. As usual, speed was imperative. But, seven feet down, the boring tool struck a stratum of flinty pebbles. It was making a fearful grating sound which Cowan said later could have been heard in Berlin. He decided to stop boring, filled the hole as it was with fifty pounds of ammonal and tamped it down with clay. A timed fuse was set off and they retired to safety. But nothing happened. On inspection the fuse appeared to have burned through normally. Had the Germans heard them and simply removed it? Cowan delicately re-opened the hole and removed the tamping. Peering down, they could see the zinc canister and when they punched a hole in the top of it the nail came out covered in white ammonal powder. It was a mystery. For good measure they packed another twenty-five pounds of ammonal down the hole with three electric detonators. The result was spectacular. A crater thirty yards across was created. Huge amounts of earth and sandbags were hurled into the air and the fifty yards they had retired was nowhere near enough to save them from a painful deluge of heavy debris. They had blown the German mine as well as their own.

Firebrace's four diversionary mines were fired at four-twenty in the morning of 25 September, destroying about 150 yards of German trenches, killing over a hundred of the enemy and triggering the start of the massive autumn offensive further south known as the Battle of Loos. It would drag on until November. Only months before, the British had protested bitterly about the German use of chlorine gas at Ypres – it was 'damned unsportsmanlike' – but at Loos they brought it into play themselves without compunction. 5,243 heavy cylinders were mounted ready in the front trenches, but the autumn air hung dank and still. Gas was an impotent weapon without a favourable wind. But at 0515 General Haig spotted a rustle of leaves in the poplars and ordered the release of 150 tons of gas. There was a panic when it was discovered that most of the spanners issued did not fit the cylinders and gas-men rushed about borrowing adjustable tools from all and sundry. And then the gas, which was successfully released, obstinately drifted back slowly over the British lines. The British did manage to push the Germans back beyond Loos, but at fearful cost. Winston Churchill said later that

"Victory was to be bought so dear as to be indistinguishable from defeat". The First, Fifteenth and Forty-Seventh Divisions were all thrown into the line, with the 15th Highland Division's piper, who won the V.C. wailing 'Scotland the Brave'. By evening one dressing station alone, at École Jules Fery, was inundated with 2,000 walking wounded, including many gas cases.

At last the knives came out for Sir John French. He had stationed his HQ twenty-five miles behind the line at Lillers, without so much as a telephone to stay in contact with his commanders in the field. He had held back his reserve troops far too long and his overall tactics had incurred heavy criticism from Haig, Robertson and especially Kitchener, who had made no secret of his hostility to him ever since the Boer War. He was given a title and posted home, to be replaced by Haig. The amazing thing was that French had survived so long, resting entirely on the laurels won by his out-dated cavalry at Kimberley and Paardeberg.

Most probably it had been a lack of detailed paperwork which had caused Jack's suggestions for a 'big blow' along the Messines Ridge to fall on stony ground in Fowke's office. Better presentation would, doubtlessly, have given it a better chance of winning approval. As it was, all he had submitted comprised a few short notes accompanied by a small thumbnail sketch, which in turn was crude to say the least. But that is not to say that he had not formed a more professional plan *in his head*. He envisaged the three-and-a-half-mile stretch to be blown being divided into three sectors, each commanded by an officer whose performance had been impressive and had already earmarked the men for this. Their names were Captain Clay Hepburn, Lieutenant Horace Hickling and Captain Gordon Hyland.

Hepburn was in command of 172 Company. He was a thirty-seven-year-old colliery manager from Monmouth and, as an early civilian respondent to Jack's advertisements for recruits, he was somewhat of a rarity in having a company command. It had been Hepburn who was showing Jack around the time he slipped from the plank to fall into the shell-crater latrine. And it was Hepburn, together with Hickling, who had originally suggested 'going deep' to escape the problems of tunnellers working beneath the filthy seepage from such craters. Firm clean blue clay

164

was to be found sixty feet down. They had started way back on 7 May, but once again the Germans proved that they were up to the pace when in June two British sergeants broke through the end of their fifty-foot tunnel to find what they least expected sixty feet beneath Hill 60 – a German mine. Hepburn tore over to see for himself, to find them calmly examining the cache of 1,000 lbs of high explosive *by candle-light*! One spark would have sent the lot up. Apparently, no other system of lighting was available, which seems incredible, because electric battery flashlights were in general everyday use. Be that as it may, they spent two days gingerly clearing the charge away. Hepburn was not one to waste good explosive, so he transferred it to a five-mine spread of his own at St Eloi, which was highly successful. He and Hickling fired the five mines by going from terminal to terminal with their exploder box, connecting up the wires and blowing each one singly, ad hoc, rather than make a concerted explosion of all five. They reasoned that this would have a far more demoralizing effect on the Germans, and they were right. As the fifth explosion of the giant 'jumping jack' rent the air, the Germans, not knowing how many more the British had to fire, emerged from their trenches and began running to the rear, pursued by heavy machine-gun fire from the British positions. That was the type of forethought that earned Jack's admiration of these men. He was particularly impressed with the way that Hickling had laid and tamped the charges.

Indeed, Hickling was to receive his praises for his work in general:

15 July 1915.   Visited 172 Coy. 2/Lt Hickling who has been stationed at Dickebusch with his Section since 172 Coy started has with 2/Lt Gardner done exceedingly good work. The CE and Corps Commander has I understand put his name forward. The Gs have made repeated efforts to get at us – Hickling has blown them off each time and succeeded in getting around and blowing them. 14/4 Gs blew first and killed I think from memory 2 of our men. Since then Hickling has had them each time. He blew them on 23/4, 24/4, 3/5, 17/5, 26/5, 28/5, 5/6, 10/7.

Tuesday 2 September 1915.   The mining reports of 2 Army are not encouraging.

165

177 – cold feet   } { these 2 coys might well start a new
175 – nil to speak of.   } { branch undertakers to the B E
Force.

172 – Lt Hickling the 'live spark'! Has 2 deepshafts down 60 feet without tacking into clay and going for St Eloi under craters with 55 feet head cover. Beyond this, this Coy is in petty defensive work.

171 – Live show. Keen on big things if given the chance.

A year into the war and Jack's hectic recruiting activities still continued apace. More and more men was his constant cry. And when they came he was faced with the task of sorting the wheat from the chaff. In mid-October sufficient numbers had been found to allow for four new Tunnelling Companies to be formed, 250, 251, 252, 253. He went to Rouen to inspect the 600 odd men, most of whom were new recruits, but some had been drawn from 184 and 185 Companies:

12 October 1915. Arrived Rouen 3pm. Commenced inspecting and sorting 4pm, finishing with the Cornishmen at 6.30. Evening spent discussing ways and means with Drummond.

13 October. Parades.
250 Coy. Officers. OC Lt. Cropper suggested. Lt Bottom. 2/Lts A S Holmes, A E Champion, G H Roberts, R W Picken, H A T O'Connor.

114 Scotchmen from England.

17 odd details from Front for transfer.

20 Welshmen from England to be built up into a Welsh Section.

251 Coy. Cornish Company Officers - OC Capt Bullen. Lt C O Deacon 2/Lts P N Whitehead, F R Richards, F A Schneider, W V Pettit.

This unit appears to be well organized and have a good looking lot of men. All miners. Some china clay workers. Propose suggesting to C E 1st Army that it would be wise to draft a few experienced men and officers from other Coys in the 1st Army into this Coy and then I think it should do well.

252 Coy. Officers. OC Lt Trower (this OC had not yet arrived, but I understand he is en route.) Lt Haines. 2/Lts A W H Deane, G A Cunnack, F Dickson, E Trower.

136 Yorkshiremen from England.

55 from front for transfer.

253 Coy. OC Lt du pre Lance not yet arrived. 2/Lts E E Currie, L P K Fisher, F W Greaves, E S Cunningham.
37 from England.
11 odd details from front for transfer.
To fill this Coy up in 3rd Army.
Lt F C C Ferres detailed for this Coy was left at Southampton sick – presumably from an epileptic fit, but his brother officers at the base say DTs was the real cause. I submit that either complaint would not make him a suitable officer.

Nevertheless, he still managed to find time to make comments in his diary that seem to be in a light-hearted vein. A civilian mind may even have considered them to be humorous, but there are situations that cannot be passed over lightly if military etiquette is to be satisfied. Others still may think that the following anecdote tells of a situation where a sledge-hammer was used to crack a nut.

18 October 1915.   It appears that W. Miller and A.E. Fowler who were recommended for and given Temporary Commissions and posted to 174 Coy, were sent here from Armentières and arrived dressed as privates, being joyfully greeted by Danford's cook to 'Come here you blokes and wash up these bloody plates!'
   To avoid repetition of cooks training new officers in this manner I suggest in all new nominations for Temp Comms leaving out the postings until their arrival at the Base in order that officers may have time to go and buy some clothes. Owing to the strained atmosphere produced by the non-cleansing of the said plates I think the re-posting of these officers is advisable – Fowler to 183 and Miller to 184, which Major Danford approves.

The year of 1915 was grinding to an end. It had been a catastrophic time for the British. They had lost 375,000 men – the equivalent of their pre-war army, with almost nothing to show for it, plus hundreds of merchant ships to 'the U-boat menace'. Every individual sinew of their fighting arm now came under close scrutiny in the Halls of Power, and this, of course, included the Tunnelling Companies. If the truth be told, they had recruited and employed about 20,000 men who had courageously sweated underground in fearfully dangerous and

167

unpleasant conditions. True, they had killed some Germans and blown a few localized holes in the ground, but the front line was not too far removed from where it had been a year before. And some infantry commanders were now asserting that these holes in the ground were actually an impediment to their efforts. Once a crater had been blown, they pointed out, it gave the advancing infantry the task of holding it. And it was far more difficult to hold a hole than a piece of high ground. Jack had quickly seen the remedy for this situation. Don't wait for the enemy to recover from the shock of an explosion, he urged. Send the infantry over the top instantly the 'blow' erupts, even if it means advancing through the falling debris. And don't run *into* the crater. Run *around* it. Indeed, the Germans were already doing just that.

But there was no proper plan, nor any centralized organization, which was a situation that Jack had deplored from the beginning. Indeed, it was the lack of such basic essentials that had required him to tear hither and thither trying to be in umpteen different places at once, with no real recognition or definition of his authority for months on end. And privately Fowke had been in agreement with him for some time. Clearly, the War Office thinking machine had been pondering the same problem. Towards the end of December a letter arrived on Fowke's desk at St Omer mentioning the concern that was being felt in London. It asked him to appoint an Inspector of Mines, who should be a high-ranking officer, with overall control and co-ordination of the Tunnelling Companies, under whom would work a Controller of Mines for each of the British Armies in the field. Fowke could see that this would mean the creation of a new Department. He asked Harvey to formulate it. Now Harvey and Jack, as we saw earlier, had each other's confidence, and Harvey had been quietly subjected to Jack's persuasive charms, with not a little success, over a big Messines Ridge 'stunt' for months. Therefore when Brigadier-General Robert Napier 'Ducky' Harvey, a robust square-jawed forty-seven-year-old with a greying moustache was duly appointed as Inspector of Mines as from 1 January 1916, it gave fresh hope to Jack's idea.

16

GREEN LIGHT FOR THE BIG BLOW

Harvey was of much the same stamp as Jack. He was deceptively iron-willed and did not see himself at all as a mining technician but as a manager. The job of a manager is to make things happen. First, there was a plethora of muddle to cut away, and to standardize procedures. Not least was the supply of equipment in that regard.

Out went the last of the Crimean War gear and in came modern pumps, surveying instruments and dynamo lighting sets. Jack's diary for 11 May 1915 says: "Particulars of 'Holman' pump rec'd. Right idea, double action. Pulling out and pumping in at the same time. Want one. If any difficulty getting will ask Oakes send it if we give it to him. Oakes' 'quick union joint' quite a success for borers."

Three days later he had cause to criticize a piece of equipment known as the 'Roots Blower'. "From the two tests I have made recently at mines it is certain that Roots blowers and fans of any kind will have to be stopped. Iron piping where used to conduct air is a conductor of sound too. Rubber and zinc piping is best. At the Monmouths' mine yesterday a Roots blower was put into use to enable me to get into mine. I could hear the rotten thing at the heading. So could the Gs through the broken ground caused by their craters."

Evidently he had also given the question of listening devices some more thought. "To deal with mining by the enemy," he wrote, "each infantry battn should be supplied with one standard earth auger with 20ft rods. A Tommy could be shown in half an

169

hour by mining co. how to use it. They are cheap and its use will often satisfy OCs infantry whether mining is or is not going on."

Cambridge University had been working on a reliable electrically operated listening aid, as had one or two private firms, but the tunnellers favoured a simple stethoscope held against a heavy French Army water bottle, filled with water and laid flat on the ground, until Jack came up with an improvement on the same theme. On a visit to Paris to inspect some equipment, he was shown a device that had been developed by students at the Sorbonne. It consisted of a pair of wooden discs filled with mercury and faced with mica, which were attached to the ear nipples of the stethoscope. It produced amazing results. They called it the geophone.

On 19 May Jack was in England, recruiting and researching improvements in equipment and as usual riding roughshod over military etiquette where he considered expediency to be more important for the winning of the War.

"Arrived Birmingham 6.45. During evening conference with Prof Cadman and Prof Frankland. Prof Cadman is the Organizer of all the Rescue Stations throughout Midland Districts. There is at Dudley a firm who make what is known as Brattice Cloth – which is universally used for Mining ventilation. Made in rolls and hung cheaply and quickly for airing purposes. In both big and small tunnels. All collieries in the neighbourhood use this. The smallest hand pump will keep a considerable distance well ventilated. As this is important work will ask Major Oakes to order from this firm some of this Brattice Cloth, without waiting to refer to E in C."

Another of Harvey's early developments was a special training school for tunnellers, which he set up near Armentières, where specialists in digging, timbering, listening, rescue work and fighting underground would provide an intensive ten-day course for selected individuals.

But all the time the main object of Harvey's drive was the idea of the huge mining offensive on Messines Ridge. Jack had worked well on him and he, in turn, had now got Fowke himself on side. Then out of the blue, on 6 January 1916, all three were summoned to attend a conference of top brass. Now was their chance to submit their case in the appropriate forum.

Jack did most of the talking. It was his pet subject, on which he could have expounded all day if need be. Unfazed by the beribboned display of pipe-sucking grey-haired Generals before him, he tore into his presentation with his usual energy and lack of military deference. His plan, he told them, would save the lives of 10,000 British soldiers in the attack, and afterwards, he promised them, they "would be able to walk to the top of Messines Ridge smoking their pipes"! They would not so much be blowing the top of the Ridge as 'earthquaking' it. This was perfectly feasible because it was "virtually one big hill of sand sitting on blue clay." The generals listened thoughtfully, then to Fowke and Harvey as they added their contributions.

Then they rejected the whole thing out of hand. The three returned to St Omer in utter dejection, but late that night Fowke's telephone rang. The generals had changed their minds. Messines Ridge could be 'earthquaked' after all!

The reason for the reversal of decision was Top Secret, known only to a select handful of high-ranking officers. An all-out Anglo-French offensive effort was planned for the coming July. Hopefully, it would result in a breakthrough which would signal the end of the War. It would be what was to become famous to history as the Battle of the Somme. And it had occurred to the generals that an 'earthquake' farther north would serve as a perfect diversion. It would be a magnified version of the diversionary function that the 175 Tunnellers had performed to the north of Hill 60 for the botched and bloody Battle of Loos the previous September. They had just six months to get it ready.

On the Thursday after the electrically charged meeting with the generals, Jack was promoted Temporary Lieutenant-Colonel. But he knew in his heart that with the new Inspector of Mines hierarchy in being, there would soon be less room for him even though he was considered, unofficially, to be the Inspector's assistant. And perhaps it was this thought which drove him towards another inspiration – something of a grand finale effort to close his contributions to the underground war.

He had seen mechanical borers at work in British coal

mines, driving tunnels through coal seams, and he knew from his own professional experience that similar but larger machines had been adapted to drive through the London clay for the underground railways. Basically, they consisted of a wheeled chassis with rotating cutters on the front which were driven by a two-stroke compressed-air engine. Power for the engine came from a generator on the surface. The spoil was fed back by the blades of the cutters as they screwed themselves into the work-face ahead.

It seemed perfectly sensible to him that they should be used to tunnel under Messines Ridge. With his usual boundless enthusiasm, he put the idea to Harvey, urging that several of these machines be ordered – urgently. Just ordering one, for trial, he gushed, would be a waste of time. He would say four, or even half a dozen. And he rattled off on his fingers a list of reasons why Harvey should agree with him, the two main ones being speed and more speed. Harvey knew Jack very well by now, and although he found himself almost invariably in agreement with him, he had learned to modulate his own impetuosity when faced with one of Jack's infectious ideas. He refused to cave in completely to Jack's eloquent bullying and agreed to a compromise. They would ship over one machine.

The giant tool, known as the Stanley Heading Machine, was manufactured in Nuneaton. The makers would have to design and produce a special cutting head for the hard Flanders clay, but they promised delivery in six weeks. Jack wanted it to be assigned to the newly formed 250 Tunnelling Company, commanded by a dour Northumberland mining engineer, Captain Cecil Cropper. Jack was very impressed with Cropper, who had shown great initiative in finding a path through some very difficult sub-soil, and whose overall plans seemed to fall in very neatly as part of the 'big idea'. He went out of his way to develop a cordial relationship with the man. Privately, however, Cropper did not like Jack at all, seeing him as a bit of a 'showman who threw his weight about', although he was astute enough to keep his thoughts to himself.

Jack and Harvey called on Cropper to inform him what had been decided. They already knew that part of his plans were to drive a long four-gallery system towards the Ridge. But as they talked, it seemed to Cropper that Jack had taken over the idea as if it were his own, except that he had doubled the length of Cropper's already huge planned drive to an astounding 6,000 feet, or all the way to Wytschaete village. The hard-headed Geordie was professionally affronted. The difficulty was, of course, that he could be told nothing about the major Somme offensive planned for July, or that it was somewhat of a coincidence that his own ideas fitted in, very neatly, with the overall scheme. Nevertheless, Cropper was a professional through and through. He agreed to take delivery of the boring machine and, pending its arrival, to dig a preparatory shaft, known as Petit Bois, or SP13, down which it could be lowered.

Jack was back in Cropper's office on 10 February, and was unhappy with progress, although for him that was nothing new. Cropper, it seems, had been pressing on with his usual clay-kicking work, but had hardly made a start on the special shaft to receive the boring machine. Jack turned on the charm, although this time it was more of a veiled threat. "Kitchener," he told an admonished Cropper, "is personally interested in this." Then, by way of encouragement, a crate of port was lifted from the boot of the much-abused Rolls just before it sped away on its next errand. The unfortunate thing was that Cropper was to all intents and purposes teetotal.

On Wednesday 12 February Jack left for London. He wanted to meet up with the machine and accompany it personally to Boulogne, trusting nothing to others on such a vital mission. Two lorries were to meet the boat on the French side and would be waiting from two o'clock onwards on the following Monday at the quayside. He was delayed all night, waiting for mine-sweepers to clear the channel, and did not arrive at 3 Central Buildings until early on the Friday, to find two worried representatives from the machine's manufacturers waiting to see him. There was a major problem over shipping. The machine was lying at Marylebone Station, ready for onward transit, in twenty-four packets of components weighing a total of seven and a half tons. Nobody, it seems, had made arrangements to get it across London and down to Folkestone. Jack was determined to keep to his original schedule. He flew across to the War Office and was ushered in to see a Royal Engineers Colonel

Brady. There he found more bad news. The shipment would be too bulky to go on the mail boat on which Jack had booked it. But Brady saved the day by reserving space for it on the next ammunition boat from Newhaven, which would sail the following night. It would have to be at Victoria Station by four o'clock the next day.

A typical Jack-type flurry of pell-mell activity started. There were lorries to organize, clearance to arrange for the shipment to leave Marylebone Station, and to find a skilled engineer who was able to come to France and assemble the monster. From somewhere or other a man named Carter was found and Brady made hurried arrangements for him to be given a temporary commission. At the same time a Mr Talbot was signed up as a temporary sergeant to travel out and 'drive' the machine. Clearly, Jack's decision to go to London to oversee matters had been a wise one. With typical gratitude for anybody who had 'pulled out the stops' for him, he wrote to Harvey "Brady is a splendid man, and has done lots to unblock. I want you to . . . thank him." Last of all, he ordered a supply of specially designed wooden shuttering to keep the moisture which would be created and thrown out by the machine from getting into contact with the clay. The efficiency of this shuttering would prove to be crucial, as things worked out.

The welter of inept confusion the next day must have driven him to despair. First, the lorries did not turn up, and then when he ordered some more from the Great Central Railway at his own expense both convoys arrived together. And at noon the official paperwork was still awaited at Marylebone. In the end the shipment was lugged aboard the afternoon train to Newhaven and was safely on its way to France.

Jack travelled back from Folkestone, but mines in the channel again delayed his boat, this time for a whole twenty-four hours. After a very rough crossing, he was relieved to see three lorries on the dockside at Boulogne, loading up the precious machine. He was unable to get to see Cropper for two days because of other commitments, but when he did arrive at Petit Bois it was to see that Carter was still in the process of assembly and testing. Carter reckoned that he could have it going, eighty feet down, within forty-eight hours. But Jack was laid low with a temperature:

28 Feb 16. GHQ. Bed at 1 after going to hospital for injection. Temp 101.2.

29 Feb. Hospital 11. Temp normal. To Boulogne 12. 10 tons of well lining sent forward Monday. Cropper rang and states that only 25 more sets arrived, viz, 50 in all. This is only 3 or 4 tons. Shipping Co wire to BC stated 10 tons on shipping documents. This for checking later.

Dentist went to bed after giving me his cold and apparently everybody else he saw that day! Result jaw unfinished. Very annoying. No news of hoists or oil.

At last the monster cutting machine was started up on the night of 4 March. And it ran well, making a steady two feet an hour and boring a neat round tunnel which was a roomy six feet across. The problems started each time it was stopped, or rather when they tried to restart it. The special wooden shuttering was simply not doing its job in protecting the clay from the moist air. In turn, the clay was absorbing the moisture and expanding all around the machine and trapping it securely, making it impossible to move forward. Therefore, each time a restart was necessary, first came the job of digging out the machine. The electric motor on the surface blew its fuses so frequently that the supply of fuse-wire became exhausted. An uninitiated sapper substituted some barbed-wire, which pulled many more amperes through the circuit than was prudent and the motor burned out.

And, worst of all, there was a perverse proclivity on the part of the machine to dive. "We never discovered why," said one old tunneller many years later, "but this machine showed a complete disinclination to proceed towards Germany, but preferred to head to Australia by the most direct route." Carter and Talbot sweated and strained to get the thing to cooperate, with advice ringing in their ears from all around, not least from Jack. The motor was wrong, he contended, and so was the dynamo. They had never been intended for work of this nature. And the cutting tools were badly adjusted. And the tendency to dive was the fault of the wings on each side of the machine which braced it against the tunnel walls and were designed to keep it from rotating on its own axis. But he refused to lose faith in the machine. In fact he was badgering Harvey to order more. But the truth had to be faced. All their efforts had been to no avail. The Stanley Heading Machine had foiled them. By the time it had reluctantly clawed its way forward, in fits and starts, for two hundred feet, Carter and Talbot had lost heart, packed their bags and gone home. Harvey was of a like mind. The foot of authority had to come down on this unfortunate episode. He ordered that it should be abandoned. Its corroded carcass is still there today, eighty feet down, in the firm embrace of blue Ypres clay.

20 March saw Jack chasing spares, with all the normal frustrations. He must have been fully accustomed to such irritations by then:

> 8.30 am to Dunkirk. No rings reported. Eventually with help of base Commander they were found to be on SS *Whimbrell*. 2 hours moving cargo before uncovered. They got Capt Betts to take me to IT Office. There arranging after sundry stories of Piccadilly fame etc to get self-propelled barge to take to Arques. Started loading there and then. Remainder of material going via Les Attaques in the usual manner. Left 3pm for Calais. To follow up pushing plant. There being no signs of it at Dunkirk. Nothing doing at Calais. Proceeded to Les Attaques. Sewell away but Major Cutting located material. This had come by SS *River Thames* which left England on 25/2/16 and has since been home and is due in today with another consignment and the remainder arrived on the SS *Copeland* which appears to have arrived on the 10/3/16.

The failure of the Stanley Heading Machine was a disappointing end to Jack's efforts in Flanders. Nobody had worked harder than him, and with so little to show for it. On 21 March he put in an application for two months' leave, explaining that he needed to attend to some "personal obligations of considerable importance". Fowke, who had since become Adjutant-General, had no hesitation in granting his request. At last he found time to sort out his dental problem in Boulogne, having a fresh mould taken of his jaw, and also went for an X-ray for a complaint in his nose.

On 29 March, the day before he was due to leave for home,

Jack made his final liaison visit, this time to 171 Company. He arrived early in the morning to find the commanding officer, Captain Henry Hudspeth, still in bed. Red-faced and profuse with apologies, Hudspeth threw on some clothes and jumped into the Rolls. On the way to the front, he found Jack less probing than usual into the work that was going on. He seemed relaxed to a degree that Hudspeth had not seen before. It was almost as if he had detached his mind from the war altogether. And he took a lot of photographs, in contravention of strict regulations. He even took one of Hudspeth himself, promising to send a print to his mother. True to his word, he wrote to her on 12 April:

> My dear Mrs Hudspeth,
> I promised your most excellent brave boy I would send you the accompanying picture of him. It is a small token to one who is doing invaluable work – great work, and if you only knew you would be very proud of him. I left him in the best of health, jolly and looking very fit. Believe me,
> Sincerely yours,
> Norton Griffiths.

Then he went up to Hill 60 for a last look at that scene of so much terrible bloodshed. It only remained to pass a battered Rolls-Royce over to Harvey and go home.

The 'earthquake' did not erupt as planned by the Generals as a diversion for the Battle of the Somme, even though all the tunnels for it were prepared in time. Another year would pass before the 'big blow' took place. In the meantime the fighting continued among the mud and the filth, the rats and the lice, and the shells and bullets and mines around Messines Ridge. The tunnellers continued to burrow, making endless attacks and counter-attacks many feet underground, and the maggot-rotten corpses continued to pile up in no-man's-land and in the trenches. Hundreds of men were buried alive far below the surface of Flanders, where to this day their ghosts keep company with the Stanley Heading Machine.

Jack would have another adventure before the earthquake, and it would be the most hair-raising of all. In an age before inter-national air-travel, his globe-trotting life had taken him to an amazing list of countries. He had been to South Africa, Rhodesia, Mozambique, Ivory Coast, Gold Coast, Angola, U.S.A., Canada, Argentina, Chile, Bolivia, Peru, Australia, Russia, France and Belgium. But it is doubtful if he can ever have envisaged going to the place which would see the climax of his war: Rumania.

17

OPERATION ARSON

Rumania, sitting on the rim of Balkans stewpot, had so far been able to keep out of the war. In fact, she was in many ways torn between the sides. She had strong ties with the Central Powers, relying on Austro-German imports and capital, and her Royal Family were part of the Hohenzollern dynasty. In Bessarabia thousands of ethnic Rumanians were suffering under the heel of the Tsarist regime, creating general hostility towards Russia, Germany's foe, by most Rumanians.

On the other hand there were considerable forces drawing her towards the Allies. There was a strong Francophile element in Rumania, where it had become common practice for promising young men to go to Paris for a university education, and Princess Marie was the daughter of the Duke of Edinburgh and therefore Queen Victoria's grand-daughter. She was married to the nephew of King Carol, Crown Prince Ferdinand, the heir to the throne of Rumania. At the same time, there had recently been something of a warming towards the Russians as a result of Austria's support of Bulgaria against Rumania in the Second Balkan War of 1913, which had culminated in a visit to Constanza by the Tsar in June 1914.

Most importantly, there were another 3,000,000 Rumanian 'exiles' living in Austrian Bukovina and Hungarian Transylvania who were suffering persecution and political discrimination which threatened to destroy their national identity and ensure continued domination by the ruling classes. And what was perhaps the last straw had been the attempt by the Central Powers to browbeat Rumania into mobilizing her army at the outbreak of war and march against the Russians. This had been

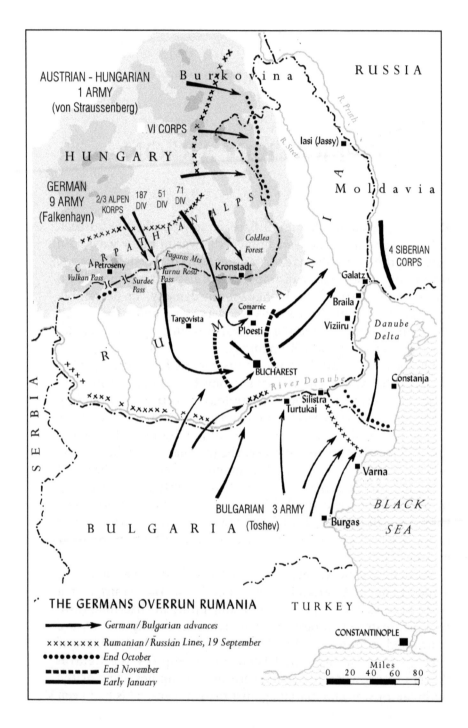

AUSTRIAN - HUNGARIAN
1 ARMY
(von Straussenberg)

RUSSIA

Burkovina

VI CORPS

Iasi (Jassy)

HUNGARY

GERMAN
9 ARMY
(Falkenhayn)

2/3 ALPEN
KORPS

187
DIV

51
DIV

71
DIV

Moldavia

R. Prut

R. Siret

CARPATHIAN ALPS

Coldlea
Forest

4 SIBERIAN
CORPS

C A Petroseny

Fagaras Mts

Kronstadt

Vulkan Pass

Turnu Rosu
Pass

Surdec
Pass

Galatz

Braila

Targovista

Comarnic

Ploesti

Viziiru

Danube
Delta

R U M A N I A

BUCHAREST

River Danube

Constanja

SERBIA

Silistra

Turtukai

Varna

BULGARIAN 3 ARMY
(Toshev)

BLACK

SEA

Burgas

B U L G A R I A

THE GERMANS OVERRUN RUMANIA

TURKEY

CONSTANTINOPLE

→ German / Bulgarian advances

×××××××× Rumanian / Russian Lines, 19 September

•••••••• End October

▬ ▬ ▬ End November

▬▬▬ Early January

Miles
0 20 40 60 80

staunchly resisted, with the universal approval of the Rumanian Crown Council which met at the King's summer palace at Sinaia on 3 August 1914. They had no desire to see Rumanian blood shed to defend the 'odious Magyar regime in Transylvania'.

The two warring sides each began to woo Rumania with bribes. The Russians, who very early in the war had overrun Galicia and Bukovina, promised to recognize Rumania's right to annexe the Austro-Hungarian territory inhabited by Rumanian majorities, thereby dangling the carrot of an invitation to join the winning side. But the Central Powers countered with an offer of Bessarabia and promises to reform the situation in Transylvania. The French-educated Rumanian Premier, Ion Braniatu, recognized the dangers of either path, saying that it would be better to wait and see how matters developed. It appeared as if he intended to pledge Rumanian support to the highest bidder in an auction of territory. By the spring of 1915, following the Gallipoli invasion and the Treaty of London, the scales of war seemed to have tipped in favour of the Allies. Sensing an opportune moment, Braniatu took his demands to St Petersburg, anticipating a welcome with open arms and an easy assent. But he had asked too much. Russia and Serbia also coveted some of the Hapsburg territory he wanted and he came away empty handed. But then came a series of setbacks for the Allies. The Austrians broke through the Russian lines at Gorlice on the same day that Braniatu arrived in St Petersburg, the Allies reached stalemate at Gallipoli and the Bulgarians were on the verge of smashing Serbia. Intense Anglo-French pressure was brought to bear on the Russians, who quickly acceded to Rumanian demands.

But by August 1915 the Russians were on the retreat. They had evacuated Bukovina, Galicia and most of Poland. This was no time for Rumania to enter the war on their side. And the Allies had grown to mistrust Braniatu. Early on in the war he had performed a valuable service to them by blocking the transit of German armaments intended for Turkey and banned the export of Rumanian oil and grain to the Central Powers. But the overrunning of Serbia by Austro-German-Bulgarian forces in October 1915 constituted a threat which he could not ignore and he now attempted to appease them by negotiating large sales of these commodities to Germany and Austria-Hungary.

Throughout the spring and summer of 1916, the bloody epics at Verdun, the Isonzo, the Somme and the Russian General Aleksei Brusilov's offensive seem to have galvanized Braniatu's thinking. He sensed that Russia was weakening and that she may have played her last card. At the same time he had begun to suspect war-weariness within Austria-Hungary: in fact he had heard rumours that the Hungarians might be willing to negotiate a separate peace. Most immediately, there was the alarming fact that Rumania now found herself surrounded on three sides by the Central Powers and their allies. A telegram from Marshal Joffre pointed out to him that "it was now or never". He hesitated no further and agreed to mobilize his army.

Now that Rumania was committed, Britain, Russia and France all immediately arranged for shipments of munitions. But there were still interminable delays before any formal Rumanian declaration of war, caused by Braniatu's apparent inability to do anything positive without a protracted period of 'wheeling and dealing'. Weeks were lost while more and more tedious conditions were thrashed out with the Allies and all the time the Sword of Damocles hovered over Rumania.

During the last week of Rumanian neutrality the military build-up intensified. Convoys of motor-lorries, wagons, guns and columns of marching men clogged the roads. Against them a contraflow of motor-cars, mule-carts and peasants pushing hand-carts laden with their belongings trudged away from the frontier areas, hoping to find better safety in the interior. Troop trains, some half a mile long, full of blue-uniformed men ran day and night, rushing troops to both the northern and southern frontiers. Muslim soldiers discarded their bright red fezes for drab grey ones and street-lamps were dimmed against Zeppelin raids. Sweethearts married in haste and excited people avidly scanned newspapers. Rumania, it seemed, was ready for war and anxious to get on with it.

At 8.45 pm on 27 August 1916 Edgar Mavrocordat, the Rumanian minister in Vienna, delivered his country's declaration of war to the Austrian Foreign Ministry.

Exactly twelve hours before, the new King Ferdinand (King Carol had died on 10 October 1915) had convened the Crown Council at Cotroceni. Braniatu had spoken eloquently, assuring

182

his colleagues that their new Allies, comprising some of the world's most powerful nations, would recognize their claims to Transylvania. "You should not look at the immediate results, gentlemen," he said, "but . . . the destiny of this nation and go forward with decision along the road which is indicated by the national conscience." King Ferdinand echoed these sentiments, but he was no politician and was therefore able to express himself rather more concisely. "Forward with God!" he intoned as he closed the meeting.

Rumania possessed a massive army of twenty infantry divisions, which, with cavalry and artillery, meant that she could put 564,000 men into the field, with artillery pieces numbering 1,300, which included 700 modern Krupp 75mm quick-firing field guns. Geography provided her with considerable natural lines of defence. To the north and west lay the thickly wooded Carpathians, which cut off the Rumanian-Translyvanians from their compatriots. There were only a few easy passes over these 8,000-foot mountains, whilst the southern border with Bulgaria and Serbia was marked by the Danube, three-quarters of a mile wide in places. And she had a strong flotilla of armed vessels, including four monitors, eight patrol boats and a mine-layer on the river to reinforce that line of defence. Chief of Staff General Zottu planned to throw the bulk of his troops against Transylvania, whilst keeping sufficient forces in the south to hold off any Bulgarian attacks. With insuperable optimism, he hoped to see his main army in Budapest within six weeks.

But the Rumanian army, large as it was, had no experience of modern heavyweight warfare, and that was true from its generals right down to its greenest private. Against them would be forces containing thousands of battle-hardened veteran troops, fighting under proven leadership.

At the beginning Zottu enjoyed some of the success he had anticipated. Throwing 369,000 troops against only 34,000 of the Austro-Hungarian First Army under Baron Arz von Straussenburg, he hurled the enemy back, taking Kronstadt on 30 August. Further west, Rumanian troops swarmed over the Vulkan Pass to take the long-coveted rich coal mines around Petroseny. By mid-September they were forty miles beyond the Carpathian passes and Zottu's optimism was appearing not to be quite so far-fetched after all.

But suddenly the Bulgarians struck in the south. Beefed up by German and Turkish infantry divisions and assisted by the Austro-Hungarian Danube flotilla, they surged towards the Danube crossings in the far south-east. With the vast bulk of their troops tied down in the north-west, the Rumanians had no immediate ability to counter this and by mid-September the Bulgarians had taken the fort at Turtukai, killing or wounding 3,570 and taking 28,000 prisoners at minimal loss, captured the Danube bridgehead at Silistra and were advancing up the Black Sea coast, crushing the Rumanian-Russian-Serbian army in the process.

King Ferdinand called an emergency meeting at Army HQ at which General Averescu, the dynamic commander of the Third Army, suggested that his forces be detached from the Transylvanian front, make a strong crossing of the Danube downstream of where it swung north into Rumania itself, thus being in a position to attack the rear of the advancing Bulgarians. The remaining forces in the north-west were to be ordered to stay on the defensive for the time being. The Rumanians' opening plans were, therefore, about to be completely reversed.

From mid-September the German General von Falkenhayn was appointed to lead the German Ninth Army and, in conjunction with the Austro-Hungarian First Army began a counter-offensive in the Carpathians against the weakened Rumanian forces on that front. They threw the defenders back over the Vulkan Pass and the elite German Alpine Corps began to advance through the inhospitable Czibin Mountain region, thus cutting off the Rumanian First Corps at Hermannstadt. The battle raged for three days until, at nightfall on the 28 September, the First Corps found themselves besieged at the northern entrance to the Turnu Rosu (Red Tower) Pass. Now completely demoralized under such overwhelming conditions, the inexperienced Rumanians began to lose their discipline. In desperation, their vehicles and artillery pieces began a wild retreat through the Pass, in the dark at reckless speed, with German machine guns spraying them with a withering fire. By some miracle, most of their guns were saved, while their confused and shocked infantry was left to straggle back by way of obscure forest border paths across the Fagaras Mountains. For the Rumanians the situation looked bleak. They had gone to war confident of early victory, but in the course of a few short weeks had suffered a series of bitter defeats. Their troops were badly shattered and their Generals had lost heart.

In London British Intelligence was well aware of the developments in Rumania and of what would be the immediate consequences of a successful invasion by the Central Powers. They would become the *de facto* owners of much oil and grain, both of which were sorely needed for their war effort. Prior to their entry into the war, the Rumanians had agreed with the Allies to destroy their oil and grain in case it fell into German hands. In the event, as soon as the possibility of this happening transformed itself into a likelihood, and then into a practical certainty, the Government and the high-ranking military fled. That left nobody to order or carry out the task of destruction. In fact, there was a plethora of relatively minor officials who were determined that the oil fields should not be damaged at all.

Germany and her Allies were engaged in total warfare against Britain, France and their Allies. German submarines were sinking British ships wholesale as they approached the British Isles laden with essential supplies of food and materials. Winston Churchill had said that it was not invasion that he feared, but starvation. Even Britain's fishing smacks were not safe from attack. As for the Germans, their ports were securely blockaded by the Royal Navy. Their only easy exits were from their ports on the Baltic to destinations in neutral Scandinavia. Thus, it was probably true that the German war machine, as well as her hungry civilian population, was finding life in wartime even more difficult than their enemies. Britain at least had several sources to which she could turn for supplies of vital oil, even though the tankers carrying it ran a dangerous gauntlet to bring it home. The Germans were fast running short of friends and had no such luxury, even if they had been able to break through the blockade. To allow the Central Powers access to the Rumanian oil now, to say nothing of the grain, would be to concede a major piece on the chessboard of the war. This had to be prevented at all costs.

Jack, who on his return from France had been reinstated to his rank of Major, had been 'resting' at the Ministry of Munitions.

He received notice on 4 November that he had been appointed again to Temporary Lieutenant-Colonel and was ordered to report to the Department of Military Intelligence. On arrival at the hush-hush temple of shadowy deviousness, he was ushered into the office of General McDonough, head of MI 17b. He sat impassively as he listened to the General describing the mission that had been assigned to him. They wanted him to go to Rumania to destroy the oil!

"You are a skilled engineer, Colonel. You will have men there, working for the oil companies, who will do the work, but you must direct it. Any questions?"

Jack was still a little dazed with surprise. The only thing he could think of was to say, "What regiments do I take, sir?"

"You go alone," replied McDonough, as if he were passing some remark about the weather, "You may take only your batman."

Then he went on, "You will first go to St Petersburg and report to the Tsar, then on to Bucharest where you will report to the Rumanian Government. Try to enlist their co-operation. The French are having little success. Here is your Passport and your Orders."

He handed Jack a piece of white vellum, beautifully embossed and scrolled, and a sealed manila envelope. Clearly everything had been carefully cut and dried.

"And what do I tell the owners of the oilfields?"

"You may say that the British Government undertakes to pay for the cost of restoration at the end of the war. You have been granted plenary powers by Mr McKenna, Chancellor of the Exchequer. Goodbye, Colonel, and good luck."

We do not know how and on whose instigation Jack had been selected for this dangerous task. We know that he was taken by a British destroyer to Bergen in Norway. Quite how he travelled from there to St Petersburg we do not know, except that it was via Sweden and Finland. But a mere eight days after his briefing by McDonough, and they must have been a hectic eight days, he was in Petrograd. Russia was by that time not only fighting a major war with Germany and Austria-Hungary, but was also in the throes of a domestic crisis, ridden with strikes and civilian unrest. Jack described his uncomfortable journey through the midst of this hellish confusion to Rumania in a series of letters to Gwladys.

13 November 1916. Petrograd. After a great scramble I got into this train yesterday, and after all got a cabin to myself, but I have kept Finch in with me. His mystic shoulder-chains apparently pass him for any rank, otherwise he ought to be huddled up in Third with a crowd of unwashed. Busy day yesterday. Saw General Arenkof, who is Head of Rumanian Affairs in Petrograd . . . Nothing doing. He said the man to see was Batioff at the Rumanian H.Q. Difficult travelling where only Russian is spoken. We're not sure if we have to change at Kief. Tremendous crowd . . . train packed with soldiers and officers all ranks. Sir George made a timely speech. There seems to be a strong German propaganda going on "England is only using Russia . . . trying to grab etc etc." Strikes and shouting.

14.11 16. Arrived Kief 6.30 a.m. Fortunately I got a very nice Russian officer to go with me to the station commandant and there I got fixed up in a coupé. Train supposed to get away at 8.00. Finally departed at 9.20, people and soldiers fighting to get on. Steps full with hangers on, women crying, men yelling, not a pleasant sight. However, here we are. Rotten carriage, nowhere to wash, everything filthy beyond words, men, women and children asleep on their luggage, rich and poor alike. I got someone's cold yesterday, but managed to heat some water with matches, six it took. This part of the world is full of germs. We passed a few minutes ago the first signs of defence works, stakes ready for barbed wire.

I hear it may take days to get to Bucharest. The Russians have rushed several divisions into the country and there seem to be only two lines of entry.

2.0 pm. The train keeps stopping, the jam gets worse but no chance of getting out to get any food, so we began the chocolate you gave me. It won't do any harm to go a couple of days without food – probably do our interiors a power of good. The country we are passing through now looks like reclaimed bog. Soil as black as ink, but fairly well ploughed and planted.

15.11.16. 10 am. I believe we are due at the Frontier about 3.00 or 4.00. We reached Kichenev about 12.00 Yesterday at 4.00 stopped for an hour at a big junction. The crowd was immense, about 2,000 or 3,000 people all eating at once in a big domed hall. We eventually got hold of a little boy who fetched us things. French seems to be of no use, broken English more in evidence. I met a waiter who had been in the States and an officer who had been all round the world in an English ship. We had lunch, dinner and tea all in one. Quite a good meal. No blankets or sheets on our bunk so I sleep in my rug but get into my pyjamas and this morning I shaved out of a small glass of mineral water I got yesterday

The country is slightly undulating but still black soil and huge stores of grain at various stopping places and huge stacks of hay. Another stop – just a station in the wilderness. We have just passed a troop train in a siding. A complete regiment I should say. I don't think the people here ever wash. I've seen no signs of it since leaving Petrograd.

16. 11. 16.   We have done 30 kms since 8.00 last night. We go the length of the train, then stop for half an hour or more. The line is all troop trains, crawling along one behind the other. I suppose we are about 20 miles from the Frontier, but it could take some four hours or more. We had to come down to a ration of your chocolate - ¼ of a piece each. I fear things don't look promising in the food line today. As far as I can see the line is all troop trains crawling along one after the other. We are now at the head of a troop train (closed trucks) to which we have been attached. I managed to shave this morning. Had a rotten night, vile cold on my chest. I feel like a boiled owl. Country very hilly now, bare, black soil a few people plowing, villages almost like those in West Africa, only a little better, firewood and corn stacked on the roofs of their houses.

From 4.30 to dawn we were in complete darkness except for my flashlight which I use sparingly. We have done about 50 km in twelve hours. We are now at the head of a troop train. We got one meal yesterday but I don't think there is much chance today, so we shall fall back on your chocolate. I am *very* unhappy at the way we have neglected our interests in Russia and I think it is a real danger in the war. I think the Rumanian position is very rotten as far as I can see. They have no guns or machine guns or barbed wire and that is the only answer to German attacks with spadework. However, of this I hope I shall be a better judge later.

17.11.16. 4pm. Rumania at last. A bad time yesterday – we dilly-dallied all day and got to the frontier (Iasi entrance) at 6 pm. Not

188

a bite to eat all day to be had, but got quite a decent meal at 6.30. Left frontier at midnight, arrived Iasi at 3 am. The Rumanian Minister had wired and the R R officer i/c did me well, gave me tea and coffee. It began to snow at 2 and has snowed since, a good 6" and still going on. Every station and siding is full of troops. The R. officer at Iasi put me in a coupé with instructions we were to be got to Bucharest as soon as military exigencies allow. This train is full of Rumanian and Russian soldiers and with luck we get to B tomorrow. We stopped today and had a vegetarian lunch at Pascain so we are going by the western route. They stoke a little fire under the carriage whenever it stops, so we keep fairly warm. This rough weather I should think is good, as it should give the Rs time to make their dispositions. Running into Bacan now – many Russian troops here already disembarked.

18.11.16.   8am. Just running towards Bucharest – I suppose 10 miles outside. Shaved at six in icy cold water. Not so much snow here but freezing.

They had spent a solid week on a train, and it was only a fort-night since Jack had been shown through the door of MI 17b.

He spent the next week interviewing the military authorities and appraising the situation. It was far worse than he had expected. It seemed that nothing now could stop the German Army from over-running the oilfields. General Avarescu's Third Army was fighting some brilliant rearguard actions, but was rapidly losing ground all the time. The only consolation was a small one. The oilfields were congregated in the east of the country, around Ploeşti and Braila, which meant that the Germans would have a little further to advance. But time had almost run out. On 23 November the Rumanian Government appointed a Commission of Rumanian and French officials to oversee the destruction of the oil stocks. Jack was co-opted as a member. The oil companies, as such, had ceased to be able to take responsibility for their own properties. Jack could see that the Commission was little more than a sham. There was absolutely nothing to stop its members from siphoning off the oil for the benefit of their own companies. Indeed, some had already begun to do so. In a rage, he left for Targoviste where the refineries of Rumanian Consolidated Oil were situated. He found time to dash off a quick note to Gwladys:

189

I'm off to try to deal with one big lot but doubtful if I can get there. Hung up for cars. Am trying to get some machine guns and armoured cars from Odessa. The Boches will have Bucharest before long. The Russians are so slow to move, and these people *hate* the Russians; that's the trouble.

He managed to round up a few Englishmen and arranged to have them put into khaki. How he was able to get them into uniform so far from home is a baffling question. They were engineers working for Consolidated Oilfields, a British-owned concern, the men whom McDonough had promised would be there to "do the work". The British manager at Targoviste, William Guthrie, was arrested for his efforts to support Jack, but was immediately released amid profuse apologies. Jack then set off on a rampage of activity, in typical style, haggling and hustling sometimes till two or three in the morning to get things done. In his report to the Director of Military Intelligence, he described his operations in the Targoviste area.

SECRET. 22 January 1917. Jassy. (Iasi)
TARGOVISTE – the following refineries were destroyed:-
Rumanian Consolidated Oilfields Ltd. – This refinery had a working capacity of 350 tons of crude oil per day. Storage capacity 35,000 tons, distributed over an area of 14 acres. It contained a battery of 6 stills, with ephlegmators and preheaters, refining and rectifying plant, electric light installation, 120 hp boiler plant, workshops and stores. Stocks in reservoir when fired, 18,000 tons.
   The preparatory measures taken for destruction were as follows:-
Dams were built round each reservoir.
   Channels were cut from storage tanks through the refinery to the large reservoirs.
   Communication trenches were cut to the various buildings containing plant.
   All machinery, including lathes, motors &c were smashed by sledge hammers.
   The laboratory was demolished by sledge hammers.
   All reservoir valves were opened and the oil allowed to flow into the dams *surrounding* the reservoirs and along all com-

munication trenches and ignited, burning and exploding the reservoirs and constantly feeding the trenches; these led to the plant and machinery and thus helping to complete the destruction.

This refinery being situated in the immediate vicinity of the railway station, through which divisions of infantry were retreating, special precautions had to be taken in order not to interfere with their only line of communication. At the last moment, and just before firing, the local General Commanding sent definite orders not to fire, he being influenced by the prevailing belief that the ensuing explosions would wreck the town and cut his rail communication. No heed was paid to these orders (beyond sending word that I would guarantee their safety) and before we could be stopped the refinery was blazing. Neither the town nor the station suffered.

Haiman. A small old refinery recently enlarged to a working capacity of 35 tons per day. Storage capacity 3,500 tons, distributed over an area of about 1½ acres. Contained 3 stills, refining and rectifying plant. Stocks in reservoirs when fired were 2,000 tons. A large dam was built outside the refinery and a trench cut to the storage tanks which were inside the refinery. It was here that the first work of the Rumanian Commission was seen to consist of an uphill gradient resulting in the flooding of the refinery.

Grigorescu. A small refinery recently enlarged to a working capacity of 60 tons per day. Storage capacity 4,000 tons. Area about 2½ acres. Plant all fairly old. Stocks when fired 1,300 tons. The refinery was situated immediately on the left bank of the River Jalomita. The authorities fear the escape of oil down the river and a special dam had to be built around the refinery before it was fired. Ditches were carried into the workshops and pump houses to convey oil for firing purposes after pumps and all machinery had been smashed with sledge hammers. The oil was then fired and the reservoirs exploded, firing the adjoining buildings.

Aurora. A very old and obsolete refinery, originally owned by a Dutch concern but now controlled by the German Steaua Romana group who some years ago advanced the Dutch Company an important sum of money on mortgage, which is not yet redeemed. Working capacity 100 tons per day. Storage 6,000 tons. All machinery old and the buildings in a state of ruin. The refinery contained 2,700 tons of oil, of which 780 tons were lubricating oils. In view of avoiding the possibility of exaggerated claims for compensation, I decided not to fire but to run off the oil, allowing it to percolate into the ground and wrecking machinery of any value. I understand, however, that the refinery and dams were fired by the rearguard of the Rumanian Army the following night as it passed. All these fires lasted several days. The smoke hung heavily over the town and the flames, which at times rose to great heights, illuminated the neighbouring districts, thus allowing the enemy for the first time to become aware of our work. The roads were becoming impracticable with the passing of the refugees and the retreat of the Rumanian convoys. The traffic was held up for hours at a time, causing us serious delays in our movements, and on several occasions it was necessary to take over its organization.

Now the German planes came droning overhead, dropping bombs and panicking an already terror-stricken population. By the end of November Falkenhayn's troops were on the Glavacioc, barely two days march from the oilfields. And they were about to meet up with Mackensen's forces sweeping up from the south-west.

As far as the British assurances of compensation were concerned, Braniatu had steadfastly refused to listen to a word Jack said on the subject, and officials of the Royal Dutch and Standard Oil Companies tried to buy him off. The Commission seemed prepared to see the oil stocks destroyed, but baulked at any suggestion that the wells and equipment should be touched. Jack fumed. There was no more time for delay. Now was the time to show good leadership. The only way the problem was going to be solved was to play the game his way.

"If I can get hold of a few things I want, I can do some good work here," he wrote.

The 'few things' he had in mind were more sledge-hammers and a boxes of matches, and the 'good' was to blow 1000 square kilometres of oil-fields sky high, causing millions of pounds worth of damage to what was essentially private property. He had hammered out an agreement with the Consolidated Oilfields officials. He could destroy their refineries and wells, and they would provide assistance to him to destroy others. In return he signed an assessment of the value of their property on behalf of the British Government.

192

The destruction continued as refinery after refinery was engulfed in spiralling flames. The workers and their families were evacuated from each area. Trenches were dug to the refinery and flooded with petrol. Acid was poured into the boilers to corrode them. Jack had learned to trust nobody. Where possible, he threw a lighted match into a trench himself. Instantly, there was a crr-rump and within seconds the entire landscape was a mass of roaring fire. Then they turned to the equipment, cutting down derricks and throwing them down the shafts, destroying bore-holes, pipelines, dynamos, tanks, engines and motor vehicles with dynamite, fire and sledgehammer. The sledgehammer was rarely out of his reach for days on end. Where something could not be burned or blown up, a few swipes with the sledgehammer could usually render it useless. There were dramatic scenes, with great columns of smoke and flame, loud explosions, and men, their faces blackened by smoke and their clothes pocked with scorch holes, destroying and demolishing round the clock until they were exhausted.

In his report to the DMI he described his methods of plugging an oil well. At the time he was operating in the Ochiuri Rasvad field, to the east of Targoviste. This field was producing from a depth of 380-450 metres in the Dacian formation, which was covered by Levantine beds. All the drilling had been done by way of the Canadian system and nothing but Canadian tools had been found on the field. With these confiscated, and the existing bore-holes plugged at depth, experts agreed that it would take the Germans at least a year to make fresh bores.

These were the first wells encountered and his object was to plug them – burn the oil stocks and stores and destroy by hammers the workshops and plant. This field was equipped with large numbers of steam and belt pumps, large electric motors and steam engines, besides a vast amount of drilling, fishing and bailing materials and tools.

The plugging of the wells was commenced and the following course adopted:- Bailers were dropped down together with their wire lines (from 1 inch to 1¼ inch diameter) which were released from the drum and allowed to 'run away' and drop to the bottom of the hole. On top of the wire line, (always about 300-400 metres in length) other available tools were dropped in inverted form which jammed further down the wire line. The tools dropped from the top of the holes consisted of bits of the same diameter as the casing, varying from 6-inch to 12-inch fishing hooks; tool wrenches, pulleys, iron bars and bolts, which would pack and jam in between the bigger tools. In addition, small material in the way of brass fittings (babbit metal, copper, tin and small connecting joints) were also thrown down the holes. After this we smashed the engines, pulleys and other vulnerable parts in the derrick which was then fired. It should be stated that the production on this field was obtained by bailing – there being no natural flowing wells.

Several times Jack came close to death, catching his clothes and his hair alight in his haste. At Moreni he was nearly trapped in his own fire, being stunned by the explosion. It was only the quick thinking of the loyal Rumanian aristocrat Captain Prince Antoine Bibesco, future husband of Prime Minister Asquith's daughter Elizabeth, who dragged him clear at great risk to himself, that saved his life. In between 'jobs' Jack would snatch a few minutes' sleep in his car as it raced across the snow-bound landscape towards the next scene of destruction, bulldozing his way past the officialdom which set out to hamper his efforts. But he was too quick to be caught by any Government preventative measures. His mission was all-important.

On 1 December the Germans pushed Averescu's forces back to the valley of the Dambo Vita, an area of difficult broken country with no made-up roads, which gave Jack a few vital hours to blow up refineries there and in the Prahova and Campina valleys with gelignite. Officials were waved away with a gesture of his revolver. "I don't speak your blasted language," he shouted at one of them, "My Chief is the British War Cabinet and the War Office in London. If you want me to stop, cable them!" At Bana he was arrested by a member of the Commission, but managed to fight his way free with his fists. And on another occasion, when confronted by a particularly difficult individual, he promptly drew his revolver and shot the man dead. The Germans were now so close that twice their cavalry patrols cut in behind him. It was only by the speed of his car that he was able to escape. Rampaging

194

through the Doltana, Comarnic and Tzintea valleys, demolishing wells and refineries as he went, often his car was scarcely out of sight as the first German patrols came on the scene to find a lake of fire and a twisted tangle of toppled derricks. Ploesti, the major oil town, was clogged with crowds of refugees and wounded soldiers, but there were also 50,000 tons of oil to destroy and the huge Astrea and Steaua refineries to wreck. Impatiently, he paced up and down waiting for the town to be cleared as the minutes ticked away. Then, leaving nothing to chance, he personally set the gelignite in the main machinery, flooded the complete area with petrol and ignited it. A great maelstrom of fire erupted over the town. It was so powerful that he was almost sucked into the vacuum it created. The heat was so intense that a family of gypsies camped just outside the town was choked to death. On 6 December the Germans entered Bucharest and turned towards Ploesti, but they were too late. All they found were blocked wells, blazing tanks and acres of plant thoroughly destroyed. Towering columns of dense black smoke still climbed into the sky over an area of 100 square miles, creating a pall so thick that it shut out the daylight.

But Jack's work was not yet done. There was still the grain to deal with. He had destroyed all the grain he had encountered so far in his orgy of destruction, but there remained much more. At Braila, at the head of the Danube delta and connected to the Black Sea by the Sulina Channel, were 54,000 tons of wheat stored in gigantic granaries – at that time the biggest in the world. The Germans were keeping these covered with their heavy guns, but Jack worked by night, laying charges of dynamite which shook the town of Galatz over twenty miles away. By the time Braila was finally taken by the invaders in mid-January 1917 he had demolished or contaminated the lot.

10 December 1916.   Braila. Here I am arrived last night after continuous work morning , noon and night. A more complete debacle you cannot imagine. I told General Varesco commanding the most important position that it was madness not to retire. The position so desperate, no time to arrange anything . . . I had to personally do the oil . . . my hastily formed force did the trick. Day and night we worked over large areas, everyone running like

195

hares when we began to fire. I burnt my nose . . . blown out of a large engine house through the door. We wrecked millions of stuff and machinery. The Boche will get nothing. I am dead beat but well. Once or twice we nearly got cut off by the cavalry sweeping in behind. Hayward escaped by the skin of his teeth. Good boy.

The position is deplorable. The Rumanian army is no more to speak of and they have nothing in guns, material and so on – the Boches simply made rings round them, and will continue to do so. The next two or three days I am going to try and sink barges on the Danube at night, as our bank is generally covered by their guns. I have had awful rows with the Rumanians who wanted to save the oil and works for the Boche – two of my own officers were arrested, but I kicked up such a Hell of a row they let them go. One obstacle of a blighter – a Rumanian official – I tried to trap in 20,000 tons of benzine. I watched him go, I hoped in the right direction, he not knowing that I was going to fire, but the swine escaped. However, I scared him off the next show and he has not been seen since.

5.12.16.   40 km south of Braila. Yesterday we were between the lines burning corn – the Russians retired to a new line on account of Boche pressure from the NW. In great haste, but I am well and very fit except for swollen eyelids, from the corn dust I suppose. Colonel G. now destroying corn Tatarul area south of Braila. Russian troops now co-operating, 5,000 tons destroyed the first day and work proceeding. Railway hopelessly blocked, consequently very little chance of saving any. 100 horse wagons engaged in transporting to Braila. The line is reforming on a line from Shancuta Filiul, about 6 km south of Vizirul.

Yesterday we were between the last rearguard and the Germans, burning, but it was quite safe as the Russians were retiring on account of the pressure on the Rumanian front at Buzan. I am not hopeful that Braila can be retained. Please excuse these hurried notes but time is of the greatest importance. Today we have a lot of work in Satarul area, which is in front of the new Russian front, if it can be done.

22.12.16.   Here I am at the new HQ of the Russians and Rumanians, after a continuous front line of burning and wrecking between the Danube and Buzau – road impossible, and movement sometimes hopeless.

I have just left two cars stuck, and got a passing Russian Cavalry Regiment to give us horses and I have used their saddles as pack saddles, and we have been riding two nights and days. Railway hopelessly congested – took 22 hours to do 60 km and that only by telegraphing repeatedly to HQ. Trains block every siding – oddments of Regiments and Divisions rolling along to reform – Russians going in to the front. I slept in the corridor of a filthy carriage last night, and woke up like ice. The roads are worse for movement than Africa.

I see General Sakaroff tomorrow at 10, the new Gen. (Rumanian) afterwards to press them to continue the work which I have begun with the aid of Russian troops which I have had to borrow. The Russians should do all the work themselves now, and they want to, but they want some definite order from HQ, which HQ not only won't give, but the day before yesterday sent out new instructions not to destroy, after Sakaroff had given me a most splendidly worded authority which I got from him myself. This authorized me to call on any Russian Division for assistance etc. I don't think they have ever seen such a 'move on' before.

Tell General McDonough that [name erased] has shot his bolt, and he really ought to send a good pukka General like Sir John Maxwell or a big-wig invaluable just now, but [name erased] was always with [name erased] who wrecked the army and [names erased] don't count with the Russian colonels. It's a General who would count and render invaluable service. It's English they really cry for, French swarm everywhere. I can't emphasise this too much. I beg CIGS to do this in the interests of our country. Tell the General it's go night and day, and I cannot wire him secretly, and I'd better not write – I have to be at it all the time to override obstacles. I've not been to bed for four nights.

On Christmas Day I shall be right in the Russian front between the Danube and the Buzău. It's awful here, retreating and retreating, but I think now for the first time they will soon be stopped. Tell General McDonough that corn is most difficult. The Russians have never been instructed to destroy it. There are stacks yet that I am shoving back into wagons and carts, tons and tons of it, and I am going to try to sell the remainder to the Russians. I destroy as the last line comes back, mostly at night when we can't be seen, but it covers so much ground – still we have done much in the time. While I was in oil they stopped the men I sent out and nothing was done until I went out and simply overrode all authority. I am off now to Braila which may fall at any minute.

197

It is difficult to put an exact figure on the damage that Jack and his handful of men had inflicted in Rumania, but it was probably around £55 million at 1917 prices. All oil production had been halted. Against this can be measured the effects of the American bombing of the same targets in 1942 and 1943, when at a cost of fifty-four aircraft only half the production was lost.

It was time to go home again. From Iasi, near the frontier, he wrote to Gwladys on 19 January, ". . . The oil has been a complete success but to achieve it meant Benguela tactics all over again. Night and day, personally driving all the time, riding roughshod over everybody in the pandemonium, generally raising hell in the absolute hell of terrific explosions, smoke, gas, the day as night once thousands of tons of oil were well under way, bursting reservoirs and always the uncertainty of the Boche cavalry cutting in behind us, which they did more than once. I can assure you that the revolver played a part on one occasion. It would have been short shrift if they had caught us ....I have flouted all authority here and the politicians hate me, but I think they are afraid of offending the British Government by taking any action against me, otherwise I should have been arrested over and over again."

It was at Iasi that he found friends in the Rumanian Royal Family, who had fled there from Bucharest on 2 December. Queen Marie was working with the Red Cross, helping to organize hospitals for the many wounded and for typhoid victims. She had been married to the inept Crown Prince, now King Ferdinand, for twenty-four years, much against her will, it was said, to avenge her Russian mother's own unhappy marriage to Alfred, Duke of Edinburgh, who had died of gunshot wounds in 1900, possibly through suicide. Marie was far from her homeland and warmed to Jack. Indeed, scurrilous rumours abounded that she was not immune to his charms, nor he to hers. But proof of anything improper between them does not exist. Moreover, Jack was so besotted with Gwladys all their life together as to make such a suggestion highly dubious. All that exists as testament to their friendship is a signed photograph, taken outdoors in the snow, with Jack in the middle of the Royal Family, with a note that Queen Marie wrote to him after his return to England:

To John Norton Griffiths,
Carlton Club,
London.

Thank you so much for your kind letter and for the seeds. I like to think of you and the work you did for us. You were one of my consolations in the very terrible winter that lies behind us. I am sure you must have mourned with me for my sister's fate*, it is cruel and unfair when she worked so nobly and loved her people so well. This war has been so cruel to the innocent and has carried off much that was great and good – but disasters are so vast one can but bow one's head. With the warm weather our own difficulties are less hard to bear and our poor little army has been reconstrued in a marvellous way. The spirit of our soldiers has become excellent. I still would like you to send me some bulbs when you can: irises, tulips and lilies – I want to plant them this autumn upon my soldiers' graves – there are so many, so many! Otherwise we are being bravely helped by England, America and France, but the unruly state of Russia is a great danger for our struggling suffering little country.

Thank you for all that you have done and are doing for us!
Marie.

Jack finalized his despatch to the Director of Military Intelligence with a section headed 'Recommendations'.

I have to mention the following members of the Mission for their untiring energy and devotion to duty:-
A. *Foreign.*

Captain Prince G.B.Bibesco (attached to me for special duty) for conspicuous gallantry at Moreni, who at great personal risk cut off an encircling flow of lighted benzine, and also behaved in an exemplary manner on other occasions when assisting in igniting and destroying vast stores of refined and other oils, commencing with the Mission until the work of destroying the oil industry was completed.

* Queen Marie had three sisters, Victoria, Alexandra and Beatrice, who died in 1936, 1942 and 1966 respectively. She is probably referring to Alexandra, who, being divorced, had been banished from Russia by the Tsar in 1917 for marrying his cousin Cyril Vladimirovich Romanov in 1905 without his permission. Cyril was also Alexandra's first cousin, so the marriage was forbidden by the Church.

Lieutenant Maurice Phillipon, engineer and chemist to the Mission Militaire Technique Française des Munitions, for devotion to duty, untiring energy and self-sacrifice at Targoviste, Moreni and particularly at Ploesti, where he narrowly escaped while lighting large quantities of benzine.

Lieutenant I. Tanasescu, Rumanian Government Ingineur des Mines, for his untiring energy and devotion to duty and for materially assisting the Mission in their work at Targoviste, Moreni and elsewhere.

2nd-Lieutenant A. Tzantzareanu, Rumanian Government Engineer, for his great and invaluable help to the Mission, often under circumstances of extreme difficulty and against the views held by so many of his colleagues. This officer ran many risks and showed great zeal and energy in carrying out instructions to destroy various distilleries. (The only two mining officers who were generally to be found at their posts at critical moments.)
B. British.

Captain Thomas Samuel Masterson, for conspicuous bravery at Moreni, Ploesti and Arbanasi; at great risk of life re-entering the main distillery buildings at the Vegas works; re-visiting the destroyed works at Targoviste, Gura Ochitza and Ochiuri to see that the works were properly destroyed; passing through the rear-guard of the retreating army and firing remaining untouched works of value, and generally for exemplary conduct throughout the Mission's work, both in oil and corn.

Captain J. Scale, of the Russian Mission, Petrograd, for conspicuous gallantry and determination at Campina where, to convince the Rumanian General Voiteanu that further delay in the destruction was dangerous, rode out beyond the Rumanian rearguard until nearly surrounded by the enemy. Then later, he stuck to his post until the work of destruction of the important refinery works, stocks of highly gaseous oils and stores, although opposed by the Mayor and Councillors, was completed, narrowly escaping capture.

Lieutenant Philip Huntington Simpson who in the face of great opposition carried out difficult and dangerous work at Campina. Although slightly wounded by an explosion and his clothes badly burnt he succeeded in carrying out the work of destruction entrusted to him. To escape capture he had to make his way across country.

Lieutenant John Thomson Hayward for gallant conduct at Moreni, Campina and Bustenari. This young officer single-handed fired and destroyed the important works and wells at Bustenari, although well knowing that the enemy were already in his rear, ultimately walking some 60 kilometres through hilly native paths to regain safety and suffering much privation until reaching Buzeu. From the commencement Lieutenant Hayward has distinguished himself for his zeal, energy and courage and is deserving of high praise.

It has been a great privilege to command such officers and I crave your special notice of their gallant conduct.

The work of the Mission in oil alone was carried out day and night without interruption for the first ten days.

I have the honour to be, Sir,

Your obedient servant,

J. Norton Griffiths. Lieut-Colonel.

Jassy, 22 January 1917.

Jack smuggled himself back over the frontier into Russia and boarded a train for Petrograd. Before leaving, King Ferdinand had pinned the Grand Star of Rumania to his breast. Russia, by now, had worked itself into an even more dire state of chaos than he had found it on the way south three months before. In towns along the way hordes of people stampeded through the streets demonstrating against the war and the shortage of food, while the aristocracy, seemingly oblivious of this state of affairs, dined on caviar and champagne. Everywhere the strains of the French revolutionary song, the *Marseillaise*, rang out. The Tsar's troops were doing nothing to maintain order. By now they were on the verge of becoming revolutionaries too. Jack arrived in Petrograd on 28 February 1917 to find almost all the factories on strike and shops being looted. The British Embassy issued him with a Passport for his return journey to London. Hopefully such an impressive document would ensure his safety. On the other hand these revolutionaries were dangerous anti-Establishment fanatics and the opposite effect could well have been achieved. Now that his mission was complete, Jack was once more travelling as a civilian, John Griffiths Esq, who was bearing dispatches for the British Government. Among these was to be a letter from the Tsar, Nicholas II, to his cousin King George V.

Jack's last orders were to make his presence known to His Majesty. Nicholas Romanov, autocratic and somewhat of a mystic, was not at all a similar character to his pragmatic consti-tutionalist cousin on the British throne. Long had he suffered from a delusion that his popularity with his people was as solid as a rock, despite a series of Revolutions against his oppressive regime throughout the early 1900s. Now there were many factions among the population, from the peasantry to the intelli-gentsia, who had grown to hate him and all the Russian Royal Family. His Queen, Alexandra, was eccentrically devoted to the mysterious monk Rasputin, who had been murdered on the night of 29/30 December 1916. Her worship of this strange man even went to the point of referring to him as He or Him with a capital H when writing about him. She had not been able to cope with the strains of war and had become unstable. Her public image did nothing to add to the security of the Romanov dynasty. In fact, she had become the most detested woman in all Russia.

Nicholas, who within a remarkably short space of time had grown old, with his hair and beard now pale grey and blue rings round his eyes, received Jack and invested him with the Order of St Vladimir. He then handed him a letter addressed to King George V. The contents of it have never been made public, but it is known that several unsuccessful attempts were made to persuade the British to grant asylum to the Romanovs. Most probably, the Tsar had at last woken up to reality and anticipated events that were shortly to occur and was making the first over-tures for help from his cousin. A fortnight later, on 15 March, he abdicated. On 21 March they came to arrest him and his family. At two o'clock in the morning of 17 July 1917 they were slaugh-tered by Bolshevik extremists in the regency wallpapered basement of a house in Ekaterinburg, their bodies taken away in a lorry and thrown down a mineshaft.

Thus Jack became the last person to be decorated by a ruling monarch of the Romanov dynasty that had been the overlords of Russia for three hundred years. His return journey was not as rapid as the outward one, but he was home by Easter, to be awarded the Knight Commander of the Bath and the French Légion d'Honneur for his exploits in Eastern Europe.

18

THE GREATEST MAN-MADE EARTHQUAKE

The original plan to use the 'big blow' at Messines as a diversion for the 1916 offensive on the Somme was never implemented. Instead, there was to be a two-pronged attack, with the British pushing on through the Messines area, and a combined British and French assault along the Somme. Both of these prongs would include a major element of mining.

Tunnelling Companies composed of troops from the Dominions – Australia, New Zealand and Canada – began to arrive that spring. Their added muscle was much appreciated as longer and longer tunnels were dug and more and more Y saps were created for more and more sealed tins of ammonal to be stacked in the ends of them.

At seven-thirty precisely by the watch of Captain Hugh Kerr of 179 Company on the morning of 1 July 1916 the epic Battle of the Somme started. Exactly one minute before, sitting in his dugout beside the Albert-Bapaume road, he had rammed down the handle of an exploder box to fire 40,000 lbs of ammonal and a giant pale grey mountain rose above the horizon into the blue summer sky over the fields of Picardy. Seconds later the mountain fell back to earth, leaving nothing but a curtain of black smoke hanging on the spot where it had been. The deep-throated thunder of a furious artillery barrage began. It would be the greatest ever fired by a British army, and went on for a week, during which 1,732,873 shells were fired.

Half a mile to the south Captain James Young had fired an even bigger mine. Twin charges of 24,000 and 36,000 lbs of ammonal, placed sixty feet apart, had made the biggest crater of the entire war at La Boiselle. It was 450 feet across and had obliterated nine German dugouts, killing hundreds of men. Altogether, eighteen British mines were fired along the front that morning. Almost an entire company of the German 119 Reserve Regiment were blown to bits.

Seconds later whistles blew and along a twenty-five-mile front to the north of the Somme the Allied infantry went 'over the top' *en masse* with fixed bayonets, to meet a solid deluge of machine-gun fire. It was to be the most costly single day of the war for the British: 57,470 men, volunteers every one, were either killed, wounded or missing. Before the worst of the winter weather arrived the tally was to approach half a million. Tragic as it was for a generation of Britain's finest young men to be wiped out, to Harvey, now promoted to Major-General, it gave time. With German forces largely distracted to deal with the Somme offensive, it left the Ypres Salient comparatively quiet, at least as far as mining activity was concerned.

The game of underground cat and mouse had never entirely let up since Jack had left for England. Attack and counter-attack, winning a few yards and then losing them, only to win them back again the next day, all became part of a grotesque drama without any apparent plot. The ground had become so churned up by repeated shell-blasts that it was quite normal for a clay-kicker to feel his spade strike a dead man's rotting body. For men living and working in such putrid conditions, it was not surprising that ill health had become a big problem. Outbreaks of boils and jaundice were common, and lice and rats were more rife than ever. Harvey ordered that even a minor scratch on some barbed wire must receive a tetanus injection.

Lloyd George had now succeeded Asquith as Prime Minister and had come to an agreement with the French that their General Nivelle should take overall command along the Western Front. Apparently the smooth-talking Nivelle had assured him that he could win the war in forty-eight hours "by means of a scientifically prepared, technically executed offensive". In essence, his plan was for Haig to launch an attack on a forty-mile front to the north and south of Arras, while he, Nivelle, would launch three French armies across the Aisne and further south in Champagne.

This, according to Nivelle's reasoning, would pull enough German reserves south to leave the British able to take Flanders by breaking through 'wherever they wished'. Haig felt able to subscribe to this plan because the British trenches ended on the Channel beaches and he envisaged the Royal Navy coming into the act by offering supporting fire from offshore as his forces advanced along the Belgian coast, knocking out the German submarine bases at Ostend and Zeebrugge on the way. Accordingly, Haig ordered General Sir Herbert Plumer, in command of the British Second Army on the Ypres Salient, to make plans for a major strategic push, rather than the series of short-term tactical rushes which had become the norm.

Mining on the Ypres front had become a case of tactical defensive tunnelling. Nineteen enormous charges of ammonal sat stacked in the main explosion chambers at various points along Messines Ridge known as Hill 60, Caterpillar, St Eloi, Hollandscheschuur Farm, Petit Bois, Maedelsteede Farm, Peckham, Spanbroekmolen, Kruisstraat, Ontario Farm, Trench 127 and Trench 122 waiting for a signal from 'on high' to blow them. These had to be defended at all costs. Tunnelling experts were expressing doubts that the sealed tins of ammonal would have remained watertight for long. Ammonal was very absorbent and was unreliable if it contained more than about 4% water. And there was the question of the effect of moisture on the firing wires. Would their rubber and hemp coatings have resisted the damp? Daily circuit tests were carried out on all the mines and one or two had begun to show signs of deterioration. On top of all these questions, there was the ever-present danger that the Germans would discover them before the order to fire came through, which did happen on one occasion.

Harvey's German opposite number, Lieutenant-Colonel Füsslein, in command of the Fourth Army miners, knew by the late summer of 1916 that something big was being planned by the British along the Messines Ridge. His men were tunnelling eighty feet deep under the outbuildings of what once had been Petit Douve Farm when they struck some wooden shuttering. Plainly it was freshly prepared timber. It could only be the supports of a British gallery. An officer and eight men were sent down to investigate. Delicately, they removed some of the timber

205

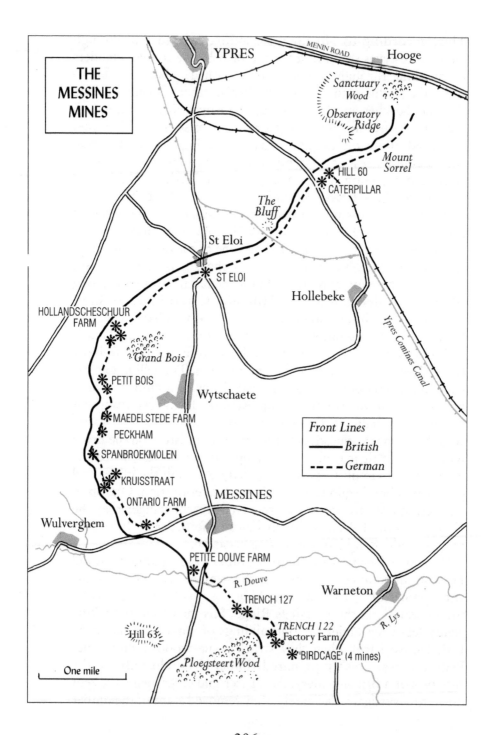

THE
MESSINES
MINES

YPRES

MENIN ROAD   Hooge

*Sanctuary
Wood*

*Observatory
Ridge*

*Mount
Sorrel*

❋ HILL 60
❋ CATERPILLAR

*The
Bluff*

St Eloi

❋ ST ELOI

Hollebeke

Ypres Comines Canal

HOLLANDSCHESCHUUR
FARM

❋
❋

Grand Bois

❋ PETIT BOIS

❋ MAEDELSTEDE FARM
❋ PECKHAM
❋ SPANBROEKMOLEN
❋ KRUISSTRAAT
ONTARIO FARM

Wytschaete

Front Lines

——— *British*
- - - *German*

MESSINES

Wulverghem

❋

PETITE DOUVE FARM
❋

R. Douve
❋ TRENCH 127

Warneton

Hill 63

❋ *TRENCH 122*
Factory Farm
❋

R. Lys

❋ 'BIRDCAGE' (4 mines)

Ploegsteert Wood

One mile

206

and found themselves looking into a vast mine chamber, stacked with thirty-five tons of ammonal. Immediately the Germans began to haul the charge out. Soon they came across the exposed firing wires and the officer moved forward to cut them. But he did not live to do so because at that exact second Lieutenant Peter King of 171 Company slammed down the plunger handle of an exploder and blew a *camouflet** close by. The German officer and his whole squad were killed.

At Christmas 1916 the shrewd Füsslein passed responsibility 'upstairs' by reporting to his General Staff that he was convinced the British were planning a surface attack, supported by deep mining. But although the German commanders granted him an extra three mining companies, they made it clear that they were not taking the mining threat seriously.

In the middle of February the Germans heard British tunnellers working under Spanbroekmolen. They had run across 171 Company, now commanded by Henry Hudspeth who had been promoted to Major. Working frantically, the Germans started to prepare a *camouflet*. Fortunately for the British, the sounds the Germans had heard had only come from a branch of the main tunnel that led to the huge Spanbroekmolen mine that Hudspeth had wired personally way back on 28 June 1916 and which had lain ready ever since. This branch tunnel was to serve a good purpose in acting as a decoy for the real thing. The Germans exploded two *camouflets*, but, although they were not precisely on target for the big mine, they did collapse about 400 feet of the main tunnel, wrecking it well beyond repair and destroying the wiring which led to the 91,000 lbs of ammonal. Hudspeth put his men to work, driving a secondary gallery alongside the collapsed section. It was especially dangerous, driving through the gas-soaked clay, with the risk that the Germans might well blow further *camouflets*, burying them all alive. And as always, speed was essential, it being rumoured that a 'big push' would soon be ordered along the Messines front.

Rumours have always abounded among soldiers. Only rarely are they true, but this time they were absolutely accurate. Haig

* Gallery to combat an enemy mine.

had ordered Plumer to organize a major attack. And Plumer, making use of a plan devised by General Sir Henry Rawlinson the previous year, saw his main task as the capture of the Messines-Wytschaete ridge, which would enable an advance to be made over the high ground north-eastwards beyond Ypres. In April first the British and then the French attacked as per Nivelle's scheme. Then, north of Arras, the Canadians took Vimy Ridge in an epic action. But then the French push ran out of impetus. Casualties were colossal and the French Army was on the verge of mutiny. Nivelle, stubborn and egotistical, was sacked, to be replaced by Pétain, the saviour of Verdun.

Haig called a meeting of his army commanders at Doullens on 7 May. He asked the white-haired Plumer when he could be ready to attack Messines. "A month from today" came the precise reply. Everything Plumer said was always precise. At last there was a committal to blow the Ridge and a date set for it. "There is now an end to the uncertainties concerning the summer," Haig told the meeting, and went on to explain that the plan of co-operation with the French had been abandoned, as they had made but very limited advances and were displaying much un-reliability. A heavy blow was to be struck on the Ypres front. They were to prepare to capture the Messines-Wytschaete Ridge by about 7 June and begin the next phase in Flanders soon after-wards. What he was describing was to be the Third Battle of Ypres. With the knowledge that the British Cabinet had become doubtful of the French will to continue the fight, he went to Amiens on 18 May to meet Pétain. The new French chief con-sidered that the British plans were too ambitious, but conceded that he would relieve 8,000 yards of their trenches in the south and that French forces would co-operate in the battle at Ypres.

For the tunnelling companies it meant a month of frantic preparation. Plumer decided that the scheme would take the form of a nineteen-charge barrage, laid from ten main shafts. (One mine had become 'lost' at Petit Douve.) But how many of them would be ready for 7 June was doubtful. Three were still being dug or loaded, and Hudspeth's men were still moling flat out to re-connect the wiring to the big Spanbroekmolen charge. Under Hill 60 there was a 53,500 lb mixture of ammonal and guncotton, while just 200 yards away Caterpillar (which was

208

simply a heap of spoil) hid 70,000 lbs of ammonal. These gigantic charges had lain in their explosion chambers for over eight months, having been placed by the Third Canadian Company the previous autumn. The Canadians had since been relieved by the First Australian Company, who did not find it at all amusing to have such responsibility thrust upon them. In fact, in the words of one of their officers, "It was getting on all our nerves".

The system at this northern end of the Ridge was now like a giant rabbit warren. It had four 'decks' at fifteen, forty-five, ninety and a hundred feet, each of which sprouted a collection of well-developed galleries. It had fifty listening posts, four of which were within ten feet of a main German tunnel. Both Hill 60 and Caterpillar had continual problems with ingress of water. Despite a crew of sixty men constantly at work on hand-pumps, water was always ankle-deep in the galleries under Hill 60 and the Caterpillar mine was completely immersed.

And all the time Füsslein's men continued probing. They knew that something big was afoot and they were desperate to locate it. The British listeners could hear them quite plainly. Numerous *camouflets* were fired by both sides, sometimes so close to a big mine that there was a very real fear that the vibration would set it off. Luckily this did not happen, although the wiring was sometimes damaged. On 9 April, a German raiding party had come over no-man's-land lugging explosives which they threw down several mineshafts. The Australian tunnellers grabbed rifles and grenades and assisted the infantry to fight them off, but it left them wondering how much longer they would be able to protect their two massive charges.

A terrible accident occurred a fortnight later. Captain Wilfred Avery was preparing a guncotton charge that was intended to be used to fire a *camouflet,* assisted by Lieutenant Arthur Tandy. They should have tested the current through the detonators *before* inserting them in the explosive, but somehow or other made the mistake of doing so with the wiring already connected up to a fifty pound charge of ammonal. Both men were blown to pieces. Their dugout was wrecked and the flash went down a passage into a store-room causing more casualties. All told, three officers and seven men died, with sixteen others suffering from the effects of gas. Captain William McBride, a big extrovert character from Adelaide, took charge of the cleaning-up operation. The dugout had been almost filled with sand by the blast and he set to, meticulously sieving every spadeful of it, picking out the fragments of flesh and bone that he found of his two friends, wrapping them in a blanket and sending them down for burial. He was awarded the Military Cross for this gruesome task.

The days crept on and the tension grew. Australian Captain Oliver Woodward was in command of the Hill 60 tunnels and he felt the tension more than most. Often he would man a listening post himself, "immovable as a piece of statuary and as cold from fear". On 5 June he was informed by Brigadier-General T.S. Lambert commanding the 69 Brigade that zero hour had been fixed for 3.10 a.m. on 7 June. This highly sensitive information, of course, had been privy only to a few selected officers. But somehow a loose tongue had resulted in a 'leak'. A young Belgian private named Victor Maes was skylarking with some girls in an *estaminet* in Bailleul that very same night, 5 June, when one of them remarked that there was going to be a large mine blown at Messines. Curious, he asked her when it would be. She replied, "Thursday, at three o'clock in the morning," and said with a giggle that she had been told this by some young British officers. Maes was uncertain whether to believe her or not. He did not have long to wait to find out.

Next day, 6 June, was a terrible day for Woodward. For weeks he and his officers had felt they were near breaking point as they listened to the Germans probing nearer and nearer. And now, with twenty-four hours to go, the electric wires still had to be connected up to the firing dugout about a quarter of a mile back from the mines. Nothing was to be left to chance. There were to be three separate circuits: Woodward's, which would send a 500 volt DC current from a lighting generator down to the explosion chambers and two 'fail-safe' lines manned by Lieutenants Bowry and Royle. The last two hours were the worst. After months of sweat, danger and spine-chilling suspense all was ready. He sat in the carefully blacked-out dugout, testing the wiring over and over again. Every reading showed correctly, but he took another, and another, just to be sure. Bowry and Royle sat beside him, their faces set in jaw-twitching anticipation. Then a thunderstorm erupted, sending summer hail drumming onto the dugout roof like machine-gun fire. Doubts began to race through his mind. What had the Germans made of the silence on the British side for the past day and night? This always heralded the fact that the enemy were up to something. Had they pulled back their troops and were waiting with reinforcements to slaughter the British infantry with machine guns as they rushed the empty craters? Oddly enough, Haig himself had had the same thoughts and was tempted to alter the time set for zero hour. He had even discussed it with Plumer. Finally, they decided to go ahead as planned.

At St Eloi the 1st Canadian Company had laid the biggest and deepest single charge of the Messines mines, even of the war, a gigantic 95,600 lbs of ammonal, 125 feet deep at the end of a 1,650-foot tunnel. The work had begun in August the previous year, but was finished only just in time, on 28 May 1917. Here twin circuits ran through a single exploder box, the handle of which stood ready to be pushed down by a young lieutenant from Winnipeg, Richard O'Reilly.

South of St Eloi, 250 Company, to whom Jack had entrusted the Stanley Heading Machine, had assembled an astounding collage of seven big mines, although their CO, Cropper, was not to be there to see them fired, having been shipped home with German measles, at that time a serious complaint. A bunch of three charges of 34,200, 15,900, and 17,500 lbs had lain silently at Hollandscheschuur for nearly a year. Three-quarters of a mile to the right, alongside Jack's abandoned boring machine at Petit Bois, rested two ammonal blasting charges of 30,000 lbs each. Next came 94,000lbs of ammonal at Maedelstede Farm, which they had still been laying only four days before. The last of the 250 Company mines was at Peckham, which had been beset with landslip problems throughout its preparation. In January the main gallery had caved in. The wooden props had been replaced with steel ones and a fresh tunnel driven to bypass the collapsed section and rewire the 87,000 lbs charge.

Hudspeth's 171 Company men at Spanbroekmolen had lost three of their number when driving through the gas-soaked clay to repair the wiring damaged by the German *camouflets*. Only a few hours before zero, finding the original circuits hopelessly tangled, he had rigged up a rough and ready wiring system, using a dynamite priming charge placed directly against the ammonal which was to be fired by an electric lighting set. But would it work? Hudspeth could only hope so. Just before midnight he had sent a scribbled note to 36 Divisional HQ in reply to their request for his report, saying that he was 'almost certain' that his mine would blow on time. It was now far too late for them to argue with him.

The longest tunnel of all was at Kruisstraat, another 171 Company operation. At 2,160 feet, its longest arm reached under the German *third* line of trenches and consisted of a three-mine 'trident' of 49,000 lbs and two 30,000 lb charges of ammonal. The last of the 171 Company mines was at Ontario Farm, a single charge of 60,000 lbs of ammonal laid 103 feet below the surface. Loose sand, deep underground, had caused endless problems here and only hours before zero the firing wires had been successfully connected and tested by Lieutenants Percy Ellis and Henry Daniell.

The most southerly of the long line of mines were two pairs. One was at Trench 127, of 50,000 and 36,000 lbs respectively, and the last was at Factory Farm (more prosaically known as Trench 122), to the east of Ploegsteert [Plugstreet] Wood, where Lieutenants Cecil Hall and George Dickson had been selected to fire the 20,000 and 40,000 lbs of ammonal. Only two days before a stray German shell had damaged an escape tunnel at Factory Farm. Hall had peered down the seventy-foot shaft, at the bottom of which lay the neatly coiled firing wires, ready to be connected. But fast-running sand was spurting from the shell-damaged walls. Soon the wires would be deeply buried. Scrambling down the ladder with a Sergeant Beer, Hall was able to repair the damage and rescue the all-important ends of the wires. He had understood from his orders that he and Dickson were supposed to fire their mines from the bottom of that unstable shaft. But it now dawned on him that they would have little chance of ever getting out of there alive, because the shock of the explosions would almost certainly bring an instant fall of tons of fine sand onto their heads. He made his fears known to Captain Urie, the Section Officer, but was kept on tenterhooks until 4 o'clock on the afternoon before zero hour, when Urie handed him his sealed orders. It was only then that he learned that zero was 3.10 a.m. the next morning and that he was *not* to blow his mine from the bottom of the shaft, but to run extension leads up the ladder and fire from a surface trench. There were just eleven hours to go! He would need every minute of them.

All that evening the British artillery mounted a fearsome pre-battle barrage. Quite why this was always done is somewhat mystifying. It did little but warn the enemy to be on his guard. The German gunners, naturally, had replied in kind and Dickson had caught the effects of a gas shell, rendering him temporarily *hors de combat*. Hall, then, was left on his own to extend the wires. He handed his service watch to Beer, telling him to keep a close eye on the time, but not to nag, while he began to scramble up and down the shaft, splicing wires, nailing them to the ladder and leading them into the trench. It was 2.50 a.m. when he finished, bathed in sweat, but at least he had been busy. Woodward, still perched with taut nerves by his box nine miles away, would probably have changed places with him quite readily.

Two fifty-five came and the British artillery fell quiet. One hundred thousand men lay against their parapets, ready to go 'over the top'. The sky was now clear and bright moonlight shone on the unearthly deathscape of Flanders, beneath which lay 933,200 lbs of high explosive. It was eerily silent, except for an odd cough or whisper along the line. Some even claimed that they heard a nightingale sing.

The Germans knew from long experience that something was about to happen and began to throw up flares, peering towards the British lines to catch any signs of activity. The minutes ticked away and still nothing happened. General Lambert had now joined Woodward, Bowry and Royle in their dugout at Hill 60. There was no conversation. The only voice to be heard was that of Lambert counting down the minutes. When it came to 3.09 he began calling the seconds. Clammy hands were given a quick wipe on trouserlegs.

All along the eleven firing points silence reigned, tense and dramatic, and eyes were glued to the second hands of watches. They had been nearly a year preparing for this moment. 10-9-8-7-6-5-4-3-2-1- NOW!

Woodward rammed his handle down so fast that his hand touched the live pole and he was thrown onto his back by the 500-volt shock. Dazed, he clambered to his feet to find that even here, a quarter of a mile away and several seconds after the blast, the ground was still heaving beneath his feet. Ahead the whole Ridge seemed to be shaking itself, like a giant shaggy dog that has just risen from a doze in its kennel. Then came the main spectacle of great surging curtains of vicious orange flame leaping from the earth all along the horizon. The strange thing was that he had not even heard any noise, apart from one of the other mines down the line, which had gone up seven seconds early.

At Spanbroekmolen Hudspeth stood and watched with enormous relief as his monstrous mine tore a crater 430 feet across and sent enormous slabs of clay, some the size of Jack's Rolls-Royce, spinning in majestic parabolas high against the moonlit sky. It *had* gone off after all. Seventy years later it would have been a fitting scene in a film of science fiction.

At Ontario Farm Ellis and Daniell were struggling to keep their feet as the ground lurched this way and that. Their mine had had a strange effect. It made no crater at all. All that remained as testament to its explosion was a vast circular lake of bubbling pulp, like a huge cauldron of porridge coming to the boil. It was still bubbling days later.

Nineteen mines had been fired on cue and nearly a million lbs of the most powerful explosives then known to man had ripped the guts out of the Messines Ridge. The drawn-out roar it created, of God knows how many decibels, was heard hundreds of miles away. In Lille, just twelve miles away to the west, citizens tumbled from their beds to rush into the street, convinced that they were about to be engulfed by an earthquake. Prime Minister Lloyd George said he heard it at home in Downing Street. Even an insomniac student called Ormsby-Scott claimed to have heard it, lying in his bed in Dublin, a distance of 500 miles.

In his foreword to *The Tunnellers*, by Grieve and Newman, published in 1936, Jack's old friend Harvey wrote, "It was Norton Griffiths' brain, as far back as August 1915, which sowed the seeds of Messines." And Sir John Norton-Griffiths, Bart, the originator of the 'big idea' over two years before, heard the

214

distant earthquake, standing at the window of his cottage in Brighton. What his emotions were he did not record.

War correspondents were hard-pressed to find adequate adjectives and metaphors as they filed copy to their editors in Fleet Street.

"The biggest man-made earthquake ever."

"Hill 60, the scene of the cruellest fights of 1915 went up in fine dust, and a million and more pounds of ammonal, of which a pound would be enough to destroy the Mansion House, went of in many mines."

"Thunderclouds of smoke rose in solid form to immense heights from Hill 60, from Wytschaete Wood and other places."

"An hour before dawn, as we stood over the dim valley where the black treetops looked like rocks in a calm sea, we saw what might have been the doors thrown open in front of a number of colossal blast furnaces."

"It was the most diabolical splendour I have ever seen. Out of the dark ridges of Messines and Wytschaete and that ill-famed Hill 60, there gushed up and out enormous volumes of scarlet flame from the exploding mines and of earth and smoke all lighted by the flame spilling over into fountains of fierce colour, so that all the countryside was illuminated by red light. Where some of us stood watching, aghast and spellbound by the burning horror, the ground trembled and surged violently to and fro. Truly, the earth quaked."

The British and Dominions troops had expected a tough fight as they advanced after the blast, but all they found as they walked past wrecked concrete redoubts which normally would have been spitting vicious machine-gun fire were demoralized and disorientated German soldiers, most of them hardened veterans, staggering drunkenly and blindly about the Ridge. Some were on their hands and knees. Many were weeping in confusion, not even knowing where they were. By breakfast time both Messines and Wytschaete were in British hands. The top brass arrived later in the day to walk on the Ridge, no doubt smoking their pipes just as Jack had promised they would be able to do.

The following day he received a telegram from the First Lord of the Admiralty, Leo Amery, who, as *The Times* correspondent reporting on Field Marshal Roberts' progress, had wired many a

215

cable from South Africa during the Boer War, "My Dear Jack, Heartiest congratulations on the success of the great coup against Wytschaete Ridge! I hope they will give credit where credit is due."

He also heard from an old colleague, Lionel Hill, who as a green Lieutenant had led the very first party of clay-kickers from the cosy shelter of their haystack and later laid three-quarters of a ton of gunpowder at Hill 60:

57, Cadogan Street, S.W.3. 10 June 1917.
Dear Sir John,

I hope you will not think it presumptuous of me to write to congratulate you in the fulfilment of your scheme of two years ago:- the mining of the Wytschaete – Messines Ridge. It has evidently been a huge success, mainly owing to the help of the artificial earthquake and the Tunnellers have been specially brought to notice in consequence, hence my congratulations to 'The Father of the Tunnellers' and the originator of the scheme. Unfortunately, I was not in France to see the fulfilment of many months strenuous work, as I was invalided home two months ago and put on light duty in London while undergoing treatment. I hope to return to France in two or three months if I get better. All the old gang were really proud and glad that you got fitting recognition for your great energy in the successful destruction of the Rumanian oilfields after the shabby treatment that you got for organizing the Tunnelling service. With kind regards and heartiest congratulations, I remain

Yours v. sincerely, Lionel G. Hill, Major, R.E.

Making an after-dinner speech in 1927, Jack said of Messines, "All we had said had come true. There was not the slightest doubt that the frontal attack without the mines would have been an absolute failure and cost the lives of 50,000 men. This stupendous artificial earthquake shook the ridge from end to end and enabled the army – as we had promised – to walk to the top of the ridge in comparative safety."

The Germans never made an official announcement of their casualties caused by the mines, but 10,000 men were listed as missing after the battle and the British took 7,354 prisoners.

Today, ten kilometres north of Lille, the narrow N366 trails like the bristles on the spine of a sleeping hog along the top of Messines Ridge, which rises about fifty feet above the flat Flanders plain, between Ploegsteert (Plugstreet to thousands of Tommies) and Ypres (likewise Wipers). The six-mile-long ridge is just high enough to give an idyllic view of well-tended fields and peaceful farms scattered with circular watering holes for their cattle. The holes are too symmetrical to be natural, but the animals do not complain. For four years this strip was a muddy cauldron of hell, with its patches of woodland broken and stripped of leaf, the few remaining trees with their branches hanging drunkenly. The whole was criss-crossed with slime-filled trenches lined with duck-boards and the scene was littered with dead bodies. The air hung with the stench of death, rats scurried hither and thither and fat blue-bottles swarmed in their millions. The background music to this nightmarish panorama was provided by the screams of men and horses, the crackle of rifles and machine-guns and the explosions of shells – and enormous mines.

Today the mine crater at Spanbroekmolen is filled with water, forty feet deep. It is a tranquil place. The forest has grown up around it. Willows stand guard over it, weeping into its depths; water lilies float on its surface, and real moles now burrow around its edges, throwing up their little mounds of spoil as if in remembrance of their human predecessors. They call it the Pool of Peace.

19

TROUBLE

On Armistice Day 1918 Jack and Gwladys signed the deeds for Wonham Manor, near Betchworth in Surrey, a low red-brick pile set in thirty-three acres plus another 129 acres of farmland. Wonham lent itself admirably to grand parties and a healthy country life. Here Jack could chop wood to his heart's content and play with his children, all within easy reach of London, so that he could travel up to speak in the House on a host of subjects close to his heart. Gwladys became a prominent member of the Primrose League and could indulge in her new hobby of breeding champion Golden Retrievers. The stresses and strains of war were behind them. But if it was a peaceful post-war life that they sought, they were to be disappointed.

Griffiths & Co. had coasted along in Jack's absence throughout the War. Several military contracts, Knotty Ash Hospital Camp, Catterick Aerodrome and Hickling Broad Flying Boat Port, had all helped to keep things going. On a more personal level, Jack had relinquished his parliamentary seat for Wednesbury, as Gwladys had been finding the continual travelling to the Black Country constituency difficult. In 1918 he stood for Wandsworth Central, the old seat of his very first mentor, the man who had purchased his release from the Army in 1888, Sir Henry Kimber, winning with a majority of 7,800.

Jack had been instrumental in forming the Comrades of the Great War Association. In *The People* of 22 July 1917, he wrote:

> At the request of many who have served or are serving in our great Army I welcome the opportunity afforded by *The People* of giving publicity to the wish felt by many of all ranks that, having served

together in this great war, we shall continue to keep in touch with one another after it has been fought to a finish. Between those of us who have spent long months, and even years, in the trenches, patiently waiting for the guns and shells which would place us on terms of equality with the enemy, there have grown up steady ties of affection and comradeship. Silently, a general determination has developed that those who have endured much together should keep together to the end, always remembering those who have fallen by the way, and a resolve has been made that we should cement that spirit of comradeship for our mutual advantage and protection in the future.

The main objects of the Association would be:-
- To safeguard the interests of members of the Forces, before and after demobilization.
- To promote undertakings for the disabled and to find employment for all discharged soldiers and sailors.
- To help discharged soldiers and sailors prepare their necessary papers to see that their pensions and allowances are in order.
- To secure the welfare of the families left behind by those who have fallen.
- To perpetuate in loving memory and affection the dead.
- To promote a grand spirit of patriotism among the rising generation.

The Association would be strictly non-political and Jack envisaged that it would be represented in every town and village in the country. The only qualification for membership was service in the Armed Forces. His remarks about the ties of affection that had built up in the trenches were very true and he was not the only person to harbour thoughts of an Old Comrades Association. Several sprang up around the country, and very soon the Comrades of the Great War absorbed three others to evolve into the Royal British Legion that we know today, and which is indeed represented in every town and village in the country.

Jack was by nature a constructor, rather than a destroyer. The task he had been allotted in Rumania, whilst it had been overwhelmingly successful from a military viewpoint and had earned

219

him many accolades, did not sit easily on his mind when he came to reflect on the fact that he had destroyed much food and fuel while the population of Rumania starved. Indeed, Queen Marie herself went to the Treaty of Versailles talks in 1919 to plead with the Allies for help for her hungry people.

"Time alone," Jack wrote, "can balance the gain against the loss and devastation with which it has been the Mission's painful duty to lay waste the land. It has certainly been a revelation, that our concept of obstructing the enemy means sacrificing the individual and the fruits of the earth."

Meantime, there was a typical bureaucratic family row 'over the kitchen sink' between the War Office and the Foreign Office as to which of them should pay the expenses of the Rumanian Mission. Jack had been handed £5,000 in an envelope by General McDonough of Military Intelligence, who had told him verbally that he had plenary powers, authorized by the Chancellor of the Exchequer. Therefore, as far as he was concerned, he had been working under the orders of M.I., which was a department of the War Office. But the War Office, guarding its budget in typical fashion, argued that, as the costs of the Mission were to be borne jointly by the Allies, this item should be more properly dealt with by the Foreign Office. This little sideshow was to drag on until late 1920, when the War Office, which had presumably paid Jack beforehand, indented the Foreign Office under Receivable Order No. 1842 for £3,191.4s.10d., apparently being expenses of £6,313.16s.2d. plus 4,900 roubles, less £5,000 'float'.

Jack's words of regret were published in the Rumanian press, but they were not enough for some. Some of the smaller privately owned wells and refineries had been ruined by his exploits in Rumania, and they sought vengeance. Most of his day-to-day records had been destroyed by fire during his hectic stampede around Rumania. The fact that he had destroyed an estimated 165 million gallons of oil, spread over an area of 1000 square kilometres in fifteen localities, was about as accurate an account of what he had done that he could produce. Obviously there had been no time to 'take stock' at each site of destruction, usually with a German patrol about to sweep into sight. For six years, therefore, the British Government engaged in an endless stream of debate with lawyers and private individuals, wrestling with the questions of liability and quantum. Some of this is documented in Foreign Office records, but often trails of correspondence appear to go nowhere. It is almost as if some stealthy hand has 'cherry-picked' the files.

A Mr E.C.Youell was completely ruined by the destruction of his firm's property, mainly agricultural machinery. Mr Pitts, one of Jack's staff, denied having had the authority to promise compensation, but a letter states, "There was never any question that property destroyed by the Mission would not be paid in full". Lawyers wrote noisy letters, still buried in FO/371 files at the Public Record Office, which were ignored as far as one can tell. The press, ever anxious to coin a headline, followed the saga as best they could. The *Daily Express* dubbed Jack the Great God Thor.

In due course Rumanian Consolidated Oilfields filed suit against the Crown. By then the smaller companies and private individuals who had been ruined no longer had the means to pursue their litigation. The loaded dice used by the legal system had rolled against them in time-honoured fashion. In Court the British Government took the position that they agreed to owing Rumania £10 million or so, but that it should be offset by Rumania's war debt to Great Britain of £40 million. Any further compensation should be claimed from the Rumanian Government. And if that Government had been bankrupted by the War that was no concern of Great Britain.

The argument revolved around whether Rumania had agreed to destroy *stocks* of oil, or the oil *industry*. Telegrams from the Rumanian Ministry of Industry and the Rumanian General H.Q. seemed to conflict on that point. Jack was called repeatedly to testify. Some of the language used in Court seems to have tried to hold him personally responsible for the debt to Rumania:

Norton-Griffiths arrived at Moreni [this was where Bibesco had dragged him unconscious from the fire] on the 27th where the most valuable wells, stores, power houses, shops, gas and water plants were situated. Norton-Griffiths had wired General Iliescu for definite orders. No answer had as yet been received, owing to confusion at Bucharest. Norton-Griffiths, however, was so convinced that he was truly interpreting the wishes of the

Rumanian military authorities that he immediately commenced the preparatory work, smashing machinery in the power houses etc in defiance of the Commission, who actually managed to stop him from carrying out the most important part of the destruction, that is, firing everything in the oilfield.

At Ploesti, it was clear he did not begin to fire the refineries until he was fully authorized in writing; therefore there should have been nothing to answer on that score, although the Standard Oil Company, as represented by the United States Government, attempted to allege that he had acted against the will of the Rumanian Government. The fact was that he had always been covered by some sort of Rumanian Government orders. The only point at issue was in the interpretation of those orders.

On 27 March 1920 Mr Justice Darling ruled in favour of Rumanian Consolidated, but the British Government had this decision reversed in the Court of Appeal on 15 December. It was said that "Rumanian Consolidated might have won their case if they had not based it on the question of a contract between Norton Griffiths and their Manager."

But the oil company refused to lie down. The case went to the House of Lords, whose verdict pronounced Mr Justice Darling right and the Court of Appeal wrong. The case dragged on to 1927. But as far as is known, not a penny of compensation was ever paid, and Jack was left vulnerable to threats of revenge.

Perhaps the most telling piece of evidence would have been a telegram he received shortly after his return from Rumania:

From Director of Military Intelligence.
    To Colonel Norton Griffiths (through Col Thomson.) 17 January 1917.
    I am directed by the CIGS to inform you that the War Cabinet desire to express to you their appreciation for the good work done by yourself and your staff in destroying the Rumanian oil wells, refineries and grain stores, and thus preventing essential supplies from falling into the hands of the enemy.

Unfortunately, he was not allowed to produce it. Ever devious, the DMI's telegram was covered under the Official Secrets Act.
It is easy to imagine Jack's bitterness at his enforced involve-

ment in all this. He had been summoned by the Secret Service, sent on a dangerous and vital mission, bank-rolled with £5,000 and invested with plenary powers by the Chancellor of the Exchequer (at least that was what McDonough had promised him), "to do everything necessary to effect complete destruction . . . at any and all cost", had carried out the operation with complete success, received a knighthood for his efforts, seen a decade of dreary legal argy-bargy about it, including some crude attempts to besmirch him personally, knowing all the time that he was barred from producing the one piece of paper that would have probably settled it. And then he had watched his country renege on its promises, the promises that he had personally given on its behalf to an impoverished war-torn Rumania.

In typical fashion, he threw himself with vigour into his work in his new constituency at Wandsworth, with too much vigour on one occasion. At a meeting at Garrett Lane School in January 1919 he promised that he would reduce the cost of the breakfast table within twelve months. A trade unionist heckler shouted out, calling him a liar, and for the second time in his political career Jack strode from the platform, stormed across the room and punched an adversary. This time it was a left in the eye and a right on the left ear. He was summonsed for this transgression and fined ten shillings, but he kept his word. The cost of the breakfast table was reduced and he increased his majority to 12,470 at the next election.

Jack's old friend Harvey, writing in the *Royal Engineers' Journal* in December 1930, referred to this incident. "He was a man of action if ever there was one; and we in the E-in-C's office were not the only people impressed by that quality. Some years after the War I was going down Whitehall on the top of a bus watching the road being broken up by pneumatic drills, which were then coming into general use for that purpose. The man next to me suddenly said, 'Well if Empire Jack had had his way they'd have been used long ago.' I said, 'What do you know about Empire Jack?' and he said that he had worked for him for some years, and added, 'but he's a terrible man.' 'Terrible man?' I said, 'why terrible?' He said, 'Well, I was down at one of his meetings in Wandsworth, and he was making a speech, and there was a fellow there interrupting and he wouldn't stop, so Empire Jack just got down from the platform, walked to the man, knocked him out, and then came back and went on with his speech. Oh, he's a terrible man.'"

On the business front the post-war scene was very different. Most of the world now seemed to have its first-line infrastructure in place. Contracts had become much harder to chase and the days of the individual contractor appeared to be numbered.

Jack, as ever, refused to draw in his horns. But in a changing world it is vital to adapt and he began to make mistakes. Perhaps he had exhausted his mind as well as his body. Certainly he got careless about whom he employed, which was not a fault he had displayed when recruiting his clay-kickers. In 1919 he landed a consultancy for a twenty-mile stretch of the Uasin Gishu section of the Ugandan East African railway – the section that climbs 3,000 feet from Nakuru (in Kenya) up the escarpment to Mau summit on the equator. It brought him in a lot of money.

Post-war social life swung into the Roaring Twenties in a frenzy of partying, weekend 'at homes' at Wonham, a house in London for the season, Ascot, the theatre, the opera, Scotland in August for the grouse shooting and trips abroad. Jack had enough work to support rows of cars and two chauffeurs. He was made a Baronet in 1922 and thereafter hyphenated his name. Daughter Ursula was presented at Court and married a young barrister MP, Captain Thorpe, at St Margaret's Westminster in December 1921. Their daughter, Lavinia, was born in 1923. She was the only grandchild Jack was to know.

They gave a big Ball at Claridges for Phoebe's coming out. When Gwladys came to pay the bill, she noticed that they had charged for two bottles of Clicquot when they had served Pol Roger.

"Charles," she said to the manager imperiously, "who had the impertinence to order Clicquot at my Ball?"

"Well, my lady, Mr Solly Joel was there. I was sure that Sir John asked him for a purpose and he is happy only when he drinks Clicquot. I thought you would like to let him have it."

Gwladys beamed with relief and gave the manager a diamond and ruby tie pin in gratitude for his perspicacity. It had been a long time since Solly and his uncle Barney had dispensed gold sovereigns to flat broke prospectors in Johannesburg in the

1880s, but obviously Jack had maintained careful touch over the years. His sources of finance had dwindled during the war. His 'House of Lords' had almost vanished. But now Solly, a diamond-encrusted figure from the past who had twice been instrumental in his good fortune, had re-emerged from history. It would not be long before Jack would be calling for his help one last time.

At about that time Hero dropped dead with Jack's son Michael on his back. The old war-horse had survived the shells and bullets of Flanders and had been enjoying a quiet life at Wonham. Gwladys had grown far too fond of him to allow him to be given to the hounds, so they gave him a proper burial in the park where he had grazed in peace. The Rolls-Royce had gone too, sold by the War Office to a gentleman in Maida Vale. Its last known owner was the editor of the *Sunday Express*.

In 1924 Jack caught typhoid. He was ill for many weeks and, when he was well enough to travel, went on a convalescence trip to Palestine and Baghdad. True to form, there was an element of business in the trip's purpose. Jack wanted to investigate a scheme to grow cotton in Diala which would involve building a dam and irrigation system. It was a fascinating journey, driving up the beach via Tyre and Sidon to Beirut in a convoy of three cars and then across the baking desert, along stony pot-holed roads, hooting at donkeys and camels which wandered across their path, through Damascus to Baghdad. Jack spent many hours in conference with the Iraqi Minister of Public Works and other officials. King Faisal invited them to join him in his box at the races. But it all came to nothing. The public did not take to the scheme, apparently because of fears that it would take water from the small farmer. Large chunks of shares were left unsub-scribed and the underwriters caught a heavy cold. Water was to be Jack's nemesis.

The great dock at Singapore was a project that took Jack's fancy. With a large entourage in tow, he and Gwladys set sail for the Far East. He had persuaded a man named John Gibson to go with them, with a view to forming a partnership. Gibson had recently completed some very fine work for Pearsons, building the Maquah and Sennar dams in the Sudan. Singapore was a booming place, crawling with prosperous rubber planters. Gwladys was in her element, spending days trawling through one

Chinese emporium after another while Jack and Gibson got to work on their tender for the dock. The financing looked hopeful, too, because Gideon Murray, Lord Elibank, one of the 'House of Lords', also happened to be in Singapore at the time.

But competition for the tender was far too sharp for Jack and Gibson. They didn't stand a chance. Dejected, Jack and Gwladys prepared to leave for home, but over a last drink before they sailed Gibson 'dropped' the news that tenders were about to be invited for the second heightening of the Aswan Dam. How did he know this? The simple answer was that Gibson was a Pearsons man, and Pearsons had already been tipped the wink about it. Jack rubbed his chin and shook his head.

"I'll help you," promised Gibson.

Jack was hooked. "Then let's do it."

20

THE FLAME GOES OUT

For Egyptians the Nile is the gift of God. When the annual rains come to the highlands of Ethiopia and Central Africa, they swell the mighty river, washing fertile silt 3,000 miles downstream each July to make a ribbon of green across the desert. This ribbon is their only garden. Villagers along the riverbanks drink the brown muddy water, scooping it up into cupped hands, crying, "*El Hum del Allah*!" "Praise be to God!" They discovered, thousands of years ago, that it contains a medicinal bismuth which cures many of their ailments.

In an average year the Nile will rise well over twenty feet during the flood. At the peak of flow, around the second week in September, up to 712 million tons of water come rushing down each day. The Fellaheen spread out along the riverbanks, one man every hundred paces, to form a human chain 350 miles long, stretching from Esna to Alexandria. They guide the silt-laden water into pre-dug canals and basins. At the first sign of a bank bursting everyone rushes to help repair it. Not a drop of this liquid gold must be lost. The flood allows them to grow five crops a year, the silt provides bricks for their houses and it washes away the snail that carries the unpleasant parasitic disease, bilharzia. The surplus silt builds up in the Bay of Alexandria to create rich fishing grounds.

In spite of this wealth, nineteenth century Egypt had been bankrupted by her extravagant Khedives. She had colossal debts, particularly with Great Britain and France. Something had to be done. An Anglo-French Commission, the *Caisse de la Debt Publique*, was set up to look after Egypt's finances and make sure her debts were paid, and after some military and diplomatic scuffling, Great Britain finished up occupying Egypt, appointing Lord Cromer as the first Consul-General.

At the turn of the century the Egyptian population was outstripping agricultural production. Cromer saw immediately that a dam on the Nile would be a means both of feeding her people and making money for Egypt to pay her debts. Irrigation independent of the flood would enable cotton to be grown, there would be increased agricultural output to avert famine and harnessing the power of the Nile would permit the generation of hydro-electricity to develop industry. But the *Caisse* refused to finance such a scheme, and Great Britain refused to re-invest any of the profits from the Suez Canal in Egypt. Then, in 1896, the Sudan fell under the control of the Mahdi. Security of the Nile was threatened, which was seen by British Prime Minister Lord Salisbury as a serious state of affairs. He sent an Expedition under Kitchener to recapture Khartoum, but made it clear that if Egypt wanted a dam, she would have to pay for it herself. This, of course, was impossible.

Cromer, undeterred, carried on seeking sources of finance. In the end a complicated deal was done with Cassel's of Cologne. The firm of Airds won the tender and after many difficulties and disasters, the first Aswan Dam was opened in 1902, 500 miles upstream from the Mediterranean Sea. But Egypt's needs were still growing and it was clear that whilst the new dam was a money-spinner, it would soon need heightening. The First Heightening was started in 1907 and completed five years later, increasing the reservoir capacity by 250%. Cromer had retired and Kitchener was appointed British Agent and Consul-General in his place.

There then arose a bitter squabble, involving complex technical matters which do not need to be explained here, between Sir William Willcocks, the Head of the Department of Irrigation and Sir Murdoch MacDonald, who had been appointed by Aird as Engineer for the heightening project. As a side issue, MacDonald and Kitchener supported the Sudanese in their claim to have a dam built on the Blue Nile at Sennar. This infuriated the Egyptians, who feared that they would lose water to the Sudan. After a series of law suits, MacDonald sued Willcocks for defamatory libel and won. The Sennar Dam was eventually approved and work was completed in 1925. And Egyptian resentment over the Nile water goes on to this day.

It should not be overlooked that Sir John Gibson had been appointed Contractor for the Sennar Dam by Sir Murdoch MacDonald and it was against the background of this political morass that Jack walked innocently to Aswan, encouraged by Gibson.

Jack had been interested in Aswan since 1914, when he had visited Kitchener in Cairo and demonstrated some of his 'twopenny' party tricks. He wrote to Prime Minister Ramsay MacDonald in 1924, lobbying for support for a second heightening of the Dam, suggesting that it would be a means of conserving more water for the Egyptians, who were concerned about losing water to the Sudan, and saying that in his opinion it was not a scheme which could be funded by private capital alone. The reply was non-committal. The understanding of capitalist ventures has never been a *forte* of Labour Governments.

In the winter of 1928 news was out that tenders for a second heightening were about to be invited. Jack and Gwladys left for Egypt immediately. Jack was in his late fifties. He wanted to retire on a high note. Here was the opportunity to close a magnificent career with a final prestigious flourish. Gibson joined them in Cairo and took them on a tour of his work in the Sudan. They stopped on the way to look at the dam at Aswan, then went on to Khartoum, travelling on Kitchener's railway and to Wadi Medani, where Gibson had his HQ. Finally they visited Gibson's dam at Sennar, 207 miles upstream from Khartoum. Jack had never built a dam, and was able to see first-hand what dam-building was all about. He drank in everything he could from Gibson's know-how. The heat was 42° Centigrade.

They started to discuss the setting-up of their new Company. It was to exist specifically and purely for the Aswan project. And right from the start there was friction. Jack wanted to call it Norton-Griffiths, Gibson & Sons. They each had sons to think of. But Gibson would not hear of it. The firm would be called simply Gibson & Griffiths. "Patently absurd," sniffed an incensed Gwladys, "when one thinks of Jack's world-wide reputation. And as for Gibson, he is a very ordinary little

Yorkshireman with a strong accent and could never pass as a gentleman, however clever and brilliant he might be."

Back at Griffiths House, London Wall, Jack pored over the Specifications, searching for traps and looking at ways to cut his margins, while he waited for Gibson to arrive: "Concrete: 354,900 cubic metres. Granite: 15,000 cubic metres. It may be quarried from the surrounding district at sites approved by the Resident Engineer, subject to restrictions imposed by the Mines Department. Rubble masonry: No stones weighing less than 30 kgs shall be used. Cement: Only the best quality Portland Cement. A 4% deduction shall apply for Societé Egyptienne de Ciment Portland. In every dispute, the Resident Engineer's decision is final."

Gibson did not show up. Jack called for his car and went to see Solly Joel. Since the War money had become scarcer and Solly was no fool. Even the Joel pockets had bottoms to them. But Jack's charms worked, up to a point. He came away with an agreement that Solly would finance the Dam up to £495,000. It would be enough to set up the plant, but no more.

It was July before Jack heard anything from Gibson. A terse letter arrived on his desk, stating simply, without any pre-ambular pleasantries, that he would not be able to help Jack on the Dam after all, as he had promised his wife not to work in Africa any more. Jack was stunned, but undeterred. He would just have to soldier on alone. There were only two months left before the tender deadline. It meant burning much midnight oil, but in the end he reckoned he could clinch it and make a small profit.

The tenders were submitted on 27 September 1929 and opened on 1 October, just three weeks before the Wall Street Crash. Had Solly seen it coming? It was more than likely. Jack's tender was for £1,997,000. It was £300,000 below the next lowest. Sir Murdoch MacDonald sent for Jack. He was deeply concerned.

"Do you want to pull out?" he asked.

"No," Jack replied, "I can do it."

"Don't!" implored Gwladys, "I beg you."

Many of his wide circle of friends all beseeched him to withdraw, but to no avail. His mind was made up. Gwladys came down with shingles.

The contract was signed on 27 January 1930. It was amazing that the Egyptian Government approved of Jack's involvement. It specifically stated in the Instructions to Persons Tendering, Clause 17, page 91: "Tenderers must have previously executed work of a similar nature . . . and must supply . . . satisfactory evidence that they have executed works of approximately the same kind." The expertise, of course, was to have been supplied by Gibson. Jack's job was to find the finance.

He flew out to Egypt to get things moving. Three months had slipped by since the last flood and only six more remained until the next one. By mid-July everything would have to be cleared away and then floodgates opened to await God's gift to Egypt to come roaring down from Ethiopia. It was to be Jack versus the clock again, just like it had been at Benguela. But pure brute force and will power would not be enough this time. The contract specified that the Dam was to be lengthened by 170 metres and heightened to 35 metres. This would result in a giant sweep of stonework, one and a quarter miles long and a hundred feet high straddling the Nile, dominating the desert scene. The first task was to take down part of the existing dam to prepare it for deeper supporting buttresses. This was as far as the work had progressed when July came. In a normal year work would have had to be suspended until October when the flood had subsided, but this was not a normal year. The 1930 flood did not come in its usual force. The winter rains had failed in the Highlands. For once it looked as if Jack had been lucky. He would not have to stop work, provided the workers could survive the summer heat.

Four thousand men, with skins ranging from sallow yellow to coal black, swarmed over the dry aprons of the Dam, just as they had done over the Pyramids some millennia before. Most wore an amulet strapped to his right arm. The remorseless sun beat down between their shoulder blades and six tall cranes raised their heads towards the cloudless sky. Wagon loads of rubble were pushed along a rail and a warning cry of *"Oh-a Rasak"* rang out as each one was tipped and its contents rumbled and crashed down a chute into the core of the heightening blocks, to be followed by a skipful of concrete which had dangled, waiting to be manhandled, on the end of a crane. "Concrete shall wherever

231

possible be deposited by means of skips. In no case shall concrete be dropped from a height." The temperature rose and rose. The reading on the face of the Dam was 100° Centigrade – the boiling point of water. The water content of the concrete was evaporating before it could be poured. The reservoir was nearly empty and there was trouble at the quarry, which was run by an Italian workforce. Details of the exact nature of the trouble were never made clear, but possibly it had been fomented by the Wafdists, a left-wing reactionary group who were lobbying for constitutional reform in Egypt. "Cowsons!" Jack yelled at his agent, Baxter. In the aftermath of the Wall Street Crash, there was a world slump. That, plus the low flood, had caused the price of Egyptian cotton to fall from £20 a *kantar* to £12. The Egyptian Government started to be 'difficult'. "Every difficulty that could be raised was raised, until the position with the Dam became critical," wrote Gwladys in her memoirs.

Solly's money was finished, the Egyptian Government would not, or could not help, and in the middle of the depression, Jack was forced to return to London to beg for more. But Solly had not become rich by backing dead horses. It was no go. On 29 August 1930 Jack and Gwladys spent a peaceful evening trying to cheer each other up. Outside there was a terrible thunderstorm. It was to be their last night together.

He sailed for Alexandria the next day and took the train up to Aswan. In a remarkably short space of time anxiety had caused his hair to fall out. He was nearly bald, with a grey sunken face. On 21 September he ordered stoppage of work. It seems that the roots of the operational problems were in the quarries, not so much in the setting of the concrete. On the 25th he made one last desperate attempt to salvage the project by writing to the Egyptian Premier, Sidky Pasha, asking him to help, then went back to Alexandria to await MacDonald who was due on the 27th. He took with him Mr East, MacDonald's representative, who was meeting Government officials in Cairo, and Signor Pizzigalli, the Italian manager of the quarries.

When the three men checked into the Casino Hotel at San Stefano, a couple of miles down the coast from Alexandria, the manager handed Jack a sealed buff envelope. On the front was scrawled "Sir John Norton-Griffiths – By Hand". He tore it open.

Inside was a single sheet of white paper, with a few hand-written words on it. Ashen faced, Jack scowled as he read it, then without a word stuffed it in his pocket.

By the evening of 26 September the hotel was crammed with reporters, quickly on the scent of a major story. They made much of the *imbroglio*. Jack was quoted as blaming 'interference amounting to tyranny' by the Government. The Wafdists blamed Jack for upsetting the Egyptian engineers. Pizzigalli blamed the Egyptian liaison staff, saying that similar problems had beset the French dams at Rosetta and Damietta. Various sub-contractors blamed the excessive incompetence of the Egyptian Government inspectors. The Egyptian Government made no attempt to hide its displeasure at the appointment of MacDonald as Consulting Engineer and the reporters blamed Jack for getting them into trouble with the Wafdists. Surrounded by newsmen, Jack said, "I'll explain things personally to Nashas Pasha (the Wafdist leader), who is dining right over there." (Evidently, as with so many with similar political persuasions, the man's left-wing reactionary politics did not preclude him from dining in top-class hotels.) But a friend tugged him back by the sleeve, saying, "Don't make a fool of yourself, Jack."

Reporters never let matters drop until they have enough material for copy. They continued to badger him for a statement. In desperation, he protested "For goodness sake! I'm tired of talking shop. I've been driven crazy by lawyers all day. I'll see you later."

The London *News Chronicle* gave the story the headline "A breathless race against time", while the *Reuters* correspondent wired his office quoting Jack as saying that "it was too late to do anything".

The next morning Jack left the hotel at 8 o'clock to go to the beach for his morning swim. He wore a bathing costume and dressing gown and had left his watch and signet ring in his room. Pizzigalli was taking the air on the hotel balcony, surveying the beach through some binoculars. According to what he said later to the newsmen, he saw Jack return to the hotel, then go out again. He handed his towel and robe to a beach attendant, got into a surfboat and began paddling out to sea. When Pizzigalli swept his binoculars back onto the surfboat a while later he saw that it was empty. (Some reports say that it was upside down.) Quickly, he alerted the hotel staff and a boat was sent out. They found Jack's body floating near the surfboat. He had been shot through the right temple, with the exit wound through the left ear. The signs were that he had been shot from very close range, but no gun was found. The body was taken to the Anglo-Swiss Hospital and viewed by a Mr Calvert, the Assistant Consul-General.

Guido Pizzigalli, an Italian subject, agent of Sir John Norton-Griffiths & Co. Ltd. at the Aswan Dam, then residing at the Casino San Stefano, made the following statement under oath at the inquest:

> I was in the Casino on Saturday morning, the 27 September last. At about 9.15 am on the 27 September, I was on my balcony, looking at a large ship arriving from the north with my field-glasses. I noticed a gentleman on a surfboat, rowing – he had already left the shore and was about half a mile distant.
>
> I re-entered my room to take up a cigarette and then went out again on to the balcony and it struck me that the surfboat was empty and the oar floating about 100 yards away, whilst there was no one swimming near it.
>
> Remembering the figure of the gentleman in the boat, it occurred to me that it might be Sir John himself. I called the waiter and asked him to see if the gentleman of Room 99 was in or not. The waiter, without moving, replied to me, "Sir John is out at about eight o'clock on a surfboat and when he left his room, he pointed out to me an attaché case which was lying on his bed and he ordered me, when I take breakfast to Mr Pizzigalli, take the bags also to him". After that, I understood that some accident must have happened and I asked the waiter to call Mr Baxter to my room at once.
>
> Realising at once what must have happened, Mr Baxter went to the hotel manager, asking that a boat be sent out to see what had happened.
>
> About ¾ hour later, the body of Sir John N-Griffiths was brought ashore. A boat was sent out from the Casino – there were three men in it.
>
> I myself went down to the shore and was there when the body was brought ashore. I don't remember whether the surfboat was brought ashore. I did not see any weapon such as a revolver or

234

pistol brought back by the men. I only saw that Sir John was bleeding from the head.

I joined the firm on 1 July last when I met Sir John for the first time in Cairo. The last time I left Sir John was at 1p.m. on Friday 26 September. My impression of Sir John's state of health at that time was that he was quite well – he did not show much pre-occupation about his own affairs when he was in my company. I would however say that he was very much worried – especially during the last three days – by his business affairs.

I did not hear any noise, when stood on my balcony or in my room, as of the report of a pistol shot.

Ernesto Marchesi, the floor waiter whom Jack had asked to take his attaché case to Pizzigalli, said he saw Jack walk up and down the corridor and back into his room five times, dressed in a bathing costume, before going out. He seemed very agitated. There were conflicting reports as to Jack's state of mind. Some said that he was his usual cheerful self, although his mind was obviously very busy, while others, including Marchesi, had it that he was 'a nervous wreck'.

His secretary, a Mr Chard, testified that he had never known him to carry a gun, but how he could have concealed such a thing in his swimming costume is a mystery. The verdict of the Inquest was suicide whilst of temporarily unsound mind.

In 1933 a letter was written to a prospective author by a Mr Ernest Cairn (?, signature partly illegible) of Bexley, Kent, who claimed to be the life president of the *Askenazim Gesellschaft* (Ashkenazim = Eastern European Jews.) The letter said that Jack had "destroyed over $40 million of our property in Rumania, for which we have anathematised him and all his family with the firm determination to pursue him to the ends of the earth . . . It was the knowledge that the Sword of Damocles was over him that caused him to commit suicide as the Ashkenazim influence, being Jewish reaches from east to west by secret channels. Where law transcends justice, something more potent and sinister must transcend law."

It was true that Queen Marie of Rumania had visited Egypt not long beforehand with her full entourage, which would have given ample opportunity to a secret service agent to stay behind. But it is known that the reason for Marie's visit was to take her daughter, Princess Ileana, abroad for a while to recover from a broken engagement, and she was, after all, a great personal friend of Jack. She took great pains to try to comfort Gwladys after his death. It is almost beyond doubt that her visit to Cairo was genuine, although of course, there is always the possibility she could have been used as a 'stooge' by a determined assassin. Perhaps a stronger clue is the use of the German word *Gesellschaft* (= Society). It was 1933. The Ashkenazi were Jewish and therefore despised by the insurgent Nazis and Fascists. Such a letter would have been typical of their methods of propaganda. Could Cairn (?) have been the nom de plume of one of them? Even the aspiring Goebbels himself?

Jack's body was brought home, aboard the *Italian Prince*, to be buried at Mickleham, Surrey, on 18 October 1930. Gwladys was his widow for forty-four years, dying at the age of 101 in 1974. She took to her grave a tantalizing secret. She had often said that Jack had "another great worry which caused him to drown himself in his work". But she always steadfastly refused, even to the closest members of her family, to divulge what it was.

APPENDIX

Appointments, Honours and Awards to Sir John Norton-Griffiths, Bart, KCB, DSO. 1871–1930

Commanded Scouts in Matabele-Mashona War 1896–7.

Captain-Adjutant of Lord Robert's Bodyguard, South African War.

Major 2 King Edward's Horse.

Temporary Colonel Royal Engineers.

Mashonaland Campaign Medal 1897.

Mentioned in Despatches – Mashona Campaign

South African War Medal – with clasps for Cape Colony and Paardeberg.

South African War Medal – with 1901–1902 clasps, 'inscribed C-in-C's bodyguard'.

Mentioned in Despatches – 22 June 1915, 1 January 1916.

DSO – gazetted 14 January 1916.

KCB – 12 December 1917.

Russian Order of St Vladimir (Third Class) – 1 June 1917.

Order Star of Rumania (Commander with Swords) – 4 April 1918.

Legion d'Honneur – officier – 7 June 1919.

1914–1918 Great War Star.

Victory Medal (with oak leaf emblem in respect of Mentions in Despatches.)

Baronet of the U.K. – 3 June 1922

BIBLIOGRAPHY

Barrie, Alexander, *War Underground*. Spellmount 1962

Bridgland Tony, *Field Gun Jack versus the Boers*, Leo Cooper/Pen & Sword 1999

Grieve, Captain W. Grant & Newman, Bernard, *Tunnellers*. Herbert Jenkins 1936

Joel, Stanhope, *Ace of Diamonds*, Frederick Muller 1958

Massie, Robert, *Dreadnought*, Jonathan Cape 1991

Middlemas, Robert K., *The Master Builders*, Hutchinson 1963

Pakenham, Thomas, *The Boer War*, Weidenfeld & Nicolson 1979

Pakula, Hanah, *The Last Romantic*, Weidenfeld & Nicolson 1985

Passingham, Ian, *Pillars of Fire*, Sutton 1998

Pauling, George, *The Chronicles of a Contractor*, Books of Rhodesia 1969

Plomer, William, *Men of Destiny*, Peter Davies Ltd. (Heron Books)

Wilson, *With the Flag to Pretoria*, Harmsworth 1901

Heritage of Zimbabwe, The Rhodesiana Society 1991

Rhodesiana, The Rhodesiana Society 1969

The Jameson Raid Centennial Retrospective, Brenthurst Press 1996

Index

Akabo, SS, 87

Alderson, Lieutenant-Colonel, 37, 39–43, 45, 49, 51, 52, 65

Alfred, Duke of Edinburgh, 179, 198

Amery, Leo, 64, 215

Arab, SS, 37, 39

Aswan Dam, 102, 226, 228, 229, 232, 234, 237

Aubers Ridge, Battle of, 115

Avery, Captain Wilfred, 209

Bailey, Miles, 151

Balfour, Arthur J., 99, 100

Barnato, Barney, 12, 20, 35

Beer, Sergeant, 212, 213

Bewsher, Mr, 4

Bibesco, Captain Prince Antoine, 194, 200, 221

Black, Second Lieutenant, 135, 137

Bloemfontein, 68, 71–73, 76–79

Botha, Philip, 39, 46–48

Bowry, Lieutenant, 210, 213

Brabant's Horse 66, 68

Brady, Colonel, 174

Brand, President, 27, 79

Braniatu, Ion, 181, 182, 189

Buller, General Sir Redvers, 67, 68, 74, 90

Cadman, Professor, 153–155, 170

Cairn, Ernest, 235, 236

Carol, King, of Rumania, 179, 182

Carter, Mr, 174–176

Cassels, Lieutenant Geoffrey, 142–144, 147, 153

Chamberlain, Joseph, 82

Chard, Mr, 235

Charter, 40, 42

Colenso, 36, 66, 67, 73, 81

Coley, General, 10, 11

Comrades of the Great War Association, 218

Consolidated Investments Corporation, 20

Consolidated Oilfields,190, 192, 221

Cowan, Major, 142, 143, 162, 163

Craddock, Lieutenant-General Montagu, 111

Cronje, General, 34, 70–76

Cropper, Captain Cecil, 166, 172–175, 211

Crown Reef Company, 21, 28

Daniell, Lieutenant Henry, 212–214

Darling, Mr Justice, 222

De Beers Consolidated Mines Ltd., 12, 69, 72

de Moleyns, Colonel the Hon F. Eveleigh, 54–55

de Wet, Christiaan, 72, 74, 76, 82

Dickson, Lieutenant George, 166, 212, 213

Docker, Dudley, 95

Dolby, Doctor, 4, 21

Doris, HMS, 70

Dunottar Castle, SS, 67, 68
Dyson, Lieutenant Eric, 148

Edgar, Tom, 63, 64
Ellis, Lieutenant Percy, 212, 214
Eloff, Lieutenant Sarel Johannes, 32
Excell, Benjamin, 111–113, 124
Eyre, Mr, 49, 50

Ferdinand, King, of Rumania, 162, 163
Fort Hartley, 52, 53
Fort Martin, 51, 52
Fowke, Brigadier-General Henry, 119, 121–123, 133, 151, 153, 162, 164, 168, 170, 171, 176
Franz Ferdinand, Archduke, 105
French, General (later Field Marshal) Sir John, 70–73, 76, 77, 79, 114, 115, 117, 118, 121, 122, 130, 148, 149, 164
Füsslein, Lieutenant-Colonel, 205

Gandhi, Mohandas, 89, 90
George V, King, 99, 109, 201, 202
Gibson, John, 225, 226, 229–231
Gladstone, William, 10, 11, 14, 25
Godley, Captain, 39
Goschen, Sir Edward, 105, 108, 109
Gosling, Captain, 31
Gosling, Acting Commandant A., 55, 56
Grand Bassan, 84, 87
Grey, Sir Edward, 109
Griffith, Major David, 130, 136–138
Griffiths, Ursula, 87, 89–91, 93, 224
Griffiths, John Senior, 2, 5, 6
Griffiths, Juliet, 3
Griffiths, Annie, 2–5, 21, 41
Griffiths, Peter, 89, 93
Griffiths, Phoebe, 93, 224
Griffiths, Michael, 95, 225
Guthrie, William, 190

Haig, General, 114, 163, 164, 204, 205, 207, 208, 211
Hall, Lieutenant Cecil, 212, 213

Harlech Castle, SS, 34
Harrison, George, 14, 29
Harvey, Colonel, 119, 121, 122, 151, 153
Harvey, Brigadier-General Robert, 168–170, 172, 174, 176, 177, 204, 205, 214, 223
Hauha Fort, 95
Hayward, Lieutenant John Thompson, 196, 200, 201
Hepburn, Captain Clay, 164, 165
Hero, 123, 136, 225
Hickling, Lieutenant Horace, 164–166
Hill 60, 126, 127, 129–131, 133–137, 139, 140, 146, 147, 150, 162, 165, 171, 177, 205, 208–210, 213, 215, 216
Hill, Lieutenant Lionel, 127, 138, 141, 216
Honey's Scouts, 36, 39, 40, 42
Honey, Wilfred, 37, 39, 40, 42, 42, 43, 48, 50
Hoskins, Brigadier-General, 142
Howard Associates, 99
Howard de Walden, Lord, 94
Hudspeth, Captain Henry, 177, 207, 208, 211, 212, 214
Hyland, Captain Gordon, 149, 164

Ileana, Princess, 236
Italian Prince, SS, 236
Ivory Coast, 83–85, 87, 88, 94

Jameson, Doctor Leander Starr, 23–29
Jeans, Surgeon, 77
Jenner, Major, 39, 42–47, 50
Joel, Solly, 35, 224, 230
Joffre, Field Marshal, 148, 149, 154, 182

Kanzler, SS, 60, 62
Katanga Copper Mines, 88
Kekewich, Colonel, 69
Kelly-Kenny, General, 72–74, 77
Kerr, Captain Hugh, 203

Kimber, Percy, 5, 6
Kimber, Sir Henry, 6
Kimberley, 11, 12, 20, 23, 24, 66,
    68–72, 114, 117, 164
Kitchener, Field Marshal Sir Herbert,
    67, 72, 73, 81, 82, 102, 110,
    113, 114, 116–119, 121, 122,
    164, 173, 228, 229
Komati Poort, 81.
Kruger, President Paul, 12, 14,
    25–28, 30–32, 35, 64, 66, 76,
    77, 81, 104, 106

Ladysmith, 11, 18, 36, 64, 66, 68,
    74, 79, 87
Laing, W.J., 68
Lambert, General, 210, 213
Lanchester Motor Company, 111
Leonard, Lance-Corporal, 133
Lindsay, Sir William, 102
Lloyd George, David, 109, 204, 214
Lobengula, King, 13, 14, 23–26, 28,
    43
Lobito Bay, 88, 90
Lock, Lieutenant-Colonel, 133
Lomagundi, 54, 62
London Rifle Brigade, 118
Loos, Battle of, 163, 171

MacDonald, Sir Murdoch, 228–230
MacDonald, Ramsay, 229
Mackilligin, Second Lieutenant, 161
Maes, Private Victor, 210
Mafere, 85
Magersfontein, 66, 69, 71–74
Majuba Hill, 10, 11, 13, 32, 36, 66,
    68, 74, 87
Makoni, Chief, 40
Marchesi, Ernesto, 235
Marie, Queen of Rumania, 179, 198,
    199, 220, 235, 236
Mashayamombe, 41–46, 51–53, 65
Masterson, Captain Thomas, 200
Maynard, Captain, 21.
McBride, Captain William 209
McDonough, General, 186, 190,
    197, 220, 223

McKenna, Reginald, 186
Messines Ridge, 116, 129, 130, 133,
    153, 164, 168, 170–172, 177,
    205, 214, 217
Modder River, 69–73
Moffat, John, 14
Morgan, Private, 124–128, 130,
    131, 135, 136, 140
Morland, Lieutenant-General Sir
    Thomas, 158
Murray, Major the Hon Arthur, 147

Nashas Pasha, 233
Natal Land & Colonisation Co., 17
Nesbitt, Captain R.C., 51–53
Nevinson, H.W., 107
Nicholas II, Tsar, 201
Nivelle, General, 204, 205, 208
Nottingham Road, 18, 36

Paardeberg, 73–77, 87
Pall Mall Gazette, 110
Pauling, Sir George, 39, 57, 88
Petrie, Brigadier-General, 137
Phillipon, Lieutenant Maurice, 200
Pizzigalli, Signor Guido, 232–235
Plumer, General Sir Herbert, 162,
    205, 208, 211
Poplar Grove, 76, 77
Pryor, Lieutenant Edmund, 154,
    157–160

Rand Club, 19
Rees, Albert, 131, 135
Reform Committee, 27, 28, 31, 35
Rhodes, Cecil, 6, 11, 19, 20, 34, 52,
    63, 69
Rhodes, Frank, 35
Rhodesian Mining & Development
    Co., 62, 65, 83
Roberts, Field Marshal Lord, 67–73,
    75–81, 102, 112, 113, 215
Roberts, Freddie, 67, 81
Royal West Kents, 139
Royal Dutch Oil Co., 192
Royle, Lieutenant, 210, 213

241

Sawers, Corporal Basil, 146
Scale, Captain, 200
Schneider, Feldwebel Michael, 134, 135
Second King Edward's Horse, 110, 111, 113, 115, 117, 147
Selous, F.C., 24, 42
Simpson, Lieutenant Philip Huntington, 200
Sirhind Brigade, 117
South Wales Borderers, 124, 126
Standard Oil Co., 28, 192, 222
Stanley Heading Machine, 172, 176, 177, 211
Steyn, President, 77–79
Stoneham, Herbert, 83

Talbot, Mr, 174–176
Tanasescu, Lieutenant, 200
Tandy, Arthur, 209
Tharsis Gold Mining Co., 29
Tulloch, Nina, 19
Tzantzareanu, Second Lieutenant A., 200

Uitlanders, 14, 25–28, 30–32, 35, 64, 71
Umbria, SS, 83
Umtali, 40, 57
Urie, Captain, 212

Vancouver, 94, 95
Victoria, Queen, 12, 14, 23, 25, 28, 31, 37, 64, 104
von Falkenhayn General, 184, 192
von Mackensen, General, 192
von Straussenberg, Baron Arz, 183

Warren, Sir Charles, 65
Warrender, Admiral, 105, 106
Waterfield, A., 68, 69
Waterval Drift, 71, 72, 77
Wellesley, Captain Edward, 154, 157–159
Wetherby & Jones, Messrs, 5
White, Mr, 58, 60
Wilhelm, Kaiser, 104–106
Willcocks, Sir William, 228
Williams, Mrs Hwfa, 100
Williams, Major Guy, 124
Williamson, Lieutenant, 155, 156
Wipers Times, 126
Wood, Mrs, 83, 84, 93
Woodward, Captain Oliver, 210, 213, 214

Youell, Mr E.C., 221
Ypres, Battles of, 129, 208

Zarps, 35, 36, 63, 77, 80
Zottu, General, 183